T0067250

Health
—*and*—
Happiness

A Holistic Approach

ROBERT W. WILDMAN, II, Ph.D.
&
JULIUS M. ROGINA, Ph.D., ABMPP

Order this book online at www.trafford.com
or email orders@trafford.com

Most Trafford titles are also available at major online book retailers.

© Copyright 2015 Robert W. Wildman, II, Ph.D. & Julius M. Rogina, Ph.D., ABMPP.
All rights reserved. No part of this publication may be reproduced, stored in a retrieval
system, or transmitted, in any form or by any means, electronic, mechanical, photocopying,
recording, or otherwise, without the written prior permission of the author.

Print information available on the last page.

ISBN: 978-1-4907-6079-7 (sc)
ISBN: 978-1-4907-6078-0 (e)

Library of Congress Control Number: 2015909109

Because of the dynamic nature of the Internet, any web addresses or links contained in
this book may have changed since publication and may no longer be valid. The views
expressed in this work are solely those of the author and do not necessarily reflect the views
of the publisher, and the publisher hereby disclaims any responsibility for them.

Any people depicted in stock imagery provided by Thinkstock are models,
and such images are being used for illustrative purposes only.
Certain stock imagery © Thinkstock.

Trafford rev. 06/03/2015

www.trafford.com
North America & international
toll-free: 1 888 232 4444 (USA & Canada)
fax: 812 355 4082

CONTENTS

PREFACE

This book for me, Robert W. Wildman, II., was begun at a time when, for some rather unique geographic and personal reasons, I found myself unable to continue with a long-term scientific project in which I had been engaged. Looking for some scientific/literary contribution I might make under those circumstances, I found myself frequently visiting the psychology section of a book store in a mall near where I was temporarily residing. A review of the shelves of "pop" psychology books revealed to me two things. First, all of the authors had and gave "the answer," typically a rather simple and unitary answer, to the emotional and mental problems of the reader. And second, all of these answers were different!

Well, it just so happens that I received my clinical training at Georgia State University in the early 70s. While there, I went through all three of the major training programs. These were the psychotherapy training program, the behavior modification sequence and the marriage and family program. There were also, I would add just for the sake of completeness, courses on psychological testing. Anyone at all familiar with the different "schools" of psychology will recognize that being exposed to such radically different ways of looking at "mental problems" and the even more radically different ways of going about trying to deal with them, all at the same time, would be a truly mind blowing experience for a young graduate student. And it was! For various reasons, I feel fortunate to have survived. But now is not the time to go into all that.

What my clinical training did teach me was that any problem or condition can be analyzed and understood in a variety of ways. There are also a number of treatments which may be useful. If what I learned is correct, and I obviously believe that it is or I wouldn't have taken pen in hand, then it must follow that there is no single and simple solution to all of these problems. Shouldn't, I wondered, people be made aware of some of the basic information that is available from a variety of resources and traditions regarding their "mental health," as well as their physical health, and how they might improve their own adjustment to life? Over the years, I've been impressed by and appreciative of the efforts of professionals in various fields to explain to lay persons like myself some of the basic principles of their areas of expertise. Might I be able to do this for clinical psychology, particularly as it relates to that issue with which we are all nowadays so concerned, health? The answer was that I would try.

In contrast to the other things I have written, like a paper on the generalization of behavior modification procedures and my book on gambling, both of which involved extensive literature reviews and long lists of references, this book was written from the earliest drafts in what one might call a more "impressionistic" manner. I stepped back and looked at what I had learned over the years as a student and then practitioner of clinical psychology. For better or worse, what I have written literally "flowed" from that context. As a matter of fact, I have come to see my involvement in this work as something of a mid-career comprehensive examination. Given, though, that I had not meticulously followed the literature on health psychology for some time, I did read four volumes of works summarizing the status of that field. Basically, reading these writings did not in any way change my approach to the practical implications of the whole field of clinical psychology for the specific area of health psychology as summarized in these pages.

Two technical notes need to be made about this work. The first is that the use of projects or real-life assignments follows from my father's (same name just without the "II") courses at Georgia College. We reported on this technique in the 1975 Directory of teaching innovations in psychology which was published by the American Psychological Association. My additions to this chain of using real-life assignments evolved over the years from the courses I taught in Behavioral Techniques at Radford University in Virginia and in courses in Adjustment at Northern Nevada Community College in Elko and Truckee Meadows Community College in Reno.

I would beg to make here two requests of the reader, at least of those readers who actually read prefaces! Perhaps these are actually more in the way of warnings or cautions. The first is that you not take the Table of Contents too seriously. It was, almost by necessity, laid out in terms of the various problems people face. This book is NOT, though, designed to be a handbook. While each chapter focuses on a particular set of "concerns," they are not intended to be self-contained packages of "solutions." There is much overlap among the chapters. For example, relaxation training is described in great detail in one chapter, but it is also relevant to the handling of a number of other problems, like addictions and sexual disorders, which are the focus of other chapters. Hopefully, the reader will find this book worthy of being read in its entirety. Doing so should maximize one's chances of putting together a package of procedures which will help you in dealing successfully with what may be going wrong in your life and in improving its quality.

The second issue relates to the times when it becomes clear that your own individual efforts, with or without the help of this book, are not proving successful. Numerous times throughout this work it is noted that if your own efforts are not working, professional help is readily available to you. Looking back, though, we probably didn't emphasize this point enough. So I'm re-emphasizing it here. Your family doctor is probably the best guide to good mental health services in your community.

Should this book be blessed by printer's ink, it will, inevitably, be criticized. I cannot foresee all of the criticisms which may be brought to bear on this work. I can, though, be fairly confident of two. The first is that there is nothing original in this book, that what is written here is well known to all even marginally competent clinical psychologists. This is a charge to which I plead guilty, but happily so. As a matter of fact, an effort was made in my part of the writing of this book to present only materials that are so well known and accepted that they could be conveyed to the reader with great confidence.

The second potential criticism is possibly more telling. I can see a colleague of mine who happened to take the time to read this book putting it down and saying, in effect, "Thirty some years and that's ALL Bob Wildman has learned?" To that charge I have to simply plead guilty!

Finally, I would like to be permitted a personal note. I find myself very much in the position of a clergyman (which our coauthor actually is) who has just preached a sermon on living the "Good Life." There is, I think, the danger that implicit in such sermons and writings is the impression that the deliverer of the words has, himself or herself, achieved the sort of spiritual or psychological level of development to which the audience has been exhorted. Those who have been close to me over the years, and more painfully I myself, know that I have not always lived up to the ideals held up in this work, a balanced life of moderation in all things which results in a reasonably consistent attitude of calmness and contentment. All I can say is that the words I have written and their role in my own life are not presented to you as final solutions. The procedures described in this book are, rather, offered as tools which we all may use in our constant and ongoing efforts in striving for a happier, more productive and satisfying life.

In view of my empirical and scientific orientation and the limitations imposed by the same, I invited Julius Rogina, Ph.D., ABMPP, who is a clinical psychologist, a Diplomate in Logotherapy (Victor Frankl Institute of Logotherapy) and an Episcopal priest, to add some more humanistic and spiritual insights/advice to our manuscript, which I believe he has done with his characteristic blend of sensitivity and scholarship.

We hope you find something of value in what we have written.

———————

Sometime during the summer of 2013, I, Julius M. Rogina, was invited by Bob to join him in shaping and writing this book on health and happiness. My first reaction was I do not need another project! My second reaction was, after the initial reading of the manuscript, that the material in this book is practical and challenging enough that it could be helpful to someone who is curious and desirous of living a more meaningful and satisfying life. I decided to get on board and accepted the invitation.

I had the privilege to have worked with Bob in the same mental health hospital for a number of years. His intellectual curiosity and care of the patients were two salient characteristics that I remember about him.

My personal and academic and professional journey differs from the one that Bob described above for himself.

I came to the United States of America in 1972 to pursue graduate studies in theology at the Jesuit School of Theology of Santa Clara University, Berkeley campus. After completing the course of studies in theology, my interest became to combine theology and clinical psychology. I engaged the field of clinical psychology particularly as it informs the mental health of a religious and spiritual person. The Graduate Theological Union and the University of California programs proved to be the place to encounter the challenge and engage the six and a half years of "academic dance" with all its demands of completing the course work, comprehensive examinations, dissertation research, internships and sitting for the National Examination in Professional Psychology to attain the licensing credentials for independent practice.

My clinical work with patients and academic engagements with the University of Nevada, Department of Psychology and School of Medicine, Department of Psychiatry forced me to not only rethink some of my earlier professional convictions, but invited me to articulate my own contributions to the field of spiritual and mental health.

The subtitle of this book, "A Holistic Approach" sums it up best for me. I understand that the proof of the pudding is in its taste. Spirituality or religion cannot be understood adequately when apart from social sciences like clinical psychology. The reverse is also true. I believe that theology as a scientific field provides a philosophical framework for religion and spirituality. I also believe that the field of scientific psychology provides a philosophical framework for meaningful research that is applied in clinical psychology practice as it relates to health and happiness of unique individual human beings as well as communities of people with their cultural richness. We cannot get away from theory. My observation is that the field of religion and spirituality is in flux today. We have not yet agreed on a common theoretical definition. Regardless, scientific dialogue within the fields of scientific psychology and theology must create dialectical tension that, I hope, will gradually create a new synthesis, both theoretical and applied, in order to assist the individual person to live a full and meaningful life.

This book is, hopefully, a modest contribution to this endeavor. Our hope is that you find this book useful. There is no human being, as far as I know, who was raised in a perfect family with perfect parents and perfect brain structure, receiving unconditional positive regard at all times. There is only a real human being with the unique context of his or her environment and inheritance. This real human being has a healthy core, the resources of the human spirit, to assist her on the journey. As you live your unique lives, solving the everyday problems and moving to flourishing existence, we hope that this book will become a helpful guide.

Robert W. Wildman,II., Reno, Nevada
Julius M. Rogina, Reno, Nevada

CHAPTER 1
PHILOSOPHY AND OVERVIEW

Without question, the greatest advance in medicine was the work and influence of Louis Pasteur (1822 – 1895). The great French physician, it will be recalled, advanced the position that disease is caused by microorganisms, which we now commonly and over-generally refer to as "germs." At the time, his teachings were so heretical that they pointed to his fellow doctors as not only being ineffective in their treatment of the sicknesses of the patients who consulted them, but as being the very carriers of diseases. Following standard medical practice of the time and laughing at the fantasies of Dr. Pasteur, they went from one bedside to the next without so much as washing their hands.

Those of us who have had the advantage of seeing a culture in a Petrie dish and watching microbes squiggle under the lenses of a microscope are no longer laughing. We are, in fact, in awe of the great strides medicine has made in disease prevention through improved sanitation and the savings of lives through the administration of antibiotics, all flowing directly from the insights of Louis Pasteur.

But, perhaps surprisingly, there may be a "downside" to the universally accepted germ theory of disease. This "downside," the authors hasten to point out, reflects no lack of genius or wisdom on the part of Dr. Pasteur. It is, rather, a product of our wish for a "quick fix," a cure for all our afflictions wrought by an external agent and requiring no effort on our part.

According to this lackadaisical orientation, sickness always occurs when a "healthy," innocent person has the misfortune to be fallen upon by a bad, mean "bug." Clearly, no one denies that unavoidable misfortunes like birth defects do occur. But many, undoubtedly most, illnesses can be traced either directly or indirectly to our styles of living. Most obviously, smokers develop lung cancer and alcoholics are at risk for cirrhosis of the liver. Drug addicts have been known to throw themselves from apartment windows,

1

apparently believing that they were going for a swim. There are, though, less clear-cut relationships between disease and way of living. Obesity and a sedentary lifestyle are associated with well-known health risks. And there is a range of maladies that bear an even less systematic and obvious relationship to the way we conduct our lives. These mostly befall us as a byproduct of anxiety or nervousness, being "high-strung," as they say. The harried executive may experience chronically elevated blood pressure. The clergyman who goes out of his way to be kind to everyone, to turn the other cheek in the face of being provoked, may collapse in the pulpit from the effects of a bleeding ulcer. And the conscientious, overworked physician may complain of back pain for which no physiological explanation can be found.

This book focuses on the above types of disorders. It attempts to explain how they develop and to give some insight into their management. But more importantly, it addresses the issue of their prevention. However, just as health matters do not run their course in isolation, this work, of necessity, speaks of more than just the body.

It is the position advanced here that good overall health flows from a general state which professionals tend to label being well-adjusted or "normal," but which we can call for our purposes "contentment." It is further suggested that there are two major components to this happy condition, a well-balanced, goal-directed life and an intimate, open and sharing relationship with at least one other person.

Therefore and in an effort to be positive, a difficult task for psychologists, the early chapters focus on the components of a well-balanced, meaningful life. It will, hopefully, become clear during this process how other lifestyles are associated with disorders, both mental and physical. Then the book goes into the various illnesses, their causes, treatments and prevention. Along the way, "tips" will be given for dealing with some of life's problems and how to get yourself to do those things which, in your heart, you know you should do but seem to somehow never get around to actually doing. Finally, we presume to offer ideas on no less a subject than the meaning of life as a central, integrating factor in our approach to the subject at hand.

This book is a perhaps unusual blend of scientific information, clinical training and personal experiences and values. It is offered as the result of our personal struggles with the issues which are central to the lives of all of us. If you, Dear Reader, feel that we talk too much about ourselves, we beg forgiveness. To paraphrase Thoreau, we would not write so much about ourselves if we but knew someone else so well.

CHAPTER 2

LIFE IN A BOWLING ALLEY

The issues of health and happiness are complex, and they overlap with each other so much that they call into question the very matter of the meaning and purpose of life itself. Many have addressed themselves to this question. Some say that "Life is a bed of roses" or a "cabaret," while others maintain that "Life's a beach" and various alternative wordings. Someone, we can't recall now who, advanced the idea that "Life is a stage." The authors come now, tongue in cheek, to tell you that all of the above theories about life are wrong. Life is actually like a bowling ball! Now, if this proposition seems flippant and insulting to your intelligence, please bear with us.

Have you ever come across an old, long unused bowling ball in a basement or closet? It's a dull, dusty object which represents little more than something to trip over. How different it is from the shiny, black, gleaming, dynamic ball that scoots down the lane toward the pins. Perhaps there is an analogy here to human life. The bowling pins are the equivalent of goals. When we have no goals, we're like the abandoned bowling ball, just lying around gathering dust. Now, in using the word "goal," we are here talking about goals that give our lives meaning, purpose and joy. Please keep all these factors in mind in that, as we go forward, we will just use the general term "goal" to also stand for all of these higher-level facets, but we are actually talking about so much more than just, say, pursuing the "goal" of getting home for supper.

So we need goals to motivate us to move forward. We'll discuss later how one might go about selecting goals in life. As a matter of fact, this is sort of the "ultimate issue," as they say in court. For the present, though, let's just assume that we've selected some "good" goals for our lives. Given that, what might interfere with our attainment of those goals or, continuing with the bowling ball analogy, the knocking down of the pins? Even if we've aimed the ball properly, it could still be unbalanced and wobble off into the gutter.

We need, it would seem, to examine the components of our personal "bowling ball of life." Figure 2-1 is a schematic of one such personal structure. This figure illustrates just one of many possible configurations. This person's life is apparently reasonably well-balanced.

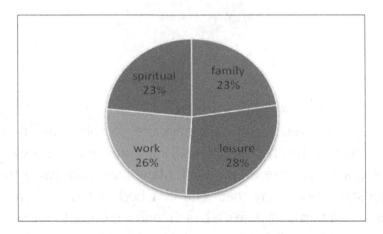

Figure 2-1. A Balanced "Bowling Ball of Life"

The individual's ball shown in Figure 2-2, unfortunately, is not so happily situated.

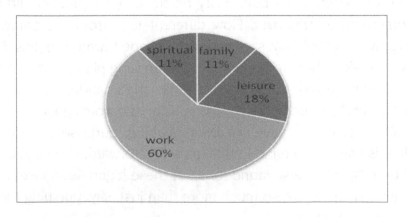

Figure 2-2. An Unbalanced "Bowling Ball of Life"

This person is what is popularly called a "workaholic." The inflated work section adds weight to the ball and will temporarily give it the appearance of movement, but it will ultimately slide off course and end up in the gutter. The goals aimed at, worthy though they may have been, will go unachieved. There are, of course, other compartments than that for work which can be oversized. Notable among these are recreation, family (usually of origin) and sex.

Moving away somewhat from our bowling ball analogy and more into the realm of conventional mental health, the psychological equivalents of "wobbling" are signs (objective indications of problems like trembling) and symptoms (subjective feelings of distress). Chief among these are anxiety, depression, substance abuse and a general feeling of unhappiness and lack of fulfillment. This is not to deny that such symptoms may be within the person, or "endogenous" as they say. People with low blood pressure, for instance, often complain of depression, and there are endocrine and gynecological problems which cause people to be anxious or "on edge." But for most of us, though, these symptoms come and go depending on what's going on in our lives and how we're reacting to these events. The specific type of problem we experience appears to vary from person to person. Why one individual develops ulcers, for example, while another drinks to excess is not presently fully understood.

Well, how do we know how to keep our lives in balance? This is a question for which there is no easy and simple answer. And to make it even more complex, the "answer" differs from person to person and may even shift over time. Rick is a high-energy individual who is ambitious and intensely interested in his profession. He has a relatively uncomplicated personal life with a wife and five-year-old son, both of whom are in good health. John, on the other hand, wants and has a closer, more intimate relationship with his wife Anne. Therefore, "intimacy" and "family" are larger components in his well-balanced life.

Given that there is no pat "answer" to the question of how to arrange one's life so that it is "balanced," as we've come to say, what are the concrete steps one can take to move toward that elusive goal? Sometimes we can glean a degree of insight into positive actions by looking at their negative counterparts. And so it may be with this issue. In the authors' experience and observations, the people who have the most difficulty with "bowling ball arrangement" are those who never even think about it in the first place. They simply drift into a lifestyle by making spur-of-the-moment decisions, usually by complying with the demands of "authority figures" and attempting to meet the expectations of "significant others." So we're going to attempt to avoid such an unhappy outcome by taking a more active role in the planning of our own lives.

The first step, in our experience, is for each person to make a list of the important things and ideals/aspirations in her/his life. This is done initially in no particular order in so far as priorities or importance are concerned. This list, it is recommended, should be written and revised over a period of time, say a week or so. You'll find that not all the important things in your life will come to you during a single sitting. Simply for purposes of illustration, Table 2-1 shows Frank's list of significant, value-anchored life factors. "Frank," incidentally, is a hypothetical person who, along with his wife "Sandra," was invented for the purpose of this book.

Table 2-1.

A Beginning Listing of Significant Value-based Factors for Frank

- My relationship with my wife
- Contributing to the betterment of the "human condition"
- Helping my children "grow" in health, knowledge and in the preparation for a productive life of their own
- Continuing in my development of an understanding of and a sense of participation with that Force which gives spiritual significance to life
- Going out to eat once or so a week
- Making love with my wife
- My family, in general, both the immediate family and extended family
- Health – being in the best possible health and the experience of moving toward that goal through exercise, proper diet, etc.
- Regular attendance at church services
- Access to books which I can use to "study up" on matters and questions of interest
- Listening to music, particularly classical music
- Dressing well – having a range of conservative, professional clothes
- Traveling and having an opportunity to experience another culture at least once a year
- An evening cocktail, preferable and almost always in Sandra's company
- A period of at least a half hour's duration and at least once a day of quiet talking and reflection with my wife
- Walks on which I can think
- Having a comfortable home

- Playing games, like gin rummy and board games, with my wife and children

We can utilize Frank's initial listing in coming up with a set of "compartments" for his bowling ball. This goal is accomplished through grouping his separate listings into general categories. Table 2-2 gives an example of this process.

Table 2-2.

Some Categories Used to Determine Bowling Ball Compartments

Spiritual – 16.66%

- Continuing in my development of and a sense of participation with that Force which gives spiritual significance life
- Regular attendance at church
- Walks on which I can think

Intimacy – 16.66%

- My relationship with my wife
- Making love with my wife
- A period of at least a half hour's duration and at least once a day of quiet talking and reflection with my wife

Family – 16.66%

- Helping my children "grow" in health, knowledge and in the preparation for a productive life of their own.
- My family, in general, that is the immediate and extended family
- Having a comfortable home

Self-improvement – 16.66%

- Health – being in the best possible health and the experience of moving toward that goal through exercise, proper diet, etc.
- Dressing well – having a range of conservative, professional clothes
- Traveling and having an opportunity to experience another culture at least once a year
- Access to books which I can use to "study up" on matters and questions of interest

Leisure and Recreation – 16.66%

- An evening cocktail or two, preferably and almost always in Sandra's company
- Listening to music, particularly classical music
- Going out to eat once or so a week
- Playing games, like gin rummy and board games, with my wife and children

Work – 16.66%

- Contributing to the betterment of the "human condition"

One is tempted at this point to establish priorities among these value-based categories, that is, ordering them in terms of importance. It is the view taken here that this step is not one that should or even can be done. The emphasis in this approach is on "balance." What good is it, for instance, if you're "famous" in your field and yet have no one with whom to share your success? Of what ultimate use is a healthy body if you're cut off from any sense of spiritual significance in life? Thus, it's not, in our opinion, possible to say that one category is more important than another in the sense that you should satisfy all of those needs first and before moving on to the "lower categories."

As noted above, a completely empty "bowling ball compartment" can cause you to wobble off into the gutter, thus effectively invalidating and destroying progress made in other areas. It is, however, possible to assign percentages or weights to these various categories, while acknowledging that at least "something" has to be in each of them, given that all of them are firmly within the individual's value system.

Frank has put in the weights, expressed as percentages, for his categories. There are several things to note about his method of doing this. First of all, he assigned the same weighting to all of the categories. This strategy reflects more than just a lack of imagination on his part. He really is unable to say that one area of his life is, in fact, more important than another. Also, the different areas are not at all mutually exclusive. They are interacting or complimentary. Specifically, Frank feels that he can pursue more than one goal at the same time. For example, going to church is something he does with his family. Thus, this activity not only contributes to Frank's spiritual development, but it also enhances his relationship with Sandra and the children. Many of the areas of self-improvement, such as traveling and reading books, are also activities shared by the family.

A perhaps noteworthy feature of Frank's listing is that there is only one activity within the category for "work," that is "contributing to the betterment of the human condition." This feature reflects perhaps a peculiarity of his attitude toward work. Frank takes no pride or enjoyment in working for its own sake. Rather, he works in order to "help" people, including those both inside and outside of his family. Therefore, he seeks employment that is aimed at providing or improving services to people, such as doing psychotherapy and publishing articles that give data and advice relevant to the treatment of various problems. The money derived from this work is important to him only in that it helps provide a comfortable home for his family and opens up such opportunities as travel and other educational experiences. Thus, much of the time spent at work is for Frank actually in pursuit of other goals, like travel and self-improvement. Undoubtedly, there are others for whom work is important for its own sake, for whom the prestige and power associated with a given position are significant factors in their lives and sense of self-worth. Similarly, the acquisition of "wealth," say in the form of CD's and stocks, is a goal of many of those who read these words. And these significant factors in their lives should be reflected in their "bowling balls."

Another important factor in Frank's lifestyle organization is the centrality of his relationship with his family, particularly his wife. As much as possible, all of the important activities in his life, as noted above, are pursued with and for his family. The specific positioning of Frank's bowling ball compartments are depicted in Figure 2-3.

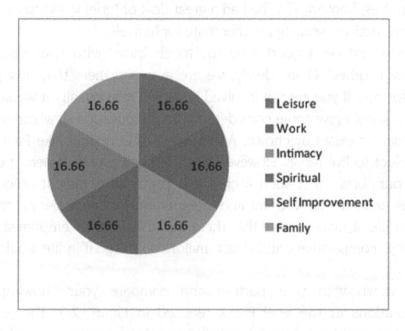

Figure 2-3. Frank's "Bowling Ball"

The great importance Frank attaches to his relationship with Sandra suggests that he should take great care with it. Some of the ways in which Frank and Sandra "take care" of their marriage are discussed in the next chapter on "Intimacy: How to find it, how to achieve it and how to keep it."

The thoughtful reader will, undoubtedly, catch a potential problem in the way Frank has organized his life. The centrality of his relationship with Sandra works well for him as long as she is in his life. But what would become of Frank should she exit his life, as through divorce or death? The former does not appear likely, and there is much that he can and would do to prevent it. The latter cause of separation, fortunately, does not seem to be more than a remote possibility for at least the next several decades. But nothing in this "transitory life" is absolutely impossible, so this matter of Sandra's potential departure is worthy of some degree of serious consideration.

After years of work in suicide prevention, Frank is reasonably certain that he would not take his own life in the unhappy circumstance of, say, Sandra's death. He doesn't think he has the biological capacity to become psychotic, to lose contact with reality. He would have to structure himself very carefully to avoid taking increasing comfort from and ultimately retreating into the abuse of chemicals. He hopes and believes that he would reorganize his personal life around: 1) a solo striving toward spirituality and 2) efforts to help the children deal with their mother's death and to be supportive of them in their efforts to build productive lives of their own. He would, in fact, very much focus on working with his children on their lives, knowing that he had a great deal of "grief work" to do before beginning actively seeking another mate for himself.

This would be a good time to "touch base" with your spouse or "significant other." Quite clearly, we are assuming here that this person exists for you. If you are not involved in such a relationship, it would seem that you should give some consideration to the question of whether or not this situation exists by choice. Admittedly, some people, like Paul in the Bible, elect to live alone. However, it is the position taken here, perhaps, again, our "bias," that such a choice is pretty rare, almost unique and requires unusual self-restraint and integrity. So for those people who are alone in life, it makes sense that there would be a great emptiness in the 'intimacy" compartment and that a major current goal in life would be to fill it.

Sit down with your partner and compare your "bowling ball" configurations at the level Frank reached in Figure 2-3. The resulting discussion could prove to be enlightening. In those areas in which the spouses are in general agreement about the weighting of a compartment, we think the question becomes: is the area devoted to that general activity complimentary or competing? For instance, say both members of the couple have a large "work" compartment. This is a situation that could drive them apart if, say, the wife is practicing law and the husband optometry. Being in the same field, Frank and Sandra have a somewhat easier time with this matter in that they do much of their work together. Their writing a book together is an excellent example. Frank is writing the first draft, while Sandra is preparing supplemental materials, like illustrations of the academic points Frank is trying to make. They go over each other's work almost daily and kindly, gently make suggestions for how the writings can be improved and how they can bring about a better "fit" between their two parts so as to better convey the central, mutually agreed upon points. So this is a project which, fortunately, brings them together both physically and intellectually. Even those work tasks that take them apart can be recast or "reframed" into things that enhance the family. Frank occasionally agrees to teach an extra class or two during evenings or weekends. "We'll take some of the money and fly to _____. As you know, dear, there's this fascinating cathedral there we've been reading about in…"

On the other hand, rather major differences in their bowling ball configurations could, theoretically, not be indicative of a problem in the marriage. For instance, one spouse might have a large work category while the other's life arrangement emphasizes, say, self-improvement, as in study. The two might well come to an agreement whereby the time one partner devotes to one activity is used by the other to pursue a different set of interests. In our opinion and experience, an arrangement in which the two members of a couple work toward most goals together is optimum. Even so, other adjustment patterns are certainly possible and may well be quite functional for some.

Obviously, should a significant conflict between the two members of the couple become apparent during this process, such as one placing more focus on "money" and the other on "spirituality," there should be serious discussion about how some type of compromise might be reached. It is even possible, regrettably, that such a wide discrepancy in life factor importance might exist for a couple that the chances for a successful marriage are greatly compromised. Ideally, an exercise similar to the one proposed here should be part of the courtship process. But even we are not grandiose or naïve enough to believe these writings will have any notable impact on the course of youthful passion!

But back to the point, Figure 2-4 shows a comparison of the two bowling balls for the Frank-Sandra couple. On a cold, snowy day which happened to be a holiday, they sat down to discuss how they were arranging their lives and the implications of this for their family and future.

A real positive aspect to their choices to emerge from this exercise is the centeredness they share in their relationship. For both of them, their marriage is the organizing "template" in their lives. Additionally, they have a great deal in common, such as a love of travel, study, etc. The alteration of the weights given to "family" and "spiritual" in the two structures appears to reflect little more than a difference in method of expression. Sandra has been engaged, for some time, in a personal journey toward a closeness with God, whereas Frank's focus is on family worship and an intellectual, philosophical understanding of spirituality. Therefore, no basic conflict between them appeared to emerge here.

Figure 2-4. A comparison of the life factor arrangements for Frank and Sandra

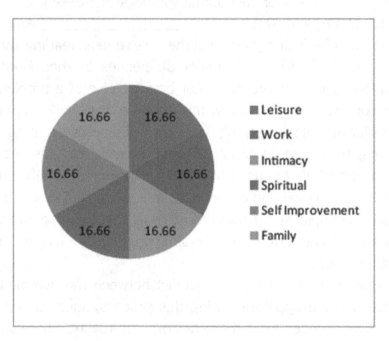

Frank

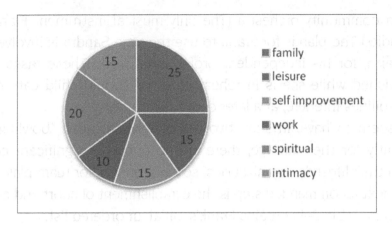

Sandra

The only potential problem area they found in the bowling ball comparison was in the "work" category, where, obviously, Frank had devoted more space. A step that helped them deal with any potential difficulties in this life sector was to break Frank's "work" into a number of subcategories, as shown in Table 2-3.

Table 2-3. A Division of the Work Category

1. The "normal 40-hour work week" expected of most husbands to maintain employment and support the family
2. Professional work they do as a couple, such as writing their book and conducting workshops
3. Extra work that Frank does to earn additional money for family "treats," such as trips to interesting places
4. Work Frank needs and wishes to do on his own, such as completing some research projects that he's been working on for a number of years

Work subcategory Number 1 is not only unproblematic but would just be expected of a dutiful husband and father. Numbers 2 and 3 involve, of course, activities which are pursued by mutual consent. Category 4 appears to be the only one having the potential for causing problems for Frank and Sandra as a couple. Following some discussion, they came to what is believed to be a workable agreement with respect to specifics which might arise in this area:

Sandra has some independent interests in which she looks forward to participating. These come under the general heading of "being well-rounded," a major focus of her life. One of these future activities is to play in a community orchestra (The only musical instrument Frank plays is the radio.) The plan is for Frank to use the time Sandra is involved with, say a band, for his independent professional work. These tasks can be accomplished while she is in rehearsal or, or should child care or work responsibilities interfere, at a later convenient time.

We seem to have, in sum, two reasonably balanced "bowling balls." Importantly for the marriage, there are no apparent significant conflicts between their lifestyle organizations, so we seem OK for team play.

Our next recommended step is the establishment of short and medium-range goals. Table 2-4 contains Frank's initial, unordered list.

Table 2-4. Frank's list of goals.

1. Obtain a temporary teaching position
2. Finish his book
3. Obtain a permanent academic appointment
4. Design and begin giving workshops on his research
5. Move to a position in his area of specialization in the Eastern United States by September 1 of next year
6. Get certain aspects of the children's behavior under control
7. Re-establish closer relations with his family of origin (long-term)
8. Help as much as possible with the completion of the children's educations
9. Travel
    A. Visit those parts of the West he has not yet seen
    B. Brief trip to the Orient
    C. Visit the four states he has yet to see
    D. Visits to South American countries to practice his Spanish, which they practice daily
    E. Return to Europe, including a stop in Greece and possibly on to Egypt

So we've set up the pins, and the Sandra and Frank Bowling Team is ready for a flourishing life!

CHAPTER 3

INTIMACY:
How to Find It, How to Achieve It and How to Keep It

This chapter grows out of the authors' personal beliefs, "bias" for those who wish to be formal, that "intimacy" with another person is a central and necessary feature of a rewarding and happy life. But what is intimacy? Whereas some psychologists might define it as a "close affectionate relationship" or a "sense of belonging together," we believe it's a lot like "love" in the sense that one can only grasp at its meaning through describing how one feels or what one experiences during the course of it. Here are a number of qualities we may associate with being intimate with another:

- A feeling of "comfort" with that person, a sense that you can tell that person everything, that you can truly be yourself with him or her
- An ongoing and perhaps "mature" feeling of fascination with the other person – everything about him or her is of importance and interest to you
- A feeling of security that the other person experiences you as being worthwhile and interesting
- A sense of feeling good or better about yourself when with or following being with that person
- A desire to "take care" of the other person. A determination to be with the other person and help her or him through life's problems and illnesses
- An ever increasing sense of longing for and missing the other in that person's absence
- Frequent surges of joy in the other's presence, the surprisingly sudden yet repeated realization that everything in life is more vivid, meaningful and fun with him or her
- A perhaps uncharacteristic lack of embarrassment with that person during "compromising" situations, such as hospitalizations and social or financial problems
- The ability to work with that person in a sustained, cooperative manner toward the attainment of individual and joint goals
- A greater concern on the part of both members of the couple for the health of the relationship than for "winning" arguments or for prevailing in disputes, as for instance in decisions relating to resource allocations. Intimate couples tend to have the ability to actually prevent arguments through, it is believed, objectifying the issues and dealing with them in a way which is characterized by empathy for the other and his/her needs and viewpoints. We'll discuss these "highfaluting" concepts later on.

Assuming that the reader agrees with the authors about the desirability of the above-described type of relationship, the question naturally becomes, "How can I get this?" At the risk of coming across as negative, we would express the opinion that most people don't have intimacy because they place themselves in a position in which it is unattainable. Some, particularly but not exclusively in youth, tend to select partners for what in retrospect appear to have been the wrong reasons. Examples are parental pressures, similarity in appearance to an admired movie star and financial/

social considerations. Utilizing these superficial criteria for mate selection, it is highly possible that two people might find themselves together in the face of wide differences in the importance to them of intimacy and in their drive for and skill in attaining it. It happens, sadly, that there are couples in which one partner is totally disinterested in, even oblivious to, intimacy as we have described it. The prospects for such a pair are not bright, to say the least.

So under the heading "how to find it," we would recommend that in the partner/mate selection process one should look for feelings of mutual comfort, joy and feeling good about oneself. We would warn you here that one's position within the intimacy dimension appears to be trapped within certain limits. You probably are deluding yourself when you reason that, "She may be cold now, but that'll change when we have our own home and live together."

Assuming that you and your spouse are reasonably consistent in the importance and effort you devote to intimacy, the next issue relates to how this kind of happy relationship can be fostered and improved. It may have occurred to the reader, as it has to the authors, that many of the features of intimacy, feeling accepted and good about yourself, feeling that the other person is really interested in you, for example, relate to one person actively listening to the other. Having your mate look you in the eye and listen attentively to what you have to say about one subject or another becomes even more of a confidence, self-esteem builder when it is coupled with gently asked open-ended questions of a sort like, "Wonder how if felt when _____" and "How do you think you might handle that?" It is particularly heartwarming, even flattering, when someone you know says something like, "You know, I was thinking about something you said last night, and I was wondering…"

Since the overriding topic here is one of interest, it logically follows that you should find a mate whom you genuinely find worthy of respect and admiration. Of course, it's important that these feelings go both ways. Much hurt has resulted from relationships in which one person feels that way about the other but these feelings are not returned.

A situation in which both spouses are concerned about the attainment of intimacy and are genuinely interested in each other is important and probably indeed necessary for the type of relationship we wish for ourselves and are trying through this and other works to help others attain. As logicians put it, "They are necessary but not sufficient conditions." Despite such favorable circumstances, problems can occur. In any marriage, there are disagreements, and we are all sometimes guilty of not being as attentive to the other person as we should. We, at times, find ourselves "cutting off" the other, as when one member of a couple gets overly wrapped up in something and tends to go on and on for a period of time. These incidents need not create serious problems if 1) they are rare, 2) the couple knows and has discussed the fact that they are really making an effort to be attentive to each other and 3) when a "slip" occurs, they both make active efforts to make it up to the other person, engaging in the process of "repairing the relationship."

So no one is perfect. And just as there may be "gaffs" in listening to one another, communication skills are part of an art which to some degree can be developed and very definitely can be improved.

At Home Client-Centered Therapy

As an introduction to our discussion on how to improve one's ability to communicate with your mate it is, we think, important to raise a question that may have already occurred to you. Why is it important, why does it feel so good to have someone really listen to you?

The person who has the most to say about the above question is the late Carl R. Rogers (1902 – 1987). In order to understand how Rogers' work relates to our topic concerning marital communications, we must digress a bit and consider the development of the human personality.

According to Rogers, the newborn person has a psychological structure he labels "The Organism." This is the "true psychic reality," what the person actually and genuinely is. Some newborns, Organisms, are naturally nurturing and artistic. Others, in contrast, may tend to be more athletic and competitive.

One of the first things a young person does and an activity that continues throughout life is to look around and try to gain an understanding and conception of the things in his or her world. One of the components of the world of which the child develops a concept is that of herself. This becomes what we popularly call the "self-concept," but which Rogers labeled simply the "Self."

The relationship between the Organism and the Self is critical for adjustment. If the person develops a pretty accurate self-concept or Self, she or he experiences a sense of self-acceptance and comfort. On the other hand, should the Organism and the Self diverge widely, the individual feels unhappy and dissatisfied with himself. Mental health professionals tend to label this latter, uncomfortable state "anxiety." Figure 3-1 shows the two arrangements possible in this early stage of personality development. Rogers calls the distance between the Organism and the

Self in the illustration on the right "incongruence." Another use of space for purposes of illustration is the depiction of the Self as lower than the Organism. This reflects the experience of people who suffer from a great deal of incongruence. They typically feel bad about themselves, unworthy and unlovable. We would commonly say they have "low self-concepts."

Figure 3-1. People and Their Self-Concepts

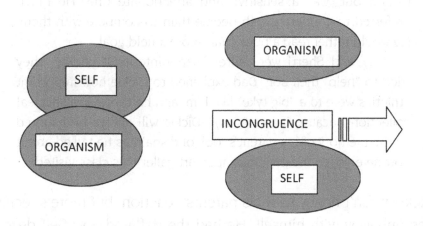

How is it that the person on the left enjoys a sense of self-acceptance and self-worth, while her sister on the right is racked with anxiety and self-doubt? This theory attributes the cause to the way people are brought up. Rogers said that parents could treat their children with either "Unconditional Positive Regard" (UR) or "Conditional Positive Regard" (CR).

Under the UR method, the parents are genuinely loving and accepting of the child. They demonstrate warmth and affection for him or her regardless of which "way of being in the world" the child might select. Please note, though, that this parenting style doesn't mean that the mother and father will smile and praise everything their daughter does. They will, in fact, have to discipline her for breaking the rules. But throughout such times they convey to the child a sense of acceptance and regard for her, if not for her behavior.

Conditional Positive Regard, however, relates to a situation in which the parents only show approval for the child when his behavior conforms to their hopes and expectations. A case study will illustrate this unhappy process:

> Dickie was born a few years ago to Guy and Sherri. Mom and
> Dad were an "All American" couple. They began dating in high

school where Guy was the captain of the football team and Sherri the head cheerleader.

They talked often during the pregnancy about how Richard, to be named for Guy's own Dad, would be "all boy" and become a "man's man." In fact, Guy bought Dickie his first football the day the sonogram revealed that Sherri was carrying a male child.

Mother Nature did not, though, fully cooperate with the couple's plans for their son. Dickie's personality (Organism), it turned out, was a sensitive and affectionate one. He much preferred to cooperate with people than to compete with them. He would rather read a book than score a field goal.

Guy and Sherri were sure disappointed! Of course, they tried to "help" their son. Dad explained to Dickie how important athletics were to a "big tyke" like him, and he threw away his leaf collection because it was "sissy." Dickie will always be haunted by the memory of his parent's look of disdain as he talked about how he enjoyed the paintings at an art gallery his class visited.

Dickie wasn't happy with his parents' reaction, but more specifically, he was unhappy with himself. He had the deflated, low Self described above. Now, a child his age doesn't have the intellectual resources to reason, "Ah, my parents are treating me with what Dr. Rogers would call Conditional Positive Regard. They don't realize that my scholarly approach to life will someday get me out of this dumpy mill town and into a professorship or practice somewhere a lot better." No, he is totally dependent on his parents and enmeshed in their perception of reality. He sees himself as having failed his parents.

But it's too early in life for Dickie to simply give up and resign himself to being a failure. Instead, Individuals typically plan and dream of doing dramatic things to earn the acceptance and approval of the people who control their lives. The child we are talking about, for example, might fantasize about scoring the winning touchdown in his senior year, or perhaps he would see himself proudly showing his parents his weight-lifting trophy. These fantasies are incorporated into what Rogers calls the Ideal Self, the conception of what you believe you ought to be. For Dickie, this Ideal Self is hopelessly unrealistic. He has the pattern shown in Figure 3-2.

Figure 3-2. Dickie: A study in incongruence

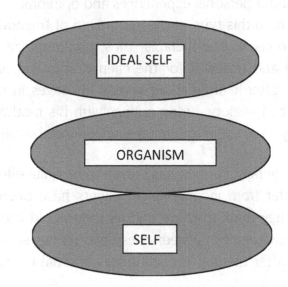

Poor Dickie suffers from a great amount of incongruence which he experiences as anxiety and hurt. His personality is not well integrated, so he is not very effective in dealing with life.

While anyone reading this book is, of course, older than Dickie, the lessons we learn from his sad history may still at least partially apply to us. First of all, many, if not most, of us were reared under CR. And, regrettably, the world we live in as adults is a pretty CR kind of place. Most of the people with whom we deal on the highways and in supermarkets certainly seem to see us more as obstacles to overcome than as people to get to know. So, most of us walk around feeling quite unattended to and lonely. We often don't feel so good about ourselves.

In extreme cases, people treated in the above fashion find it necessary to go into psychotherapy. Rogers himself put forward a system of psychotherapy to which he gave the title "Client-Centered." The purpose of this book, obviously, is not to make the readers psychotherapists. But a brief examination of how people may be helped to recover from severe mental distress might give us some clue as to how we can avoid problems in interpersonal relationships and increase the sense of closeness so many of us cherish.

The two key elements in Rogers' system of psychotherapy are:

1. Active listening. The therapist attends intensively to the client. She maintains good eye contact, consistently conveying the message that "What you are saying is of interest and importance to me." The

therapist avoids giving advice and never interrupts the client by talking about personal experiences and opinions.

2. Reflection. In this type of therapy, a kind of "mental mirror" is held up to the client. The therapist tries to summarize what the client has said and review it for the client's approval or rejection. For example, after hearing about several instances in which the client experienced anxiety during outings with his mother, the therapist might say, "You seem to often feel uncomfortable with your mother."

This type of therapy, happily, has proven to be quite effective in helping people who suffer from incongruence. Clients have been asked to rate themselves as they think they are and as they would like to be (Self vs. Ideal Self). The differences between these two ratings shrink considerably from before to after therapy, reflecting less internal distress and greater self-acceptance.

It is believed that the mechanism by which Client-Centered Therapy is effective relates primarily to the supportive, "facilitative" environment created by the therapist. This warm, nonjudgmental atmosphere allows the patient to put the details of her inner and outer life "on the table," as it were. The client is thus "given permission" to look at himself as he really is. This self-appraisal in someone concerned enough and sensitive enough to enter psychotherapy generally results in a feeling that, "Gee, I'm a much more worthwhile and successful person than I had thought." With this revelation comes an increased sense of self-acceptance, and it is no longer necessary to maintain a compensatory and unrealistic Ideal Self. The person over time goes from the distressing state depicted on the right of Figure 3-1 to the more comfortable arrangement in which the Organism, Self and the Ideal Self are quite close together or "congruent," as depicted on the left.

Below is a typical "case" from a college counseling center's files, which is illustrative of the kind of person for whom Rogers' approach is appropriate:

> Betty is a 20 year-old sophomore. She seats her trim figure in the chair across from the therapist. She pushes her strawberry blond hair behind one ear and smiles sweetly at the psychologist. He is struck by the depth of her large, hazel eyes and the warmth and genuineness of her smile. Her record indicates that she is a high-B student who is an officer in the Student Interfaith Council.
>
> What can I do for you?" he begins in true nondirective fashion.

"I...I don't know. I'm not happy, I guess."

"Hmm. I'm wondering why that is..."

"Gosh, uh...I don't know...Guess it's me...I guess I'm not happy with me."

"Gee, I wonder why."

"...Oh, there are a lot of things wrong with me..."

Over the next several sessions, Betty comes up with the following complaints about Betty:

"I hate being ugly and incompetent. That's what I am, ugly and incompetent."

"I'm fat. Well, not fat by the scales. I've got gigantic thighs and a big rear end. And to make it worse, I'm somewhat flat-chested. No wonder I don't get asked out that often. Guys want Barbie dolls. Me, I'm like a strip of bacon at the top and a side of beef at the bottom..."

"...And my face! My eyes are too big, and they don't work worth a flip either. And...my nose is like a wedge of cheese."

Dr. Johnson, even after years of hearing this kind of self-flagellation, was somewhat taken aback. Why, Betty looked to him so much like the most popular girl in his high school class.

"Damn, I hate being stupid. I was talking in the student union with some folk from the English Department. In his latest novel, John Fowles uses the term 'manage' in two ways. I was talking about the first and then couldn't remember the second! I was mortified! I'll probably flunk all my courses this semester."

Johnson shook his head all the way home. "Gee, I'd sure be proud to have a daughter like her," he summed it all up for himself.

Sound familiar? Again, this book does not seek to get everyone into psychotherapy. But the fact that people are willing to pay for this kind of treatment suggests that really being listened to is of extreme value to many. It would seem that if you can get it at home, so much the better. We might, though, facetiously ask the question of which spouse is to be the client and which the therapist? The answer, it seems, is both "neither" and "both." We might informally say that the two partners should alternate in these two roles in an informal and impure way. Certainly, it would be ludicrous to set a clock so that one spouse would be the therapist for fifty minutes and then the roles would be completely reversed for the next "session." There are clearly times when this method of interacting is inappropriate, as in discussing the grocery list. And there are many times when one's listening to the other will be interrupted, as when a child does something that requires parental attention or discipline.

Probably the best way to deal with the needs to listen to your spouse and to be listened to yourself is to make sure that there are several occasions each day in which the couple talks quietly for a period of time. This can be done as the opportunity and need arises, or, as our hypothetical couple Frank and Sandra do it, on a semi-structured basis. We much prefer a semi-structured approach because it is too easy for things that seem urgent on a short-term basis to crowd out talks like this that are much more significant.

One specific "system," one that has worked well for some couples, is to set the alarm clock for about forty-five minutes before the children need to be awakened. That gives them a half-hour of uninterrupted talking and an opportunity to read to each other from books relating to some of their current interests. They also try to carve out a little time for themselves over a glass of wine before supper, but this is sometimes difficult with kids running in and out and friends calling. So while one must admit to a preference for Bordeaux over the beans picked by Juan, we probably will have to conclude that the dawn discussions are more reliable.

Whatever time they choose, the couple makes sure that they at least touch upon the following topics:

1. Each other's plans for the coming day
2. An inquiry is always made into the physical health of the spouse
3. "How are we doing?" This is an invitation to bring up matters of concern regarding the relationship. They often make this general question more specific by asking if one of them might be doing something that is troubling to the other. This is an important but sometimes threatening component of their talks which we'll discuss in more detail later.
4. An expression of love and devotion for the other

Other points of discussion which frequently find their way into the conversation are:

1. Current events
2. What occurred during a certain period in the life of the other
3. The successes and problems of their children (at least weekly)

4. Sharing experiences of "awe and wonder"
5. Their sense of mission and purpose regarding their personal goals and their goals as a couple.

Active Listening

They always try to give the other person an opportunity to say all that's on his or her mind before moving on to another subject. This is particularly important in regard to the question of whether one of them had done or is doing something which might be of concern to the other. During the time between talks, they think about what the other person has said and their reactions to these statements. They try to make it a point to bring up such matters during their next talk.

We suggest at this point a little exercise which might help you make the talks you have with your spouse more meaningful. Try to talk with him for about fifteen minutes without saying anything. After having a laugh about how many people you know who can do that for so much longer than fifteen minutes, please consider how truly difficult it is.

As some wise wag once put it, "Most 'conversations' are really just competing monologues." When someone says, "I'm having a hard time in this physics course," it's so tempting to come back with, "Tell me about it. If my roommate hadn't been a slide rule jockey, I'd have never gotten through it myself. Course, Julian had a dark side to him…" Not very supportive was it? It's only the rare individual who says, "Gee, it sounds pretty rough." Which would you prefer?

Affirming the Other While Expressing a Different Point of View

Of course, you can't play Carl Rogers all the time. As a matter of fact, we're pretty sure he didn't himself! Merely reflecting all the time would not lead to progress in many areas because there would be no way for the other person to express a different point of view. It's here that so many couples run into problems. You see, there are at least two ways to make a point that diverges somewhat from that of your spouse:

1. Rejection of the argument:

    Husband: Boy, that Billy was a real brat at the Tomkins this evening.

    Wife: Oh, he's just an active little boy, and didn't you see how good his table manners were?

2. Affirming the communication while presenting another point of view:

Husband: Boy, that Billy was a real brat at the Tompkins this evening.

Wife: You're right I'm afraid. I keep hoping that he just has a high activity level and that he'll settle down someday, but maybe we're seeing some signs of progress. Did you notice that his table manners have improved?

Which of the two wife responses do you think felt better to the husband? The advantage of the second example is that it acknowledges that Fred had a valid point before going on to call his attention to another side of the situation. As a matter of fact, Ethel's potential disagreement with her husband about what actually transpired at the Tompkins was phrased in such a way as to give him hope that a problem, the existence of which she is affirming, is solvable.

The first response, on the other hand, made it seem almost like the two of them had wound up in different houses! Fred was probably left feeling that his viewpoint was totally rejected by the wife. If this pattern goes on and on, he may eventually come to think that she doesn't respect him or thinks he's not too bright. He may even conclude that Ethel doesn't love him. It's tough to be a good husband when you don't feel good about yourself.

Fred can deal with his wife's apparent rejection of his perspective in at least two ways;

1. He can accept the implication that he was wrong. He might then become increasingly reluctant to express his opinions to Ethel. Such a pattern of withdrawal certainly can't be good for the marriage.
2. He might "fight back":

Husband: Well, what good are table manners when he's already got everybody so upset that they can't digest their food?

Wife: You know what your problem is, Fred? You're always looking at the dark side. You can't even find anything good about your own son. You never praise him.

Husband: I'd praise him if he ever did anything worth praising. That's the boy's real problem – the way you've pampered him. Yes, Sir, he's always had dear, sweet Mom to run to when he's screwed up. It's like getting political asylum in your own home.

Wife: You're a fine one to talk, Mr. Arnold Palmer. You sure as hell weren't here to guide him along! Why, you were off…"

This couple certainly isn't going anywhere good!

Enough of this kind of rejection of the other person's opinion can turn life into a constant series of arguments. Your authors have seen couples in which this condition was so extreme that if the wife commented about what a "lovely day" it was, the husband was bound to pipe up with, "Are you kidding? I haven't seen a fouler day since Hurricane Andrew ripped through here."

One note of qualification needs to be introduced here. Like everything in psychology, this piece of advice can be taken too far. It probably isn't necessary and might even at times be tortuous, to introduce all feedback into a conversation in the gentle, affirming method recommended here. There certainly comes a point in most mature marriages when spouses feel secure enough with themselves and each other to be able to tolerate some off-hand comments. But, undoubtedly, there even then comes a certain percentage or number of such casual, potentially wounding statements, which varies from marriage to marriage, at which point there occurs a shift from comfort to outright insensitivity.

The Importance of Clarification

Another helpful adjunct to a Rogerian-like approach to marital communication relates to clarifying what the other person has said or "checking things out," as they say. Here we encounter questions and phrases like:

"You said going to the lawyer 'bothered' you. How exactly did it make you feel?"

"I'm curious about something you said last night. You mentioned something having happened in Seattle. Was that the first time you lived there or was it this last time?"

"Hmmm, what was it about the course that made you react so negatively?"

Asking these types of questions has at least two positive effects for the relationship:

1. It helps to avoid misunderstandings. Dysfunctional couples are characterized by a lot of "mind reading," concluding and assuming the other person thinks and feels a certain way without taking the time to make sure your interpretation is correct.
2. It makes you feel important, good about yourself, for someone to be so interested in what you have to say that they want to ask questions.

Dealing with Problems

Undoubtedly, the toughest part of this set of recommendations relates to the advice on bringing up "problems." Many people are reluctant to do this because they fear, or indeed have learned from experience, that to take this step will not only not result in improvements, but will actually lead to disaster. But we know, unfortunately, that saying nothing about troubling matters also has a price. If your spouse does something (or some things) that bother you day after day, the resentment will build up and up. This is not just a subjective impression. We have evidence of this from the psychological laboratory. Two groups of subjects were demeaned and insulted by one of those nasty psychologists. One of the demonstrated effects was a rise in blood pressure for the members of both groups. One group was later allowed to express their resentment to the psychologist, while the frustrated college sophomores in the other condition were denied this opportunity. Of significance for our purposes is the finding that the subjects who were permitted to ventilate their negative feelings enjoyed decreases in their blood pressure readings. The people in the other group, however, displayed continuing high blood pressure, reflecting, obviously, persisting emotional arousal. And, as we'll see later, people with chronically high blood pressure are putting their health at risk. So not only are individuals who are unable to express their anger psychologically uncomfortable, but they may be hurting themselves physically as well.

So we seem to be here on the "horns of a dilemma," as they say. To bring up "problems" in the relationship now does, in fact, raise the possibility of a disagreement right away. But holding back concerns does not, as we have seen, make them go away. They build up and come out later on, often in displaced and destructive ways. For example, a wife may feel that her husband's lovemaking lacks tenderness and a concern for her needs. She is, though, reluctant to broach this sensitive topic with him for fear of wounding his male ego, a not totally unrealistic concern. So she says nothing about the problem, and her feelings of hurt continue to haunt her. One day she walks into the bathroom and discovers that Bill has neglected to wipe off the sink after shaving, as she has so often asked him to do. She calls him a "slob" and an "inconsiderate boob." Bill is left genuinely puzzled. "Gosh, what a big reaction to such a little thing. Must be PMS." So the sexual relationship never gets the attention it deserves. And the husband may not even shape up his bathroom behavior in the conviction that Cindy should ask him nicely before he'll make any changes. Not much progress here, is there? Such problems can be "gunny sacked" for use in future arguments, as in asserting that you must be a better driver than he is because he can't even steer you to a good climax. Great logic!

To avoid the above negative chain of interactions, we advise the following approaches for dealing with potentially dangerous areas in the relationship:

1. **Objectify the problem**. Make explicit the philosophy that "we," not "you" or "I" have a problem.

This method of dealing with things is particularly important in the area of resource allocation. If Bill wants a new car while Cindy has her heart set on redecorating the house, a major disagreement could obviously arise. Perhaps a better approach would be to say, in effect, "We have certain goals and a fixed amount of money. How can we spend that money so that both of us will be as happy as possible?" All kinds of compromises are possible here. Perhaps Cindy could get her new furniture now and Bill could wait as their bank account is replenished until the year end auto sales, thus getting more car for his bucks, as just one example.

It's great if a couple can come to a workable compromise verbally. There are, though, times when the issues are so complex that it's helpful to put them into writing so they can be reviewed and "worked over." Table 3-1 presents such a "working paper."

Table 3-1. A Compromise Work Sheet

Wife's Desire Spend holidays with her parents
Husband's Desire Spend holidays with his parents

Possible Compromises
- Spend holidays alone with our little family
- Invite the Moms and Dads to come here
- Announce and begin a pattern of alternation of spending the holidays with the two sets of in-laws
- Invite the non-selected set of in-laws on an upcoming summer vacation

Other potential compromises would, obviously, be possible for the more ingenious. What is recommended is that all of the possibilities be reviewed with regard to two major questions:

1) Is any potential solution ultimately "fair" to both of the spouses and others? and
2) Will it make the partners as happy as possible under the existing circumstance that neither can have her or his way entirely?

At the risk of being repetitious, we must stress again that forcing one's own way in such potential conflicts by pouting or withholding affection will likely have the effect of converting a short-term "victory" into a long-term disaster. Enough said, hopefully!

In summary, the tone to be set here is that the relationship is more important than any individual decision. To prevail in a dispute by being obstinate and using verbal maneuvering would be a classic case of "winning the battle but losing the war." To deny that there's a sexual problem in the face of expressed dissatisfaction on the part of one of the partners is not only insensitive, but it's absurd! We really don't even have the words to characterize the position that it's okay to leave the bathroom, or any other room for that matter, a mess.

2. **State the problem as positively and non-judgmentally as possible**. Retain your judgment but take away the condemnation.

While we believe that spouses make judgments about each other's behaviors all the time, it is important to refrain from condemnation.

Try to avoid summary, evaluative, emotionally-laden judgments of the spouse. "You know, we seem to have a trash build-up problem around here" is much to be preferred to, "You're an inconsiderate bum who's too lazy to even take out the trash like a man," as an example which is clearly "condemning."

Jock Ewing of "Dallas" once put it quite nicely: "Take away a man's pride, and you've taken away everything." An event in one of the authors' lives illustrates this factor:

> As a young graduate student many years ago I was driving through a rain storm trying to scare up additional data for my dissertation. I stopped at a service station on the outskirts of Atlanta for gas. A middle-aged man with a pot belly and a chew of tobacco in his mouth lumbered up to the car. "Boy," he literally yelled at me, "you better change those wiper blades right now or you're going to be buying a new windshield."
>
> Looking, I could see the evolving scratches, but something which I didn't understand at the time caused, "Ah, I don't think so" to come out of my mouth. I paid for the gas and drove on down the street. As soon as I was out of Hayseed's sight, I pulled into the first gas station I saw and had my worn out wiper blades replaced.

Looking back on the incident, I can now see that there were, in actuality, two components to the service station attendant's statement; 1) a reasonably objective assessment of the physical situation; the wiper blades were, in fact, worn out; and 2) the implication that I was somehow "stupid" for allowing them to come to that state. But such logical distinctions are not easily hashed out in the midst of a Georgia thunderstorm! So I was left in a position of having to accept or reject the "package" of both of Hayseed's pronouncements. While I had no problem acknowledging that the wiper blades were defective, accepting the implied slur on my intelligence did cause problems. Ph.D. candidates tend to be a bit sensitive about that kind of thing!

The implications for marital communication appear to be that requests for changes in a spouse's behavior may be accepted if: 1) they are phrased in a way that doesn't appear to reflect on a central trait like conscientiousness or intelligence and 2) they make explicit or just implicit the assumption that the person is really trying but something just "went wrong." The same message might, though, be rejected if in the process of agreeing to make a change the wife has to also admit to being a "lazy, self-serving, mentally ill slut." Think about it!

3. **Deal with problems when they are small.** Try to deal with problems while they're small, as opposed to allowing them to grow into major disputes within the couple.

This piece of advice is, in actuality, little more than a rehashing of the old saw, "A stitch in time saves nine." But this very sensible step is more delicate in intimate relationships than in tailoring. As noted earlier, people are sometimes reluctant to bring up negatives in romantic relationships for fear of spoiling the mood. And thus they frequently set themselves up for a long-term disaster. So it is often necessary for a spouse to really "probe" in order to get the other to open up in this area. Couples who communicate well often find themselves asking each other, "Am I doing anything that is upsetting to you?" or "Are you concerned about anything about me or us?" Follow-ups are usually of the nature of "Are you sure?" and "You know, it'll be a lot better to get it out so we can start making it better now." Eventually, your partner will reveal any concerns or hurts. While over the short run it may be a lot more comfortable to pretend that you're perfect and that everything's just fine in the relationship, over the long-haul going through the struggle to dig out these potential trouble spots will really pay off.

"It goes without saying," is a frequently heard expression. But sometimes what is thought to go without saying needs, in fact, to be said. So it would seem to be here. As soon as a valid suggestion for change has been received, it is important for the person who has been asked to change to actually make the indicated improvements. Not to do so, obviously, is going to not only keep the other person unhappy about the displeasing behavior but will add to it the frustration and resentment of not being heard. It seems obvious that any discussion of negatives in a marriage needs to continue until both spouses are agreed as to what, if any, change is indicated and the other person has made a firm commitment to actually make that improvement.

Longer term Scheduling

Continuing with the theme of scheduling which was introduced briefly earlier, it may seem paradoxical, but we have found that some degree of pretty definite planning ahead actually adds to the spontaneous nature and fulfillment of a marriage! Part of a suggested "routine" is reproduced below:

Early Evening - A walk

Friday evening - An early bath and a drink or two. An informal supper in front of the TV (the only evening Frank and Sandra eat in front of the "idiot box." Supper on all other nights of the week includes pleasant family discussions.) Friday is their night to kick back and relax, to take a breather from what for them is usually a busy and tiring week.

Saturday afternoon – Afternoon cleanup. They then reward themselves for their exertions with a dinner for two at a "fancy restaurant."

Sunday – Church. Sunday afternoon is "kids' day." They try to take them somewhere fun, like to a pizza place with an indoor arcade in winter. The day ends with "family conference" in which they go over the things they need to take care of during the coming week and the problems they may be having with the actions or inactions of the other members of the family.

Every few months – A short, relatively inexpensive "mini-vacation," like a weekend on an offshore island

Yearly – A major week or two vacation, preferably out of the country, but at least in another and different-appearing state.

It is admitted that adopting this kind of scheduling doesn't ensure a life of perpetual joy. Such surges of joy, or "peak experiences" as Abraham Maslow called them, seem to strike at unexpected moments. But, as they say, if you want lightening to strike, it's good to make like a tree! And we've found that "penciling in" on the calendar activities that hold the potential for being interesting, relaxing and scenic is a pretty good arboreal imitation.

SUMMARY

In summary, it is suggested that the attainment of true, flourishing intimacy involves a number of factors and steps:

1. Select for your partner someone who is genuinely interested in you and in whom you yourself are genuinely interested. Warning signs that there are potential problem in this area while dating are not feeling good about yourself while with that person and the recurring sense of feeling less happy after talking with that person than you did before.

2. Develop joint goals. Work toward them together and discuss them frequently.

3. Engage at least daily in "active listening," taking care that both spouses play both the listened to and listener roles about evenly. Be sure to "affirm" the other's opinions, as discussed above, and ask a lot of questions.

4. Deal with problems in the marriage 1) objectively, 2) gently, 3) early and 4) be sure to make the improvements indicated by this process.

5. Develop and practice good compromise skills.

6. Plan and participate in frequent joint outings. And try to find some humor in things, even if things go wrong on such expeditions.

7. Finally, as sort of dessert, throwing in a surprise romantic gesture never hurts and sometimes really spices things up. Cards, flowers, candle-lit dinners, special dishes, doing a chore which is technically the other's responsibility and stuffed animals all come to mind here. As you see, such gestures needn't be expensive.

Have fun!

CHAPTER 4

COUNTING YOUR WAY TO HAPPINESS

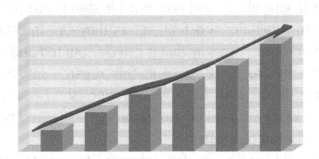

The somewhat facetious title of this chapter suggests an apparently dramatic shift in the focus of this work. But the shift is only apparent because the rather simplistic advice given in this and the next several chapters ultimately is to be used in the service of the intimacy discussed in Chapter Three. The steps outlined here would, after all, be pretty vacuous in the absence of that kind of relationship.

The line "love conquers all" appears to be more impressive to poets than to psychologists. Unfortunately, it's quite possible to have a great relationship and yet still have a problem or problems. You may be madly in love with your wife and yet smoke or drink too much. Prince Charming may come to your bed chamber at sundown, but the scales may show dramatically that you're eating too much and exercising too little. Often, problems are a lot subtler than these examples, such as not being able to get around to doing things and not being as studious as you would wish.

It's pretty easy to recognize that we have such difficulties, and most of us are "sincerely" working on them almost all the time. We frequently believe that we're doing better, and we know that we'll do much better tomorrow. Why then do these problems, which may actually erode the intimacy toward which we've been striving, never seem to actually go away?

Part of the "problem with problems" is that we tend to conceptualize them in such vague and general ways that it's quite difficult to know exactly what the problem actually is. It's even more difficult to know how bad a given problem may be and virtually impossible on a day-to-day basis to know whether it's getting better, worse or just "keeping on keeping on."

If, for example, you're concerned about not being an "intellectual," then how much of a "meathead" are you? And how will you know when the metamorphosis from meathead to intellectual has, in fact, taken place? While the authors have spent much of their lives in academic settings, we must admit that we can't, just off the top of our heads, tell you what or who an intellectual is. In point of fact, to refer to yourself as an intellectual on a college campus is one sure way to evoke snickering from your colleagues!

What we need to do, it would seem, is to get down to specifics. What exactly are we talking about and how does it stand with us? We need to come up with an "operational definition," as they say. In other words, we must define the problem in a way that it can be counted and measured.

Some problems are pretty easy in this regard. Smoking serves as a good example. It doesn't take a rocket scientist to count butts in an ashtray. You can weigh yourself on any bathroom scale, and booze is easily quantified with the aid of a jigger.

Adjustment difficulties which appear to relate to enduring characteristics of the person pose more difficulties in measurement. We would cite "scholarship" and "procrastination" here. But such apparent difficulties must be faced and overcome. The all too human tendency to delude ourselves into the false belief that a problem is improving is all too pervasive otherwise.

Some tricks for measuring what at first blush would seem to be un-measurable are to ask such questions as, "What would I actually do if I were (or were not) like that?" or "How would things be different if I had that quality?"

Take scholarship as an example. What, in your opinion, do scholarly people do? Some of the things that occur to us are:

Read books
Go to concerts
Read "good" magazines, like Atlantic Monthly,
and listen to Public Radio

Many of these activities, assuming that the reader accepts them as characteristic of the quality under consideration, will require further refinement. What books count, for example? Presumably, Harlequin Romances would not, but that's a decision left up to each individual self-improver. Can Judas Priest put on a concert? How many books or hours of public broadcasting should an intellectual be exposed to over any given period of time? The fun in coming up with operational definitions is never-ending!

Procrastination is another excellent topic for us. How would things be different if you weren't a procrastinator? There would be no more last minute cramming for exams, you might answer. This improvement would require that a certain percentage of the indicated reading and reviews be accomplished each week. Or, alternately, perhaps a fixed list of household chores would be taken care of each and every day. Again, these choices are all up to you.

So we're to down things you can count, like number of cigarettes smoked every day. And let's say your figures look like what's shown in Table 4-1. What does it mean? Kind of hard to make much of it, isn't it? Obviously, we need some device for summarizing such information or "data" in an interpretable and meaningful fashion. Entering into the picture now is one of the psychologist's favorite play things...The GRAPH.

TABLE 4-1
Day-by-Day Record of Number of Cigarettes Smoked

Day	Number
Monday	35
Tuesday	37
Wednesday	40
Thursday	30
Friday	36
Saturday	18
Sunday	17

There are two elements to what we know about this person's smoking, the number of cigarettes smoked and when he did it. So on our graph, Figure 4-1, we'll plot number of cigarettes on one axis and time, in this case days, on the other. By convention, number or amount is plotted on the up and down axis or vertical axis, the ordinate to be technical, and time is plotted on the horizontal axis, the abscissa.

Now, we've already begun to learn something about the smoking. It appears to be improved during the last two days, Saturday and Sunday.

Why? One possible explanation relates these variations to the specific days of the week in which records were kept. Assuming that you work a "normal" Monday through Friday week, then it looks like you smoke more at work than at home. Could this be because you smoke in an effort to relieve some of the work stress? Or maybe your job is just so boring that you feel the need to do something with your hands? Both explanations are possibilities, and you probably have some idea as to which might be correct. Of course, if the increase in smoking had taken place on weekends, then one would look into the possibility of tension or boredom being a problem at home. See how much fun we can have with graphs!

Figure 4-1. A Beginning Graph of a Smoking Cessation Program

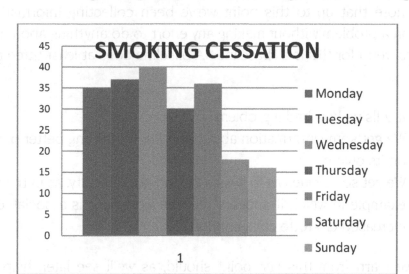

A totally different possibility is that, just maybe, the smoking is getting better, going away on its own. Not likely after a quarter of a century of puffing on the weed, you say. Granted. But from a scientific perspective, it's enough of a possibility that now wouldn't be a good time to try to do something about the problem. Someone looking at Figure 4-1 might say, "Why go to all that trouble, Bert? You were obviously giving it up before you even started your 'treatment.'" So let's count a while longer. And we wind up with Figure 4-2.

Figure 4-2. We Continue to Count

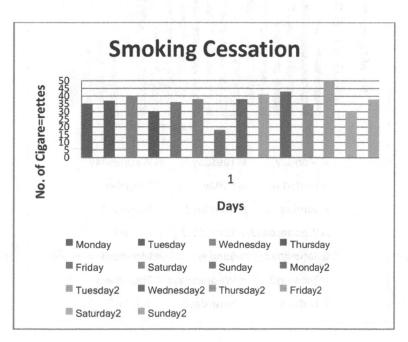

No, unfortunately, the smoking has not just gotten up and gone away. Please note that up to this point we've been collecting information or "data" on a problem without making any effort to do anything about it. The technical term for this is a "baseline." A baseline does at least three things for us:

1. It tells us how bad a problem is.
2. We get some information about whether it's getting better or worse on its own.
3. We get some clues as to what's behind our difficulty, as in the above example in which it appears that the workplace is associated with increased cigarette consumption.

What we learn from this last point should, as we'll see later, help us in devising an effective treatment for the problem.

It takes us ahead of our story a bit, but let's assume that we have developed an effective treatment or "intervention." Our data might look something like what we see in Figure 4-3.

Figure 4-3. We Treat and Continue to Count

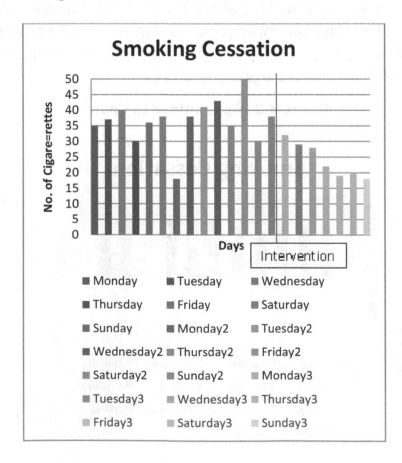

At some point the data may become so complex and confusing that we can't make much out of it. At times like this a good thing to do is to average the data by weeks. To do this, we simply total the number of cigarettes smoked during the entire week and divide through by 7. This step gives us a smoother graph and thus a clearer picture of how things are going, as shown in Figure 4-4.

Figure 4-4. A Smoother, Neater Graph by Averaging Across Weeks

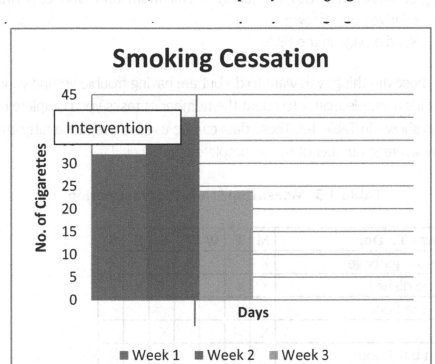

Our self-improvement project becomes more complex when we attempt to deal with more global adjustment difficulties, like not being scholarly or procrastinating. Again, the trick is to ask what would I do, expressed in definite time periods, if I were not, say, a procrastinator? One hypothetical person's answers to this question are contained in Table 4-2.

Table 4-2. Things a Non-Procrastinator Would Do Each Day

1. Take out the garbage
2. Do the dishes
3. One of the following
   a. Mop the floor
   b. Dust

    c. Vacuum

    d. Clean the bathroom

    e. Clean out the refrigerator

    f. Clean the oven

    g. Bathe the dog

    h. Wash the car

4. Read ten pages of the textbook for my American Literature course
5. Communicate with my family – call Mom and Dad or write to relatives out of town
6. Read a page in the Bible

If these are things you want to do but are having trouble getting yourself to do, it's a simple matter to count the number of tasks you complete each day, as shown in Table 4-3. These data can be used to prepare a nifty graph, of, say, average number of tasks completed each week!

Table 4-3. Measuring "Non-Procrastination"

Things To Do:	M	T	W	T	F	S	S
Take out garbage	X			X	X		X
Do the dishes	X	X		X	X	X	X
Mop the floor		X					
Dust	X				X		
Clean bathroom			X				X
Clean oven						X	
Wash dog	X						
Wash car						X	
Read 10 pages of textbook	X	X		X	X		X
Read a page in Bible	X		X	X		X	

The practice of graphing things may seem like going a bit too far. But if you think about it, perhaps you'll agree that measuring something is "half the battle." All that's left at this point is to keep trying different things until something works, as shown in Figure 4-5.

Figure 4-5. Your First Attempt Won't Always Work

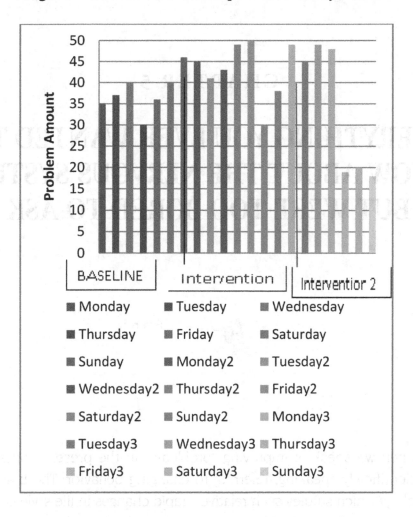

As shown in Figure 4-5, "try, try again" usually pays off in the long run.

CHAPTER 5

EVERYTHING YOU EVER WANTED TO KNOW ABOUT THE NERVOUS SYSTEM BUT WERE TOO BORED TO ASK

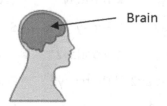

Brain

When we speak of improving "problems" in the present context we are, scientifically speaking, referring to changing behavior. The branch of psychology which studies such relatively rapid changes in life style is called "learning theory." Learning theory, as a matter of fact, is the general topic of this and the next two chapters. The intent of these chapters is to begin to give you some definite tools you can use to make rapid improvements in your life.

The part of our bodies which is involved in making short-term adjustments through learning is the nervous system. The nervous system is probably not the most fascinating topic to include in a "pop" psychology book. Perhaps that's why we're tempted to call this "un-pop"! But it is, regrettably, important to have at least a basic understanding of this rapid electro-chemical communication and coordinating apparatus of our bodies. Table 5-1 outlines the various components of the nervous system.

As shown in Table 5-1, the nervous system is composed of two main parts, the Central Nervous System, or CNS as it is so frequently abbreviated, and the Peripheral Nervous System, which for some reason is never referred to as the "PNS." The Central Nervous System is composed of the brain and the spinal cord. The brain, of course, is the organ in which we do our thinking and decision-making. The spinal cord's role is to carry the brain's decisions to the body. Fortunately for us, we don't have to consider these highly complex structures much further in order to understand the matters before us at present.

TABLE 5-1

THE NERVOUS SYSTEM

I. **Central**
   A. **Brain:** The "executive" organ
   B. **Spinal Cord:** Carries the brain's decisions to the body
II. **Peripheral**
   A. **Skeletal:** Controls the "voluntary" muscles of the body, such as the arms and legs and mouth
   B. **Autonomic :** Controls the "involuntary" functions of the body, e.g., heart and digestion
      1. **Sympathetic:** Activates the body into the "flight or flight" reaction. Such functions as heart rate and blood pressure go up.
      2. **Parasympathetic :** Calms the body into a state of relaxation. Functions such as blood pressure go down and digestion proceeds.

The most obvious part of the Peripheral Nervous System is the section labeled "skeletal." This part controls the so-called "voluntary" activities of the body, like walking, writing and speaking. Behavioral changes which we discuss under the heading of "operant," "instrumental" or perhaps "Skinnerian" conditioning are, technically, the products of learning involving this specific component of our nervous systems. Here again, we need only a vague and general knowledge that this particular part of our bodies exists.

Much, much more complex is the "Autonomic Nervous System," which controls, basically, the body's internal organs. The term "autonomic," incidentally, refers to the fact that it works automatically or out of the person's conscious control. But just because we can't simply will changes in this part of our bodies doesn't mean that we have absolutely no way to influence it. As we'll see later, we can, indeed, affect what goes on in the Autonomic Nervous System, but we can only do this indirectly and with some difficulty.

As shown in Table 5-1, the Autonomic Nervous System is divided into the Sympathetic and the Parasympathetic. Just to show you that these are not just "up in the air" theories, it is possible to specify exactly the anatomical locations of these parts of the body. The Sympathetic system emerges from the spinal cord with the nerves that come out of the thoracic and lumbar spines, the middle of the back, roughly. For this reason, this part of the nervous system is properly referred to as the "Thoraso-Lumbar System." The Parasympathetic is sometimes called the "Cranio-Sacral" nervous system because its nerves make their appearance directly from the brain, principally here the Vagus nerve, and from the sacrum, down near where we seat ourselves.

TABLE 5-2

A Comparison of the Sympathetic and Parasympathetic Portions of the Autonomic Nervous System

Organ	Sympathetic	Parasympathetic
HEART	Increases heart rate	Decreases heart rate
	Increases blood pressure	Decreases blood pressure
LUNGS	Increases rate of respiration	Decreases rate of respiration
DIGESTIVE	Suspends digestion (Generally)	Promotes digestion (Generally)
EYES	Tends to restrict focusing to distant objects	Allows focusing on close-up objects
HAIR	May cause hair to stand on end	---
MUSCLES	Creates tension, tightness, trembling	Promotes relaxation
SEX		
Female	Inhibits responsiveness, lubrication and orgasm	Promote responsiveness, lubrication and orgasm
Male	Inhibits responsiveness, stimulates ejaculation	Promotes responsiveness, erections

Table 5-2 compares the general functioning of the two components of the Autonomic Nervous System. As you review them, you will see that they are very opposite in effect. But not only are they opposite, they are also "antagonistic." This means that, in effect, they work against each other. Specifically, when the amount of stimulation in one branch increases, activity in the other declines proportionately. Much has been made of this feature of the nervous system in dealing with problems generally labeled "anxiety," among others, as we shall see.

Perhaps the question of "why" we're wired up as we are is of importance only to eggheads, but it might be interesting to speculate. And this process could even help us in understanding ourselves and becoming more flexible and creative in facing the various life difficulties with which we are confronted.

Assuming the general validity of Darwin's Theory of Evolution, we take the position that we are the way we are because a given structure or arrangement of our bodies was associated with some type of "evolutionary advantage." In other words, it contributed in some way to the survival and continuation of the species. A good example here would be our upright postures. This is most convenient for a creature who counts more on brains than brawn for survival. The erect position enabled our ancestors to make good use of their increasingly clever hands to manipulate objects to their advantage.

Returning to the nervous system, a little story, apocryphal of course, may help to illustrate how we came to be as we are:

> Return with us now to the scary days of prehistoric times. Og and Ug are walking down a jungle path. Out jumps a saber toothed tiger!
>
> Og responds to this threat with increased blood pressure and heart rate. His muscles become active. Digestion stops, so that part of the body's energy is directed to other functions. Blood comes out of the face, hands and feet and remains in the body's center. Og breathes more deeply, taking in more oxygen. These changes allow him to fight more fiercely or, as in the case of the authors' ancestors, to flee more rapidly. And if in the process Og is injured, the fact that his vital blood supply has been largely withdrawn from the outside of his body means that he'll lose less of it. This Stone Age gentleman will live to fight on other days and, not just incidentally, to reproduce between fights.
>
> Ug, on the other hand, is one laid back caveman. "Like man, a kitty," sums up his reaction to the fanged feline.
>
> By way of sparing the reader the gruesome scene, it suffices to note that we are the descendants of Og!

So we've made it to the beginning of the Twenty-First Century. But that doesn't mean that the picture is entirely rosy. Darwin selected us on the basis of our capacity to respond to physical threats. Unfortunately for modern man, most of the threats to us now are directed at our sense of self-worth, prestige or pocket books. Events like being asked to make a speech, being criticized by the boss at work, and that ultimately negative experience of being the object of special attention by the IRS come to mind here.

As we sit in front of the IRS agent peering at us over her granny glasses, our heart pounds within our chest, breathing becomes labored, we perspire and tremble, our hands and feet are like ice. You could do a super job of throttling the old hag, but that probably wouldn't be a good idea! What you're experiencing is a pattern of arousal in the Sympathetic portion of the Autonomic Nervous System. And it doesn't help us. It actually hurts us. We're too aroused and upset to do a credible job of presenting our well-planned out and eloquent explanation for why our dog is a legitimate business expense. We open our mouths, and our brains fall out, so to speak.

We hope that this admittedly dull chapter on the nervous system will give readers some insight into how we are "wired up," helping you to better understand why your bodies are responding as they are in different life situations. We really believe that such an understanding will help you exert more control over yourself, the ultimate aim here being to give you more flexibility in pursuing a comfortable and meaningful life.

CHAPTER 6

LEARNING ABOUT LEARNING

Psychologists have spent decades running rats through mazes and watching pigeons peck disks in "Skinner Boxes." Most of these experiments have been conducted in order to prove one or another theory as to how the behavior of organisms is modified through the process we call "learning." This chapter adopts a much less pedantic tone and seeks only to give you some information about the processes of learning to assist you in making desirable changes in your own lifestyle. The good news here is that such changes are possible in spite of past learned, unhelpful behaviors/relationships.

Continuing with the evolutionary perspective we adopted in discussing the nervous system, it is, quite obviously, adaptive, it has importance for survival, to do things that result in "good" things happening to us. A good example here is picking up the phone to order a pizza when we're hungry. Shortly after this action, a delivery person appears at our door and gives us a steaming, tasty pie which, at least in the short run, improves the quality of our lives. We say, technically, that the behavior of calling the pizza place to put in an order has been rewarded, or "positively reinforced." The fact that the delicious food was, in fact, brought to us shortly after we phoned in the order makes it more likely that we will repeat this action the next time we feel the pangs of hunger. That's how "Positive Reinforcement," or just plain "reward" if you prefer, works. It increases the probability that whatever behavior it follows will be repeated in the future. We've learned here to phone a particular restaurant when we're hungry.

But this habit of calling a certain pizza place isn't necessarily "written in stone." What do you think would happen if one day you phoned the restaurant and ordered your favorite pizza, and yet an hour went by without the deliverer appearing at your doorstep? Certainly, you'd be frustrated, perhaps even angry. You'd probably phone up the restaurant and suggest in your own way they "get on the stick." But still no pizza. At this point a call to another pizzeria would seem to be in order.

Would you ever call the "No Show Pizza Joint" again? Maybe. You might figure that they, like everyone else, just had an off night. So you might give them a second chance. But if they repeated their no show performance several times, that particular Italian restaurant would, without doubt, be off your speed dialer!

The purpose of the above example is to show you that learning, or "conditioning," tends not to bring about an eternal change in one's behavior. Just as you learned by being reinforced by the pleasure of eating a delicious pizza to call a particular Italian restaurant, you went on to learn not to call that restaurant when they let you down several times. Psychologists, by the way, call the process of learning not to do something you had previously learned to do "extinction."

The other side of the picture is learning not to do something you might naturally be inclined to do. Og, our great, great, great...grandfather was walking down the jungle path, alone now after Ug was eaten. He was hungry, and the red berries looked pretty good to him. So down they went. But pretty soon they came back up again, accompanied by some reasonably severe digestive complaints. No more of the red berries for Og! He had learned not to eat them. As we say, he was "punished" for downing those red berries.

Thus far we've introduced the two great principles of learning, reward and punishment. Of course, there's nothing too dramatic in what's been presented here. These facts of human behavior are so well known that they're sometimes called "Grandma's Laws." After all, she knew from long years of experience to give you a piece of her wonderful cherry pie after you did your chores and not before. And if you did something seriously out of line, there were consequences!

But while the general principles of reward and punishment are quite straightforward and simple, many of the details are not. These learning phenomena are, in fact, so complex that there are times when they don't appear to work. For example, good academic work is rewarded with A's and sometimes money and treats by parents. Why, then, don't kids do better in school? On a longer-range basis, the completion of higher education is strongly associated with higher earnings. Why don't more people stay in school? Speeding on the highways is punished with expensive tickets and higher insurance rates. Then why do we see so many speeders on the roads? Excessive drinking brings about hangovers and physical problems like liver disease. Overweight people get fewer "strokes" than do their trimmer peers. Why then...well, you get the idea.

But before we get into some of the apparent contradictions between how we would expect things to work and how they actually do, there are several more learning phenomena we need to discuss.

We have seen that reinforcement is the process by which the future probability of a behavior is increased. The specific kind of reinforcement we've been looking at is "positive reinforcement." This is when you give a person something she or he likes following that person's doing something positive. Grandmother telling you that you're a "good boy" and giving you a piece of pie when you hang up your coat after school is a perfect example of positive reinforcement.

But there's a different type of reinforcement called "negative reinforcement." This is not punishment. Embarrassingly, even some psychologists get punishment and negative reinforcement mixed up. Remember, reinforcers make activities more likely to be repeated, and punishers make them less so. Negative reinforcement is in operation when a certain behavior enables you to escape or avoid something unpleasant. These two types of negative reinforcement are called "escape" and "avoidance" learning. Don't psychologists apply clever names?

A child who doesn't like school and frequently complains of vague aches and pains may be an example of escape conditioning. She has probably learned that griping about a stomach ache is good for a trip down to the nurse's office and sometimes all the way back home. In either case, she's allowed to escape, if only briefly, from the classroom environment she seems to experience as being so oppressive.

If this kid plays her cards right, she might even graduate to avoidance conditioning. If she catches on to the idea of raising the issue of her physical problems before first bell, she might even avoid school altogether!

Table 6-1 summarizes the main types of learning for your future reference.

TABLE 6-1. The Main Types of Learning

I.   Reinforcement: It increases the likelihood that whatever behavior it follows will occur again in the future.

   A. Positive: A "desirable" object or event that has reinforcing properties when it follows the desired behavior

   B. Negative: The removal or avoidance of an event or condition is the reinforcer.

      1. Escape: The behavior is reinforced by permitting the individual to remove herself from an unpleasant situation.

      2. Avoidance: The individual learns to take action to avoid entirely some unpleasant situation or condition.

II. Punishment: The delivery of an undesirable stimulus or situation which decreases the likelihood that the person will repeat the behavior which preceded the punishment

Well, you might say, if it were that simple, then it should be a pretty easy matter to arrange the world so that people "do right." But, as we've seen, most of us "fall through the cracks" of learning at one time or another, sometimes in major and disastrous ways. Some of the reasons that we frequently don't make our behavior conform to the "rules" of life with their seemingly clear and powerful rewards and punishments are:

1. Inconsistency/Lack of Clarity: This problem comes up most dramatically in the rearing of children. A kid may be genuinely taken aback for having been called down during an adult's visit earlier on during the evening. He may not, indeed probably wouldn't, have recognized that the turned around collar the soft-spoken elderly man was wearing was a signal that his parents wanted and expected a higher degree of angelic behavior than during Uncle Jack's frequent drop-ins during the cocktail hour.

    The "beastly brother" of such a lack of clarity is inconsistency. This is where, for instance, one parent has one set of rules and the other parent enforces an entirely different set of standards. But, as we'll see, such inconsistency can also exist within the very same "lawgiver," giving rise to even more devastating effects.

It doesn't take a rocket scientist to understand how lack of clarity and inconsistency make the disciplining of children an impossible task.

After all, if the rules keep changing, no pattern of behavior the child might display is going to always be rewarded. Sometimes, what was "good" yesterday will actually meet with negative consequences today. And children lack the cognitive complexity to recognize that one set of rules is in effect now, but another will be operative later. Unfortunately, it appears that the capacity to make such distinctions, or "discriminations" as psychologists phrase them, does not automatically spring forth on one's eighteenth or twenty-first birthday.

The "worst case scenario" of parental inconsistency is the substance-abusing mom or dad, an all too common kind of parent to be assigned to by fate. The reactions of, say, an alcoholic parent are more determined by her or his blood alcohol level than the child's behavior. When Dad has a hangover, as he does on a lot of mornings, even practicing the piano will be greeted with, "Cut that infernal racket out, you little _____!" Not a very high level of either art appreciation or encouragement, is it? But let the Old Man get tanked up and everything tickles him. This includes writing on the wall and using the crystal punch bowl in little Johnnie's coin-tossing game. How's a child to adjust? He can't.

We've gotten now into something which has, deservedly, attracted a great deal of attention in recent years, the matter of "Adult Children of Alcoholics (ACOA)." The authors have had occasion to work with a number of ACOA's, and it seems to us that they share a number of strikingly common characteristics:

1. Low "self-esteem"
2. Frequent and sometimes alarming bouts of depression
3. A haunting sense of guilt
4. A feeling of uncertainty and lack of optimism about the future
5. Frequent periods in which it is difficult to motivate oneself to "get going," as it were
6. The belief, often in the face of overwhelming evidence to the contrary, that one is incompetent
7. An all-pervasive sense of helplessness

Why do all these undesirable and excruciating mental problems befall someone just because a parent happened to regularly ingest an intoxicant? Part of the answer to this question may relate to Rogerian incongruence, which we discussed in the chapter on intimacy. Clearly, a parent in the throes of an addictive disorder would not be a sensitive and active listener, to put it mildly. Additionally, an alcoholic parent may affect a child's thinking about himself directly. All too frequently, substance abusers descend to the level of openly blaming their children for their problems in life, including and specifically their pattern of substance abuse.

But it seems to be in the area that we're considering now, learning theory, that we find the bulk of the answers to our questions about the cause of the problems of the children of alcoholics (as well as other substance abusers). In order to understand what appears to be happening here, we must take a detour into the animal lab. Martin Seligman (1942 -) and his colleagues conducted a series of studies which help us explain rather neatly what befalls on ACOA.

The psychologists utilized in this experiment a piece of apparatus called a "shuttle box." The basic experimental procedure involved placing a dog in one side of the box. At some point, the grid floor was electrified. The dog, of course, will hop to the other side of the box. If you're keeping score, this is "escape conditioning." A variant on this study is to illuminate a light on one side of the box a few seconds before electrifying the grid floor, thus warning the subject of the impending unpleasant experience. A clever dog will, obviously, jump to the other side upon seeing the light, thus demonstrating "avoidance conditioning."

A modification in the shuttle box allows us to see the effect we are interested in, which Seligman labeled "learned helplessness." A plexiglass screen was installed above the barrier. Thus, the dog could see the safe area on the other side but was prevented from reaching it. Some of the dogs were placed in the shuttle box with the screen up. This was their initial exposure to the device. They were, thus, shocked with no opportunity to avoid or escape this unpleasantness.

When the screen was removed, a startling and instructive thing occurred. When the dogs were shocked, they didn't jump! They simply crouched on the floor and whined. Because they had been exposed to a situation in which the shock was inescapable, they continued to act like they were still trapped, even though it was not so. Seligman had taught the dogs to be helpless, to accept an awful situation without making the least effort to improve it. The animals, in fact, looked depressed.

Seligman's studies give us a reasonably clear model of what happens to the child of a substance abuser. Since the child is treated on the basis of the level of the abused substance in the parent's system instead of the boy or girl's own actions, there is no way to reliably earn rewards and avoid punishments. So the ACOA was exposed to the same kind of unavoidable unpleasantness that the dogs had experienced. And they tend to respond in a similar, helpless fashion. This helps us understand why we see the bright young lady moping around her apartment when all of her friends can and do suggest so many things that she could work on to improve her lot in life. Her friends may not even know that her mother went on "toots," and if they are aware of this they probably don't see any connection between that and Judy's depressed lassitude. Perhaps we can now discern such a connection.

Unfortunately for the off-springs of "dry" parents, it isn't necessary to be a substance abuser to be an inconsistent disciplinarian. Inconsistency in the use of rewards and punishments, whatever its cause, is ineffective and may, as in the case of Judy, have seriously negative long-term consequences.

A particularly devastating form of inconsistency can even teach children to scream and demand things they're not supposed to have. Witness the following supermarket scene:

"Mommy, can I have a candy bar?"

"No."

"Why?"

"Your room is a mess. I told you to pick it up. You always want me to do things for you, but you don't do anything for Daddy and me. You just don't take responsibility for your own behavior. And you're almost eight years old. I'd be ashamed."

"I'm hungry. You didn't feed me enough lunch."

"I took you to Burger Heaven and let you order anything you wanted."

"You didn't give me time to finish."

"Yes, I did."

"I'm hungry."

"Sh-h-h…"

"I want a candy bar. WAAAAAA"

"Oh, if you're going to be that way about it, take the blankity-blank thing. Here!"

So Mom tosses a candy bar to Junior. She's also tossed away one lesson and tossed another his way. Can you guess what these lessons were?

This mother is going on the concept that her son should just immediately accept what she says when she says it. Consistency has gone out the window. What she has actually taught Junior is persistence… persistence at demanding what he wants. Note that he didn't get the candy bar the first time he asked for it. He had to demand, yell and scream. Next time he wants something he'll do the same thing because he's learned that nothing less is effective.

Is that what Mommy wanted to teach Junior?

By way of summary, one of the major reasons that rewards and punishments appear not to work is that they are applied inconsistently and in an unclear manner. What we need to do, clearly, is to make sure the "rules" for ourselves and for others we are in a position to ask changes in behavior from are 1) clear to all concerned and 2) applied in a routine and invariable manner. We'll have more to say about all this later on.

2. Competing reinforcers: Unfortunately for our purposes, parents and teachers don't control all of the reinforcers in town. There are other rewards available to our children, and these other positive reinforcers often compete with the ones we are offering to them.

There are two facets to this problem in the use of rewards and punishments, or the "contingencies" as they are technically called. The first of these involves simple and direct competition. Practicing the piano may, indeed and for example, be rewarded by praise and an ice cream cone, but playing football outside with the boys is even more fun. So out Billy goes. We have to make sure that whatever reward we are offering is more powerful than its competition. And we know that when it <u>works</u>. No one in his right mind would clean a bathroom for a penny, but a thousand dollars would work for most of us "Everyday Joes," to use an overdrawn example.

The other and overlapping factor relates to what is termed the "gradient of reinforcement." This component of what we know about learning refers to the fact that the more immediate a reward is the more powerful it is. An informal but "classic" experiment illustrates this phenomenon nicely. An adult went to every class in an elementary school. She offered all of the kids the following deal, "I'll give you a nickel if you'd like. Or, I'll come back tomorrow and give you a quarter. Which will it be?" Many of the children chose the nickel now even though they were being offered a five hundred percent interest rate over a twenty-four hour period. What's interesting is that more of the younger children than those who were older passed up this phenomenal investment opportunity. Wonder how little Donnie Trump handled that one?

So opting for the quarter, or "deferment of gratification" as our friends over in the Department of Sociology call it, increases with age. Even so, not all of the youngsters, even in the higher grades, were willing to defer the joy of having something to put in their jeans <u>today</u>. And it's probably fair to say that none of us gets totally mature in all areas. Otherwise, we'd all be in outstanding physical shape, have plenty of money in the bank, etc. So one person may be able to scrimp to near-starvation in order to get through medical school but be unable to force himself to exercise. Another person, though, exercises regularly but can't make it through a survey course in junior college. We're all different and unique, but, again, it's probably safe to say that we all have trouble delaying gratification in one area, if not more.

In summary, then, the rewards authority figures offer are frequently ineffective both because there are competing reinforcers available in the natural environment and also because these unplanned reinforcements are quicker than those offered by, say, teachers.

3. Ratio strain. This is a frequently overlooked cause of failure in the reinforcement contingencies set up by our society.

In order to understand ratio strain, we have to know about a little wrinkle in the use of positive reinforcement. The standard device that behavioral scientists have used for decades in studying learning was invented by B. F. Skinner (1904 – 1990), who christened it an "operant conditioning chamber." Everyone else calls it a Skinner Box. One of these is pictured at the beginning of this chapter.

The two main features of this apparatus are a lever which a rat can press and a food tray in which the subject can be rewarded for doing so. The simplest rule for delivering rewards, obviously, is to give the rat a food pellet every time the lever is depressed. Since the reward is delivered every time the bar press response occurs, this is called "continuous reinforcement."

It is, though, possible to induce such laboratory animals to perform tasks without delivering rewards on a continuous basis. After a number of rewarded lever presses the experimenter may change the contingencies to where only every other press is reinforced with a pellet of food. Your standard university albino rat is able to adjust to this shift in reward schedule quite nicely. At this point, it's possible to shift to a schedule in which only every third or fourth bar press is rewarded with a food pellet. And from this level, it's possible to slowly and progressively "lean" the schedule of reinforcement to where hundreds of bar presses are required to obtain a single pellet of food.

But what would have happened had the psychologist simply shifted the schedule from continuous reinforcement to one in which three hundred bar presses were necessary to get any food? Following such a radical shift, our four-legged subject would press several times and, in the absence of what he was looking for, "give up." Even though food would have been forthcoming after the addition of a mere 296 bar presses, the response becomes "extinguished." Skinnerians like to say that "The rat is always right." Certainly in this case, the experimenter was decidedly "wrong." Something was demanded of the rat that it simply wasn't up to delivering. The animal had fallen through the schedule of reinforcement "cracks," as it were. We might say by way of summary that too much was expected of the little beast. This is "ration strain."

The closest thing to a Skinner Box for humans is our educational system. One possible way to look at instructional techniques, it is argued, is on the basis of schedules of reinforcement. The early years, say kindergarten and first grade, entail a very generous and rich pattern of rewards. Early elementary teachers are known for their continuous streams of "That's great!" and "What a beautiful horse you've drawn!" They must own stock in the companies that print up those little smiley faces.

The other end of the pole is graduate education where the rewards, we can testify from personal experience, are few and far between. Perhaps the extreme of a lean schedule of reinforcement for a human is the way students are dealt with, reportedly, when they attempt to get doctorates from British universities. They are given a list of books and told to come back in a few years for exams!

In general, the years between kindergarten and Ph.D. training are marked by less and less immediate reinforcement of academic behaviors. Teachers increasingly encourage "independence," which may actually be another way of saying the same thing. This, for a variety of reasons, certainly appears to be a good and appropriate way to deal with these issues. After all, we'd raise our eyebrows if the professor stuck an orange happy face on the cast the senior medical student had just placed on our ski-busted leg!

But what happens if the schedule of reinforcement in school is leaned suddenly and unexpectedly? Might ratio strain set in? The authors believe that we've actually seen this occur, so we would answer "yes" to that question.

When one of us started college at the University of Georgia way back in 1964, in his classes were a number of kids from small Georgia towns. They had been graduated from high schools in classes as small as five or six students. They were regarded as "brilliant," and everyone in their communities openly expressed the hope and belief that Sally or George would "put our little town on the map." Their teachers had worked with these students daily, even hourly, in their efforts to help them along in achieving such ambitions. They were the recipients of lavish measures of attention, praise and encouragement.

But things were radically different at the University! These youngsters found themselves in two or three hundred seat lecture halls. There were only two tests during the entire quarter. And you wrote your student number, not your name, on the answer sheet. I was 94375. And I had to show my student ID to the proctor to prove it, too!

I saw many of the kids from places like Comer and Willacoochee lying around their dorm rooms looking quite depressed. They should have been in class but weren't. Some never even made it back for Winter Quarter. The shift from constant structure and warm support to the impersonal state university atmosphere was too much of a shock for them. Many had fallen victim, we now realize in looking back, to ratio strain.

The last two mentioned factors, competing reinforcers, particularly when the gradient of reinforcement is figured into the equation, and ratio strain raise a general point for our consideration. There are so frequently in life goals and changes in styles of living that are so obviously desirable that it would be so wonderful if we had, in fact, achieved them. Losing weight, the completion of a program of exercise and finishing a degree program are examples that come readily to mind here. But despite their extreme worthiness, we just don't seem able to accomplish them. And we're often puzzled as to why. "I know I want to practice law like crazy, but I just can't get myself to wade through that book on torts. What's wrong with me?"

What's wrong with Mike is that, as we might put it, too much work is being asked for the reward currently and visibly being offered. "They only put in a nickel, but they want a dollar song," is the reaction here.

We'll see that we quite frequently need to "trick ourselves" into persisting at long-term projects. The primary manner of accomplishing this goal is to break such seemingly insurmountable tasks into small steps and devise and work into our lives rewards for the accomplishments of such "baby steps." This set of techniques will, in fact, be a major focus in our later consideration of the usefulness of applied learning theory.

A Touch of Subtly

Like in most fields, the early days of approaches to human problems based on what we've gleaned from the results of studies from learning laboratories involved some rather crude techniques. Children were rewarded for sitting still with pieces of candy and Kool-Aide. Head-bangers were punished with shocks from cattle prods.

Increasingly, efforts are being made to make both rewards and punishments less dramatic and contrived. This is important not only because it makes the development of contingencies more convenient and less expensive, but also, for a number of reasons which go beyond the scope of this book, the use of such naturally-occurring and appearing consequences promotes the transfer of what is learned to other times and settings.

The obvious rewards, things like food, are called "primary reinforcers." They are thus called because they directly satisfy a basic, primary need, a "tissue need" if you will. But we've learned over the years that you don't have to feed someone to reward them.

The first type of more subtle reward we will consider is called "secondary reinforcement." This type of reinforcement is in use when we give some easily transferrable object which can later be exchanged for specific goods our learner might desire. Money, come to think of it, is an excellent example of a secondary reinforcer.

Systems of secondary reinforcement in schools, hospitals and even in homes are frequently referred to as "token economies." This is so because the original forms of these systems used metal tokens as the secondary reinforcer. Whenever a staff member observed some desirable behavior on the ward, the patient would be slipped one of these metal objects. When enough tokens had been accumulated, they could be spent at the ward token store for whatever the individual might choose.

The use of this type of secondary reward has two obvious advantages: 1) it is clearly more convenient than carrying around a bag of primary reinforcers and 2) it allows the same delivered reward to be useful for several different people. Mary, for instance, likes bubble gum, while Jane is a fruit lover. Both can have their good behavior rewarded with tokens which they can spend for whatever "floats their boat." We'll also find that a token system may enable us to break a large reward down into a number of smaller rewards. There might be a carnival in town which the children are most anxious to attend. Asking them to be good all week to earn this treat is probably expecting a bit much. It induces ratio strain. But what we can do is offer them "points" which they can get by accomplishing certain desirable tasks, like cleaning up their rooms and doing their homework. A set number of points is then required for them to be given the privilege of going to the carnival. We'll have more to say about this technique in the next chapter.

Rewards can be symbolic. Stars and happy faces are kindergarten examples of positive reinforcement that can't be eaten or played with. And yet children seem to relish them. Adults are, it would seem, particularly responsive to symbolic rewards, like keys to the executive washroom. In one firm, to show the ridiculous importance of this factor, vice presidents were rewarded with fully carpeted offices. At one point it was found necessary to move a lower level manager into an office that had formerly been occupied by a vice president. Workmen were sent to remove a strip of carpeting from around the baseboard!

The graphs we use to chart progress in overcoming some behavioral problems may even have reinforcing properties in and of themselves! There's the famous case of tricitillamania, self-hair pulling. This one woman had gotten into the habit, nervous in nature we would expect, of twisting her hair around her fingers as she studied and on other stressful occasions. In the process she had pulled out so much of her hair that she had to wear a wig. This was not a circumstance that would make her feel good about herself, of course. Her therapist instructed her to count the number of hairs she pulled out and to plot that number. When she brought in the graph of what was to have been a "baseline," it showed the number of hairs extracted declining steadily to zero. And, indeed, her hair was beginning to look a lot fuller. This outcome "blew" the psychologist's neat, experimental design, but it certainly was a wonderful thing for the client. At least part of this outcome probably related to the woman's pleasure at seeing the graph line go down, which rather directly indicated an improvement in her much-valued appearance. Another component, though, was likely to have been that counting hairs is a tedious task, and one "thinks twice" about doing something that creates such work for oneself. We'll discuss this aspect of the cure later under the heading of "response cost."

A powerful and often overlooked, and incidentally a supremely inexpensive, reward is attention. A pat on the back, a kind word, a "good going" have powerful reinforcing and motivating properties for kids of all ages. Why this form of reward is not used more often and generously than it is a mystery to most of us. It probably relates to the statistically-based illusion that makes it appear that criticism is a better way to improve performance than praise. But it isn't so, so catch someone being good and tell them about it.

Lightening the Dark Side of the Equation: Punishment

Punishment is, regrettably, a necessity in the management of human behavior. It's undoubtedly overused in most cases, but, as we'll see, there are times when it simply can't be avoided. Even when justified, though, it's unpleasant, particularly in the most spontaneous forms as in the spanking of children. This manner of disciplining children creates strains in the parent-child relationship, and it may even have the effect of teaching the child to take out his frustrations and anger at others in a violent manner. It would seem that we need some gentler forms of punishment, and that's exactly the issue that this section seeks to address.

1. Time Out. Time out, technically and instructively called "time out from positive reinforcement," is probably the first and gentlest of the subtle punishment procedures. It's theoretically pretty simple, but like so many things, it's often a lot more difficult to actually carry out. The basic principle is to punish someone by making them leave a rewarding, "fun" setting and go to one that is "un-fun." The classic self-help attempt at this technique comes into play when a child is misbehaving. The parent may send her to her room. The idea here, of course, is that this step is aversive to the child. This makes sense intuitively, but it may not actually work out like that in practice. Cindy's room may have a TV and a stereo. All her playthings are there, and she may even have a phone. This is time out from positive reinforcement? Think about it!

As we've pointed out so often, the principle method for determining whether or not you've really used time out, or any other behavioral procedure for that matter, relates back to the phrase, "The rat is always right." If banishing someone to a specific place decreases the offending behavior, then time out has, in fact, been employed. But there's always the possibility of "Throwing Br'ier Rabbit into the briar patch." This happened repeatedly to one of the authors during his days as a highly active elementary school pupil. The teacher would send him out into the hall for minor rule infractions. Out there it was possible to talk with counterparts from across the hall. You could watch the comings and goings of visitors to the office, and I became the first kid in my class to find out what the inside of a Coca-Cola machine looked like. It wasn't so bad, after all.

2. Overcorrection. This mild punishment is based on the intuitively sound idea that if a person isn't doing such a hot job of taking care of something that person probably needs practice at that particular job. A child who can't seem to hang up her coat as she comes home after school needs to practice hanging up her coat. About ten times of walking in with the coat and hanging it up in the closet should do. Janet will probably make it a point to put her brown jacket on the peg tomorrow! And it certainly doesn't look like punishment. We're weak in this area, so we're simply practicing in an effort to overcome this deficit! That's the American way of making improvements in problems. After all, practice makes perfect.

3. Increasing "response cost." This technique relies on the principle that we're less likely to do things that require a great deal of effort or some other aversive state like embarrassment or self-depreciation. A good example of increasing response cost is a technique used by many successful dieters. They only keep in the house foods that would require extensive preparation, like whole chickens and cake mixes. If they become "hungry," there are no munchies to grab. They'd have to break out the frying pan or mixing bowl in order to eat. Often, that's just too much trouble.

The Ultimate in Subtly: The Premack Principle

A psychologist, David Premack (1925 -) by name, some years ago was working with a class of children. Being a good behavior modifier, his initial idea was to give the kids "blockbuster" rewards for their good deeds, things like M&Ms and plastic animals. But, surprisingly for a psychologist, he learned by watching the kids that some of the things he wouldn't have thought would be fun or rewarding to them in fact were. One of these was that the students enjoyed pushing him around in his swivel chair!

From these observations, Premack came up with a "Reinforcement Menu." The rule was that when one of the children did something "good," like completing a math assignment or going for a period of time without creating a disturbance, that child was allowed to make a selection from the menu. It worked quite well. The summary statement that Dr. Premack came up with to put together what he had observed was, "Any low probability behavior can be reinforced by a behavior of higher probability."

Just to make sure we understand the Premack Principle, let's look at an extreme kind of illustration. Suppose we had a large room with two tables. Suppose further that on one of the tables are placed a number of math and other school workbooks. The table across the room, though, has on it the latest in toys for kids today, the GI Joes and Barbie Dolls of the Twenty-First Century, whatever they may be. When, say, seven and eight year old children are allowed into the room, to which table do you think they would go? It doesn't take a genius to figure that one out! Another way to phrase this situation is to say that playing with toys is a "high probability behavior," whereas completing workbooks is a "low probability behavior." And if, as the Premack Principle states, a high probability behavior can be used to reinforce a behavior of lower probability, then it follows that allowing the kids to play at the toy laden table can be used as a reinforcer for working on the academic materials. And that's precisely what we might do. We can say that the completion of so many pages in a workbook will be rewarded with so much time at the play table.

One of the authors used the Premack Principle in his attempts to deal with the demands of a job he once had. He was working in a mental health center which, for various reasons, had more paperwork than the Pentagon. A particularly onerous task in that job involved a long, complex form which was required to close cases. This form had to be filed out even if the person had been seen only once, or, as so often happened to him, just for a psychological evaluation. Most staff members allowed these forms to pile up until they received a nasty note from the central office. They would then have to face the unappealing prospect of spending several hours in the exquisite boredom of completing a pile of Forms Whatever They Were.

Not wishing to subject myself to that duration and intensity of pain, I vowed to fill out these forms as the need arose. But that, to put it mildly, is an easier thing to decide to do than to actually do. What I did, following the Premack Principle, was to make myself fill out one, just one, of those forms at the beginning of my free hour each morning. Then and only then would I permit myself to do something I find enjoyable, pouring myself my morning cup of coffee and reading a professional article or book for about fifteen minutes.

Apparently, this author's enjoyment of reading psychology articles and books is not universal among people in this profession. One colleague "punished" himself for high probability behaviors like smoking with the, for him, low probability behavior of reading an article in a psychology journal.

Come to think of it, maybe it's the coffee that was liked! In any case, the Premack Principle provides a promising and convenient "rule" for the modification of our own behavior, and that of others as well.

However and as powerful as these behavioral techniques may potentially be, we must keep them within the perspective of our overall holistic and promotion of self-determination orientation. As Victor Frankl said, "Between stimulus and response there is a space. In that space is our power to choose our response. In our response lies our growth and our freedom." As will be discussed later, scientific understanding and procedures are most effectively employed when we choose positive goals that enhance not only our own lives but those of others as well. We'll attempt to integrate the learning principles covered in this chapter into our overall efforts to improve ourselves and our relationships in the course of moving toward such transcendent goals as this work goes forward.

CHAPTER 7

CASE STUDIES IN THE CONTROL AND CHANGING OF BEHAVIOR

TIME OUT CHAIR

The purpose of this chapter is to illustrate the use of various principles in the modification of problems. It's hoped that the reader will be able to extract from these examples some ideas as to how to go about changing those behaviors which are causing problems for her.

A Positive Approach: Reward

<u>Primary Reinforcement</u>

3:15 PM.

School is out, and the kids come barging in. Their coats go on the floor, as usual. You're already irritated with them. Walking through the house this morning you found toys strewn all around Becky's room. And Bill's bed wasn't made, as he's supposed to do.

But you're trying so hard to make this "househusband thing" work while your wife is away on assignment. So you smile at the little darlings.

"How was school today?"

"Okay."

"What did you do?"

"Nothing. Hey, what's for snack?"

"Here's some apple pie and milk."

"Yea!" Gobble, gobble.

You go back to your drawing board to work on the plans Mr. Stanton commissioned as they have their snack while watching The Flintstones.

"I think that's what the Ol' Boy wanted," you finally conclude to yourself.

You walk back into the den. They're gone. You won't see them again until the next meal. You pick up their coats and toys. Foiled again!

Could this have gone any better?

3:15 PM

"What's for snack?"

"Nothing."

"Nothing? Nothing!"

"Yep. I haven't made you a snack just like you kids haven't picked up after yourselves."

Some minutes and the wondrous sounds of children throwing toys into baskets, etc. later...

"Here you are, fresh apple pie."

"Yea." Gobble, gobble.

This little story illustrates an often overlooked point. A parent doesn't have to yell and scream in order to get children to do what you wish. A calm, matter-of-fact and firm use of the contingencies is what's called for.

Secondary Reinforcement

Maude and Mark, the teenaged children of Myrtle and Mack, have a number of chores to do each day. The tasks are listed on the "point sheet" shown in Figure 7-1. A star is given for each completed chore. You can see how flexible the system is.

FIGURE 7-1

A Point Sheet for Maude and Mark

Maude

Task	M	T	W	TH	F	S	SU
Make bed	*	*	*				
Dress within 15 minutes of being awakened	*	*	*				
Hang up clothes after school			*				
Walk dog	*	*	*				
Vacuum house (x5)							

Mark

	M	T	W	TH	F	S	SU
Make bed	*	*	*				
Don't use poor language like "ain't"			*				
Take out trash	*	*	*				
Keep room neat	*	*	*				
Wash car (x5)							

There's a partially different set of chores for each child. This reflects the specific needs and weaknesses of the two individuals. Obviously, Maude has a problem with "dawdling" In the mornings, while little Mark's language could be cleaned up. Both have some rather standard chores to which they need to attend. The "x5" by "vacuum house" and "wash car" means that five stars are awarded for these tasks. They are, after all, more demanding and time-consuming than are the others. And they don't need to be done as often.

The way this system works evolved from the fact that Sunday afternoon, after church to be specific, was "kids' time." That meant an outing for Maude and Mark. This system dates back to their early primary school days. They were taken to a pizza restaurant that featured rides and games. The number of these activities purchased for Mark and Maude related to the number of stars on their charts. Nowadays the parents have to be more inventive. They typically give several dollars for each star. The monies help with the kids' Saturday evening dates.

Attention and Symbolic Rewards

Remember, "You're getting to be such a big boy" is always free.

For some reason, hard of comprehension to responsibility-ridden adults, children actually <u>want</u> to grow up! Thus, paradoxical though it may seem, adult-like responsibilities may even function as a reward. So a parent can actually get some mileage out of things like allowing a child to walk to school alone and taking the dog for a walk. Think about it!

On the Slightly Darker Side: Negative Reinforcement

Negative reinforcement, it will hopefully be recalled, is a reward involving the removal of an aversive stimulus. There are two variants on this theme, escape and avoidance.

Escape

Perhaps the simplest example of escape conditioning is the wise practice of some parents in requiring their children to remain inside on sunny days until they've completed their chores. Conceptualized in this way, the confinement of being inside, analogous to the electrified floor of the shuttle box, is the aversive stimulus. Completing the chores is the desirable behavior which allows little Johnny to escape.

Avoidance

Please recall that avoidance conditioning involves a situation in which desirable behavior allows a person to avoid altogether a certain unpleasantness. A good example of this type of learning would involve instructing a child that her room has to be neat and she has to be off to school on time. If these things don't happen, then she's the one who does the dishes after supper. Otherwise, Good Ol' Dad will do them. Thus taking care of these little morning chores allows Sandy to avoid entirely the later onerous task of doing the dishes.

Punishment: The dark side, but we're trying to lighten it

The procedure involved in punishment is to cause an undesirable behavior to be followed by an aversive stimulus, thus decreasing the future probability of the offending actions. Punishment is many things, but nothing is more true of this behavioral procedure than that it's overused.

Among punishment's undesirable characteristics is that it merely suppresses behavior. This means, basically, that it doesn't actually modify people's behavioral inclinations. It teaches them, rather, to restrain themselves under certain circumstances, such as in the presence of the punisher. One of the authors suffered through a most difficult year with a highly punishing teacher. She would yell at us with such intensity that the veins would literally bulge in her neck. We were afraid of her and with good reason too. No one misbehaved while she was in the room. But let her step out and "all "heck" broke loose. We had learned to fear, not to be young ladies and gentlemen!

The other undesirable facets to punishment are the interference with the relationship between the punisher and the punished and the possible instruction and perpetuation of violent attempts at controlling the behavior of others. The complaints about punishment merely suppressing bad behavior appear to be universally supported by the studies on this question which have been conducted. The other two potential problems are not so clear. It seems that they don't, in fact, occur in every case. But just the mere possibility of such devastating consequences should convince people that punishment should be utilized with the utmost of caution.

The consensus among workers in this area is that rewards should be used about four times as much as punishments. Unfortunately, most of us fall far short of that standard. The authors have seen the sign "4 x 1" in the offices of behavior modifiers. That sign is worthy of more extensive reproduction than it has thus far been accorded. But, again, given that there are times when punishment is unavoidable, we discuss below several ways to make its use less oppressive.

But a little caveat needs to be acknowledged before considering the gentler forms of punishment.

The Old Fashioned Way: Spare the Rod and Spoil the Child

One of the authors observed a dramatic experience which vividly illustrated for him the fact that the more refined punishments may not be applicable in and to all cases. A young boy (4 to 6 years old) displayed the most distressing habit of running across parking lots. This problem climaxed in the little tyke darting across a hospital parking lot. The vision of an ambulance pulling in at breakneck speed or a distraught individual hurrying a loved one to the ER literally flashed through the author's mind. The threatening of the withholding of privileges for this behavior was not considered to be, to reuse an overused phrase, a "viable option." This child had proven from other disciplinary attempts to require a number of trials in behavioral corrections. It would not be overstating the case to suggest that the little fellow would probably be in the ICU long before such a gentle process would have worked.

What the parent did in this case was to tackle the boy and apply his hand to the child's buttocks repeatedly and vigorously. The happy part of this story is that it worked, and the little boy, now an adult and in good health, later took to admonishing other youngsters, "Don't run in parking lots."

All of the above is simply by way of saying that there are those emergency situations, usually involving safety issues, in which it is so imperative that behavior be immediately suppressed that drastic "old-fashioned" punishment appears to be justified, even demanded. It is, though, advisable to take this step in consultation with and in the presence of another responsible adult. There are three main reasons for this suggestion. Firstly, speaking about the matter with a second person helps give some assurance that the punishing parent is proceeding in a justified manner and not just working out his own frustrations. The second advantage relates to the time required to enact this recommendation, which tends to allow some of the emotionality to soften. And finally and regrettable to note, in this age of legal accusations and interfering social agencies, an observer's presence affords some protection against such things as child abuse charges.

But, fortunately, such emergent situations are rare, and tamer procedures than spanking are usually applicable.

Time Out and Overcorrection

To illustrate a more subtle, less place-bound use of "time-out" (this time combined with overcorrection) than was presented in the last chapter, one of the authors once did a demonstration project in a school in which the use of punishment was absolutely forbidden. The class in which he was working took an inordinate amount of time to line-up. In fact, the children were typically late to their next class. At my suggestion, the teacher told all the class members that they obviously had a problem in lining-up. "And, of course, if you have a problem doing something then you need to practice it." Fortunately, for our purposes, this was a gym class. "This means," the teacher continued, "that every day I'm going to blow my whistle when it's time to line-up. I'll blow it again two minutes later. If you're not all lined-up the second time I blow the whistle, then you're telling me that you don't know how to do it. So the next day you'll have to stop playing ten minutes early so that we can practice lining-up."

Sure enough, the second whistle blew that day, and only half of the students had found their places in line. And they were scuffling with each other.

There was some groaning the next day when the children had their sports time cut short. They "practiced" lining-up, time and again, for what would have been the last ten minutes of their play. The look of one of the second graders bordered on being pathetic as he glanced wistfully at the motionless basketball on the gym floor.

The next day most of the kids lined-up at once upon hearing the whistle, but a few laggards prevented them from avoiding the now-dreaded lining-up practice. All went well the next day, though, and this happy situation continued for about two weeks. One day, two or three of the students dawdled to the point that the class was once again subjected to this mild punishing procedure, but after this one lapse, never again did the class have to practice lining-up.

Ironically, the school principal who had decreed the no punishment rule, happened into the gym one day as the children were being, technically, punished. She asked the instructor what was going on. The coach explained in a very matter-of-fact manner that his students were having difficulty in assuming their places in the line for their next class and were, therefore, practicing this school routine. My anxieties were greatly relieved when the principle responded, "Good, good. Thank you," and turned smartly on her high heeled shoes and exited the room!

Increasing Response Cost

One of the authors stumbled across a use of this gentle correctional technique in his personal life. While he was teaching in Virginia, he and his family had an opportunity to live in what bordered on being an Old Southern Mansion. When he would arrive home at the end of the day he typically would find his wife and daughter in a small den, up the seemingly endless two-sectioned staircase. After greeting the two ladies, he would ask them if they wished something to drink. Wife Linda usually would request a glass of white wine. He would then ask Daughter Prudence if she might like a soft drink, to which she would usually answer, "Yes, I guess so." I would then walk down the staircase to the kitchen to pour the wine and pop. It was then back up the staircase to deliver the drinks. Then, as I was experiencing some degree of thirst myself, it was back down and then up the flights of stairs. Certainly, I had no problem with doing this. Gallantry is, after all, still in fashion in Virginia, at least when I left the Old Dominion. What did, though, bother me somewhat was that on most evenings Prudence barely touched the drink I had brought her.

This author began at this point the practice of responding to his daughter's half-hearted request for a drink with, "Great! Well, Pru, come down and help me bring the drinks up." Interestingly, most evenings the young lady would say, "Well, I'm not really thirsty." Released from the Code of Chivalry! So I could go down only one time and pour Linda and myself a drink. But on those rare evenings when Prudence did request a drink and assisted me in "fetching it," she did, in fact, consume it.

Another Virginia experience of this author illustrates the use of "increasing response cost." He taught for a time a course entitled, "Behavioral Treatments." The purpose of this course was to teach education and psychology students learning principles and their use through "hands on" experience, usually through an attempt at dealing with a problem they were having in their own lives. The story of one of these students is presented immediately below, and reports of the interventions of other students are given in subsequent chapters.

> Jamie was a beginning graduate student. He was thin as a rail, but his "problem" was his perception that he ate too many snacks from the vending machines that were so readily available on that campus. His concerns were the expense of these munchies and that their consumption was not, in all probability, contributing to a well-balanced diet for him. His previous efforts at dealing with this behavioral excess through the use of will power and inflicting some later punishment on himself had been to no avail. Apparently, the immediate reinforcement of the snacks was simply too powerful.
>
> What Jamie concluded was that he was hopelessly addicted to junk food and would never be able to discontinue buying them to excess. Perhaps, though, he thought his devotion to these nutritionally vacuous eatables could be turned to his advantage. After all, he would do anything for a Twinkie! So he made a little rule for himself. He could buy and eat all of the munchies he wanted, but he required himself to do a little exercise before inserting the coin. Jamie would stand in front of the vending machine and say in a loud voice, "This is an offering to the Ding

Dong god. It must be an offering because what comes out will do me no good whatever. Praise to you, Oh Great Junkie. Praise! Praise! Praise!" Or something to that effect.

The effectiveness of this rather unique procedure appeared to have been enhanced by the fact that on several occasions Jamie received glances from passers-by that provoked in him the genuine fear that he was about to be carted off to the local psychiatric hospital! In any case, his vending machine purchases dropped dramatically from an average of five or six a day to where he never patronized the no-armed bandits more than once a day. And he was even able to go many days without buying anything from them at all.

Increasing response cost has been widely utilized in the area of treating "addictive disorders," particularly smoking. It is not uncommonly observed that keeping a record of the number of cigarettes smoked reduces that amount in and of itself. After all, record keeping is such a hassle.

But sometimes keeping records is not enough, and one has to devise more elaborate and onerous procedures. One such technique is for a male smoker to keep his pack of cigarettes in his socks. This means that every time he wants to light up he must assume a somewhat embarrassing position, not to mention revealing a hairy leg! If this doesn't work or the reduction in smoking is not as great as hoped, an even more inconvenient placement for the "weeds" can be devised. A good example of a high response cost placement for smokables is in the trunk of one's car. This means that whenever you wish to engage in this self-destructive behavior you have to leave the office or the comfort and warmth of the couch and venture out into the parking lot. And while driving, a time when, reportedly, a great number of cigarettes are consumed, this means pulling over, getting out and unlocking the trunk. Nothing could be more painful for an American driver with our get-there-as-soon-as-you-can-regardless-of-who-you-have-to-run-off-the-road attitude!

Turning to the weight issue, we see uses of the response cost mechanism which border on outright unavailability. Some dieters, for example, only keep in the house foods which require extensive preparation. This step makes a lot of sense in that we know that overweight people are more likely to eat when food is readily available. In one study, both overweight and non-overweight students were asked to wait in a room in which there was a dish of shelled peanuts. The overweight students ate more of the peanuts than did their normal weight peers, not unexpectedly.

When, however, the peanuts were still in their shells, there was no difference in the amount consumed between the two groups. Apparently, people won't actually exert added effort to make or keep themselves fat. A variant on this theme is to leave home with only a fixed, small amount of money. This step makes the purchase of excessive amounts of eatables practically impossible.

The use of making funds unavailable is common practice in the treatment of compulsive gambling. Gamblers are frequently advised to turn over their paychecks to a money manager who doles their funds out to them in small amounts which she or he can afford to lose. There is no Antibuse for gambling or overeating, so one has to improvise techniques which keep temptation from following you around every minute of the day.

The Ultimate in Subtlety: The Premack Principle

As noted earlier in the chapter on learning theory, the Premack Principle is that any high frequency behavior can be used as a reinforcer for any behavior of lower probability. As technical and off-putting as this statement might sound, it really works! There are two major implications of the Premack Principle which are frequently overlooked and cannot, at least in your authors' opinion, be over-emphasized.

The first of these implications is that it is not, in fact, necessary to use contrived and expensive rewards to make a behavioral program successful. There simply have to be some enjoyable activities in the person's day-to-day life, as well as, of course and again, a desire to change in order to attain accomplishable goals.

The second point to be made here is that most of us run our lives all wrong. We do things we enjoy first and save the less desirable activities for "later." All too often, "later" never comes, at least until one is leaned on.

What we need to do is to reorder our lives so that the naturally occurring pleasant parts of our day come to function as positive reinforcers for getting through the less enjoyable portions. A good way to begin to accomplish this is to make a list of all your activities on a typical day. It may be necessary to keep a dairy. Now, divide these activities into 1) those you enjoy doing, 2) those you dislike doing and 3) those you have no strong feelings about one way or the other. You may note that you're finding it easier to take care of things in Category 1 than Categories 2 or 3! This phenomenon reminds the authors of the story of the man whose doctor advised him to walk a mile and drink a glass of wine every day. Asked how he was doing on this regime, he replied, "In general, I'm doing great." When the words "in general" were questioned, the patient explained, "Well, you see, I'm about two months behind on the walking, granted. But I'm five months ahead on the wine."

Table 7-1 is a rather typical listing of daily activities for one student. It is simplified for the sake of illustration.

TABLE 7-1

Sam's Daily Activities

+ Positive	0 Neutral	- Negative
Watch TV	Drive to school	Study
Drink beer	Shave and dress	Clean house
Talk with friends	Walk dog	Write home
	Work at part-time job	

Sam does have some chores to perform, but he also has some pleasant, enjoyable things going on in his life. Such a pattern would seem to be associated with a well-balanced, successful life. Why, then, is this young man so far behind in his studies, and why is his apartment in such a mess?

Well, let's look at his life. His first class is at ten, so he bounds out of bed at 9:15. He just makes it to geography. Sally's in that class, so afterwards it's off to the student union for coffee with the comely brunette.

George and Harry are in Sam's next class, Math 102 at noon. As the three young men walk out of the classroom they get into a quite animated discussion of the relative merits of Fords and Chevys. After several hours of bulling out on the Quad and noting that the sun is descending in the sky, they agree to adjourn to Poor Richard's Pub for a brew or two.

As they walk across the Quad, Sam broaches an unpleasant subject. "That geography prof is professionally deformed. You wouldn't believe the list of dead and gone eras he wants us to memorize. Gotta get on that tonight."

Happily, the discussion had turned to more enjoyable topics by the time they made it to the bar's portal.

A glance at his watch made Sam wonder where the time had gone. There was just enough of it for him to rush home to catch his favorite program on the boob tube. Excusing himself with a round of "Laters" and "Take it easy," the young man made it to his car. Gotta be careful, Sam thought to himself, don't want to be pulled over with beer on my breath.

Hunger hit our young hero at the first commercial. Aren't microwaves wonderful? He could cook and eat, all without interrupting his programs.

The phone rings. Great luck! It's Sally.

The conversation goes long into the night.

The reader will note that no mention was made of Sam either studying or cleaning up his apartment. How could he? As you can see, he was so busy that there simply wasn't time!

Of course, it wasn't a bad day for Ol' Sam. As a matter of fact, it was downright enjoyable! But he's living in a mess, and his lack of attention to his studies will eventually put him in an uncomfortable position academically. So we're dealing here with yet another situation in which what is positive and enjoyable in the short-run is bound to have long-term negative consequences. What to do?

Here's a case in which the Premack Principle can help our friend out. What he might do is make a rule for himself that he won't socialize with friends until he's put in at least two hours of studying. He could accomplish that by arriving on campus just one hour early and studying in the library from nine to ten. Putting that together with the hour between geography and math would do the trick. That would mean that Sam would be free to pursue his own wishes as early as one o'clock in the afternoon.

Alternately, he could study from eight to ten and have the whole thing behind him by the time of his first class. The point to all this is not when or even how these tasks are accomplished. They just need to get done, and any way that works for you would appear to be the way to do it. But the overall principle is to use those things you enjoy doing as rewards for completing those things you are less keen about.

A good way to handle the messy apartment matter might be to make it a law that one, just one, cleaning task needs to be accomplished before the idiot box goes on.

Perhaps an aside is in order at this point. Our last example, Sam, is a student, so academic tasks figure prominently in his life demands. But all of us are students at one time or another in our lives, and getting through school seems to be a major hurdle for so many. So it's probably justified to devote some rather detailed attention to the issue of being a successful student. Two main reasons for school failure, in your authors' opinion, are the so readily available distractions from academic life and the seeming impossibility of actually completing certain assignments.

Students, of which your authors were ones for many years, have a well-deserved reputation for being gregarious folk with a proclivity for finding parties. Hence, it would seem, the complaint voiced by some that, "School is interfering with my college." In any case, on campus you can always find someone to chat with over coffee. Admittedly, such discussions do enrich the college experience, but they can get "out of hand" to the extent of leading to the termination of the college experience altogether! This is commonly called "flunking out."

An excellent self-control device to utilize in a person's attempts to deal with this problem has, from all reports and appearances, been carefully hidden from the student body. It's called the library! Just put yourself in the "quiet section" of that building and your distracting friends won't even find you. And even if they do, and even if they try to engage you in some kind of conversation, a stern librarian will shoo them away. She may not look like she'd be much fun at a party, but the old gal might just save a choice part of your anatomy, academically speaking, of course. Going to the library is a form of nonchemical Antibuse for a variety of partying behaviors. Think about it!

One of the nice things about college is that you don't get as many assignments as, say, during high school. One of the bad things about college is how long these assignments tend to be. What typically happens is that a term paper is announced a week or so into the semester. Most students go through three stages in reaction to such assignments. The first we may impressionistically characterize as <u>indifference</u>. Why worry about something that you don't have to produce a single sign of for two months or so? But as the deadline approaches to within about a month, the "indifference" may at this point become more accurately described as <u>denial</u>. Thinking about the assignment becomes so painful that you simply don't. Many students remain at this stage and receive an "F" for their non-effort. Most, though, at some point go into what we may characterize as the <u>desperation</u> phase. This is a period of frantic and panicky activity in which the report is thrown together at the last minute. While those following this "do it when the adrenalin flows" system do usually meet the deadline, the quality of the work tends not to be what could have been accomplished with more time and reflection. And one's nerves also tend to be shot into the bargain.

Again, the reasons for these debacles are: 1) the task seems initially to be too overwhelming and 2) it appears that the deadline is so far away that it will never actually come. Both conceptualizations of the matter, obviously, are false. Firstly, most students do, in fact, complete the project. And secondly, the deadline does actually and with amazing speed come.

In your authors' opinion, the key to dealing with this all too common academic trap involves breaking the assignments down into manageable "chunks," usually on a day-by-day basis. Once this step is accomplished, it becomes possible to reward yourself for the completion of that day's bit of the assignment.

The way one of your authors utilized this behavioral aid was as follows: When I was given a project, I would first calculate how many days I had for its completion. For example, it might be due in fifty days. I would then, basically, decide what would be a fiftieth of the assignment, which would become my daily goal. I recall one review I was to do which involved summarizing and trying to make some sense out of about 100 published articles. I calculated that if I read and summarized just three a day, that would leave me well over two weeks to put my summaries of the articles in order and write an introduction, connecting passages and a general overview. This plan worked great!

Once an assignment has been "broken down" in this fashion, one immediate benefit has been achieved. The task no longer seems so monstrous and overwhelming. In this case, it wasn't having to do a major review article. I was merely required to read and take notes on three articles as I rode the bus to and from school. That shouldn't be too difficult for someone in a Ph.D. program! The reinforcement involved, consistent with the Premack Principle, a pleasurable and naturally occurring event in the student's everyday life. This was going home and having a drink or two, followed by a pleasant supper. It worked. The assignment was turned in to the professor. Further, the review was subsequently published in a national journal. And by invitation, the article was later expanded into a chapter for a book.

The combination of breaking assignments down into manageable components and the use of the Premack Principle was, in actuality, both of your writers' strategy for getting through graduate school. This system's workability may be assessed by the fact that while no one has ever accused Bob Wildman of being a genius, he did, when all was said and done, receive a Ph.D. "With Distinction." As for Julius Rogina, he also joined the cohort of clinical psychologist by receiving his Ph.D. in no less than six and a half years of productive work and some play.

At the risk of being repetitive, again, the authors wish to stress again the importance of <u>charting</u>. After all, if you can <u>count</u> the problem you've got a <u>handle</u> on it. Then it's just a matter of trying different things until your dumb graph shows that something is working. We'd repeat here our pitch for the Premack Principle. It's easy, it's cheap and it really works! We wish we could get a cut every time the Premack Principle is used. Come to think of it, we bet Premack wishes he could too!

CHAPTER 8

STRESS:
'Round and Around She Goes...

As noted in the very dull chapter on the nervous system, stress can, basically, be defined as activity in the Sympathetic Portion of the Autonomic Nervous System. That's also the way we describe fear. So what's the difference?

By convention, we call sympathetic arousal which is justified "fear" and that which isn't "anxiety." What this means is that if you think the person should be afraid, it's fear. If not, the guy's anxious. So during a rash of airplane downings, people expressing reservations about flying were told, "Well, I'd be scared too." Before that and since, they've got a "phobia of flying." Pretty arbitrary, isn't it?

Yes, it is arbitrary. And the difference between fear and anxiety probably doesn't make much difference anyway. The feeling of your heart racing while you tremble and perspire is uncomfortable no matter what causes it. What is important is that in most cases anxiety is attributed to <u>things</u> out there. We call these things "stressors." Anything or anyone who makes any kind of demand on us is a stressor. Our jobs are stressors. Our families are stressors. School can be a big stressor. Even things we do voluntarily, like church and civic organizations, can be stressors. After all there are meetings to attend and reports to prepare there too. The list goes on and on.

Figure 8-1 is an attempt to illustrate the relationship between various factors in one's life and the amount of stress with which that person must deal. People tend to see their stress levels as flowing naturally from what's going on in their lives. "I'm uptight about Friday's exam." Actually, and as we begin to understand as we look at the "Stress Cycle" in Figure 8-1, the relationship between stressors and stress is much more complex.

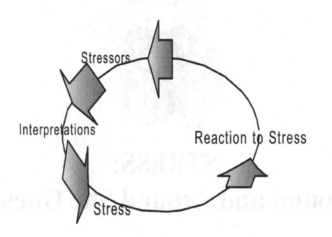

FIGURE 8-1 The Stress Cycle

We get our first hint of how complex this matter is from the everyday observation that people respond very differently to the same stressors. For example, both Joe and Earl are asked to give a speech. Joe says, "Okay" and doesn't think about it much until the night before the scheduled presentation. Earl, on the other hand, is terror-stricken from the very moment he receives the assignment. And this gets worse as time goes on, to the point that he's visibly trembling and perspiring as he delivers the address. Curiously, though, Earl has no problem with flying, but Joe is definitely of the "white knuckle school of aviation." Indeed, he once passed up an excellent job opportunity because it would have involved frequent flying.

What is different about the two men that would cause such radically different reactions to the very same common life stressors? There probably are "constitutional" factors, that is to say physical factors, in the amount of anxiety various people have to deal with. It's quite clear that some people are just more prone to anxiety than are others. Be that as it may, this factor probably doesn't have a great deal of relevance to our present comparison of these two "cases." After all, as best we can tell, they both become about equally anxious. It's just that Earl gets uptight about speeches and for Joe it's the Big Bird in the sky.

Another cause for specific anxieties, "phobias" as they are labeled in extreme cases, relates to what psychologists call "conditioning." If you've been really scared or, as some say "traumatized," in a certain situation, it often happens that you feel nervous and panicky in that situation from then on. This can occur even though there's no realistic reason to be scared, at least any longer. An example of this phenomenon was a fellow student of one of the authors. He had had the unfortunate experience of being mugged in an elevator in Cleveland. From then on, he found himself to be quite nervous when riding in elevators. But only in Cleveland!

Usually, though, such phobias are a lot more general. We might certainly speculate that Earl had once had a rough time in making a presentation, say to his second or third grade class. And Joe may as a child have gone through a patch of turbulent weather on a flight to visit his grandparents. Maybe he was even involved in a terrifying near miss. That would turn anyone off on flying!

Because of the understandability of the connection between extremely unpleasant experiences and later fears, it's tempting to assume that that's how all anxieties originate. Unfortunately and again, life appears not to be so simple for us. In many, indeed probably most, cases the patient is unable to identify a definite traumatic experience that was associated in his or her life with the phobic object. This fact does not necessarily rule out the importance of frightening experiences in causing the kinds of unreasonable fears suffered by Joe and Earl. There are many cases, as in the example of fear in Cleveland elevators noted above, in which trauma clearly was the cause of the phobia. It is also, of course, possible that the person forgot, even blocked out the memory of, the unpleasant happening.

There are two other, and more subtle, ways in which frightening experiences may play an unrecognized role in the creation of fears of things that can't really hurt you. The first relates to acquiring the fears from others. A child may observe her father acting quite tense during a flight. What conclusion can she come to other than that this is a very dangerous thing they are doing? And fear is, of course, the appropriate emotion when one is involved in dangerous activities.

The other subtle way to create a phobia is rather complex. It relates to their gradual buildup over time, called by workers in the field the "cumulative effect." Let's say that a young person is giving a little talk to a class and stumbles over a word. This is slightly disconcerting and creates a bit of anxiety. The nervousness is nothing major at this point, but it's uncomfortable. So he dreads a little bit his next speech. He goes into it already on edge. So when the inevitable little gaffs occur, the resulting discomfort adds to an already heightened level of anxiety. So our young student leaves this speech visibly shaken. He comes to dread making another speech. He will probably make active efforts to avoid invitations to present, in fact. And when Earl is forced into speaking, he's "as nervous as a long-tailed cat in a room full of rocking chairs," to quote that great Philosopher of Science Tennessee Ernie Ford. And that level of anxiety is going to make future mistakes in diction and grammar even more likely. What we're dealing with now, regrettably, is a full-blown speech phobia.

Another and overlapping cause of stress relates to the step we've inserted between "stressors" and the "stress" itself. This is the matter of "interpretations." If it seems that this factor is overemphasized, it's because this factor is probably the easiest to overlook. And if it's not, in fact, the easiest cause of stress to deal with, it is at least the easiest to begin the process of trying to cope.

People, by way of stressing a point made earlier, tend to attribute any mood state, such as happiness and anxiety, directly to events going on in their world. "I'm sure glad it's Friday." "I'm upset because Sheila turned me down for a date." "I'm happy because I'm paid so well."

At the risk of being accused of being negative, let's look at the above sentence on dating as our illustration. To flesh the example out, let's say that a college sophomore has for some weeks been involving a young lady at the checkout counter of the library in friendly conversation. Today everything was "right," the time, the mood and the occasion. So he popped the question, "How about going to the concert with me tomorrow night?" Despite all the favorable omens, the answer was "No." Oh, there was something about a pervious commitment, a family problem, as he recalled. But the answer was still "No." As Mark told his therapist later that afternoon, he was "devastated."

Let's take a look at Mark's interpretation of what's happening to him. A little graph, presented in Figure 8-2, may help us.

(Antecedent Event)   (Consequences)

A-> -> -> -> -> -> -> -> -> -> -> -> -> ->C

(Turned Down for a Date)   (Mark is upset)

Figure 8-2. Mark's Initial Interpretation of the Cause of his Discomfort.

In this diagram, "A" stands for "antecedent event, in this case, that's being turned down for a date. "C" stands for "consequence," "being upset" in this example. The line between the two shows Mark's belief that there is a direct, inevitable link between the two events. When one gets turned down, you get upset, <u>period</u> and <u>of course</u>.

Mark's therapist, a follower of Albert Ellis, sees things a bit differently. His formulation of the situation is shown in Figure 8-3.

(Antecedent Event)   (Beliefs)   (Consequence)

A -> -> -> -> -> -> B -> -> - -> -> -> ->C

(Being Turned Down for a Date) (Mark is upset)

Figure 8-3. Another way to Look at Being Turned Down for a Date

Dr. Smith believes that there's another way to look at what's taken place in Mark's life. The therapist sees a middle step on the way from "A" to "C." This is "B," which, conveniently, stands for "belief." The question at this stage of the process is what does Mark think or believe about the event? There are at least two sets of ideas or beliefs he might have about Sheila's rejection of his invitation. These are outlined, perhaps overdramatically, in Table 8-1.

Table 8-1. Beliefs Mark Might Have About Sheila Saying "No."

IRRATIONAL	RATIONAL
She thinks I'm a Nerd.	Perhaps she did have a family emergency.
I'm ugly and unlovable. No girl will ever want to date me.	Perhaps she's secretly engaged to someone else.

I'll never have a family.	Perhaps she's gay.
I'm going to die alone.	If none of the above, she certainly has bad taste.

It's pretty clear from Table 8-1 that if Mark does, indeed, interpret Sheila's turning him down in what we've labeled the "irrational" manner that he's going to be upset. Wouldn't you? It would, after all, be very discouraging to find out that you're ugly and unlovable and that you're going to die alone. Gosh, you might as well check out! What's interesting is that many, not to say most, people actually respond to life's little setbacks in this way. And that can't be realistic. Most people do eventually find someone. You just can't please all of the people all of the time.

The more "rational" interpretations, it must be admitted, may not actually be true. But they certainly are a more comfortable set of statements about what's going on. And true or not, they lead to a healthier reaction to the situation. Instead of moping around his dorm room, Mark is out searching for a young lady more deserving of his attentions! While this is getting a bit ahead in our story, it's obvious that Dr. Smith is going to devote a lot of his time with Mark to trying to switch his views of things from the "irrational" to the "rational."

We can, clearly, apply Ellis' formulation to the two cases we're looking at, particularly Earl's. In all probability, if you talked with Earl about the matter of giving speeches you would find that he has a number of irrational ideas about one's performance that are just tailor-made to make him uncomfortable. Some of these are:

> I must make a <u>perfect</u> speech. That is every word must be pronounced absolutely perfectly. No mistakes. Everyone, and I mean <u>everyone</u>, must find my presentation informative, interesting and entertaining. No dissatisfied customers. Not even one! In fact, I must make "The Great American Speech" every time out, with each speech perfect but somehow better than the last.

Assuming the reader will overlook a certain degree of exaggeration, these expressed attitudes toward an upcoming speaking engagement clearly beg the question of how realistic they are. <u>Not very</u> is the obvious answer. And anyone going into a speech with this set of irrational beliefs is setting herself up for failure and a very uncomfortable time.

Joe's attitude about speaking is markedly different from Earl's:

> I've been asked to give a speech. They must figure that I know more about the topic than they do or, quite obviously, they wouldn't have invited me. I'll do my best, but I know I can't give an absolutely perfect speech. After all, it's been shown that little slips in pronunciation, "minor dysfluencies" as they're technically called, are part of all human communications. I'm sure this group will include persons with different backgrounds. So some might regard my comments as simplistic, while at the same time others may feel that I'm talking over their heads. There's no perfect way to deal with this one, that's for sure. Also, I've noticed that some people just seem to yawn and act restless during speeches. Well, I'll just give it my "best shot." If just a few people in attendance emerge with more knowledge of my topic than when I stood up, I'll count myself a success.

With this set of attitudes, Joe is going to feel a great deal more at ease during speaking engagements than Earl, to say the last. We'll discuss the difference in these two kinds of approaches to life's stressors in great detail later in the next chapter on "Breaking the Stress Cycle."

A note, in the authors' opinion, needs to be injected at this point. Thus far, we've discussed the matters of "conditioning" and "interpretations" in the creation of fears as though they were two totally separate factors. In actuality, they very much tend to overlap, or "interact," as they say. In other words, one cause has an effect on the other and that one, in turn, comes back to cause trouble in the other direction. Someone who walks to the lectern demanding of themselves that the "Great American Speech" be forthcoming is going, as illustrated above, to make themselves highly anxious. That experienced fear, irrational and unrealistic though it may be, is going to have the effect of attaching anxiety, activity in the Sympathetic Portion of the Autonomic Nervous System, to the speaking situation. This anxiety, firstly, will further condition the speaker to feel uncomfortable when making presentations. Secondly, this state of arousal will undermine his performance. It will make him think, "Gosh, if I'm this uptight, I must be doing a pretty lousy job. I'll bet everyone can see how nervous I am and know how incompetent I am in public. I know my stuff, but I can't put it across." This kind of thinking isn't going to calm our speaker down. No, It's going to make him even more nervous, which will further undermine his self-confidence, making him even more nervous. We have here the classic "vicious cycle." Anxiety leads to negative thoughts -> -> -> negative thoughts create anxiety -> -> -> anxiety leads to negative thoughts. Not much fun! This appears to be the way in which all too minor problems in carrying out an activity lead to major discomforts and problems in adjusting to this part of life.

One final category of causes of anxiety evokes shades of FDR, "fear of fear." (For our younger readers, reference is made here to President Franklin Delano Roosevelt's 1933 Inaugural address in which he famously said, "All we have to fear is fear itself.") No matter how well balanced your life may be or how rational your thinking, stress is a part of every human life. Some people take this in stride, reasoning that everyone facing such deadlines would be feeling the pressure. Others, however, become alarmed at the signs of sympathetic arousal. "Oh, gosh," they say to themselves, "I'm uptight, on edge. I'm losing control. This is ter-r-r-r-ible..." Through such thinking people can literally work themselves into quite a state. Anxiety feeds back and becomes another stressor, yet another problem with which the person must deal.

We can now see how the stress cycle "works." People put together unbalanced lives, overloaded with stressors. They have unrealistically high expectations as to how they are going to deal with those demands. They then go on to allow, albeit unintentionally, the anxiety to become yet another stressor for them, which adds to their problems and further disrupts and impairs their ability to deal with the already present stressors. This lifestyle can easily open one up to a future of perpetual discomfort. "Around and around she goes..."

Self-help advice on breaking the stress cycle is the subject of our next chapter.

CHAPTER 9

BREAKING THE STRESS CYCLE

As described in the previous chapter, the "stress cycle" has four identifiable points: 1) stressors, 2) interpretations of the stressors, 3) stress and 4) interpretations of the meaning of the stress itself. As in any system, it's possible in this one to affect both each and every part and the system as a whole through applying force or pressure on any of the individual components. The implication of this physics-sounding statement is that in our attempts to deal with stress we can "intervene" at any of the points. The question naturally arises as to which point (or points) is the most effective one on which to focus our attention.

The best place to intervene in handling stress probably varies from case to case and person to person. Given that, though, your authors have a definite position (bias?) that people, laymen and mental health professionals (including clergy doing pastoral counseling) alike, have a tendency to pounce way too much and too quickly on one of the steps. And in so doing, we often neglect other facets of the problem. The result, regrettably, is that we may overlook long-term solutions to the problems creating anxiety.

The over-emphasized part of the system we're talking about relates to jumping in and dealing with the stress itself. Perhaps a little true-life example from the career of one of your authors will help make the point here:

Some years ago, I was working into the evening. There was a knock on my office door. Looking up from my work, I recognized a graduate student who had taken a number of courses from me. She looked very distraught. After I invited her to be seated, she reminded me of a lecture and demonstration I had given on systematic desensitization (This is an anti-anxiety technique which we'll discuss in great detail later in this chapter.) "Well, I've got this stat test coming up, and I'm scared out of my mind. I want you to do that desensitization thing with me, and I want you to do it now!"

It was a somewhat unusual request, walking into someone's office at seven o'clock at night and demanding a specific therapeutic technique. But it wasn't totally unreasonable. After all, Janet was anxious, and systematic desensitization is a well-known and standard treatment for anxiety.

But some thinking I had been doing which, hopefully, is reflected in these writings, helped me check my knee-jerk reaction of just diving in and desensitizing the young lady. It just might make a difference if we found out specifically what Janet was anxious about. Of even more importance could be the question of whether or not something might be done about the problem she appeared to be having with statistics.

Discussion revealed that she was having trouble applying the "t-test" to some data given to the class by her stat prof. And she was having trouble applying the t-test because, at base, she didn't understand the rationale behind the t-test because she didn't understand how the basic statistic behind that test, the "standard deviation, "was derived and its meaning. I decided to see how much progress I might be able to make with her discomfort level through helping her overcome her conceptual block on this statistical issue. In this attempt, I may have been helped by the fact that I am a non-statistician who at various times has been asked to teach statistics. This experience may have forced me to develop some ways to convey certain principles in statistics that don't require a great deal of mathematical sophistication. I used the analogy of two children on a teeter-totter to explain standard deviation to Janet. (Two asides at this point: I may, come to think of it, have stolen that one from my own introductory statistics teacher. I'd give him credit here, but I really can't remember his name! Secondly, not to worry, I won't bore you, the reader, with my statistical explanations!) Janet's face lighted up as I went through my little presentation. She now understood the t-test. And she was able to work a few of the problems I gave her. Any anxiety about the upcoming test? None at all!

In reflecting back on this incident, it occurs to me that if I had acceded to Janet's demand for systematic desensitization the effect would have been that of making her comfortable enough to flunk her stat test. Not a very lofty achievement!

This example, admittedly, may be overdrawn. We tend to illustrate with extreme cases when we're making a point. Even so, I can't help wondering if something akin to this doesn't happen quite frequently when people consult mental health professionals about "anxiety" and are just given pills and relaxation tapes. The premature or unwise use of these rather straight-forward anti-anxiety measures can, it is argued, enable (pun intended) people to remain for years in undesirable situations, such as in bad marriages and jobs in which totally unrealistic demands are made on them. These negative outcomes occur because nothing is done about the underlying problem(s). Now all of this is not to say that drugs and relaxation procedures have no role to play in the treatment of those suffering from nervousness. It is, rather, suggested, as will be argued later, that perhaps these techniques should be used more toward the end of treatment than right off the bat, as is so frequently the case as these words are being written.

Achieving a Balanced Lifestyle

In our opinion, in grappling with your own anxiety, the first thing you should do is look at the stressors in your life. The discussion of a "balanced bowling ball" and the suggested exercises which were presented in that chapter are what is being discussed at this point. It is recommended, strongly, that before turning to medications/drugs, whether doctor- or self-prescribed (like alcohol), you try to get your bowling ball in balance.

So at the risk of being repetitious, our first step in dealing with anxiety is to get our life in balance.

Interpretations

The second step in dealing with anxiety has to do with the matter of our interpretations of the stressors in our lives. It will help here to take a more in-depth look at the work of Albert Ellis.

Ellis was a clinical psychologist who practiced In New York City. He was trained in psychoanalysis, the set of therapeutic procedures based on the work of Sigmund Freud. In some ways, this technique resembles, roughly, the approach of Carl Rogers which we discussed in an earlier chapter, at least in terms of the relative passivity of the therapist. But Ellis grew tired of waiting for patients to come of their own accord to the solutions to their own problems. Life moves faster in New York than in Vienna, it would seem! He decided that the basic problems his clients had related to their thinking and view of the world. Specifically, he concluded that people tended to have, indeed were often carefully taught to have, a number of irrational views of the world. Simplifying Ellis' approach, we can summarize some of these irrational beliefs as follows:

1. I must be prefect and successful in everything I do.
2. Everyone must respect me and approve of everything I do.
3. Everyone must be kind and gentle to me and to every other person in the world.
4. The world must be fair and just.
5. It would be <u>terrible</u> and <u>awful</u> if things don't go just the way I think they should.

It's not at all hard to see how someone with this set of beliefs is going to have a lot of trouble at Point B in our stress cycle. The world just seems not willing to cooperate with this picture of how things should be! And if you truly expect and demand that things go just this way, you're setting yourself up for a lot of grief and disappointment. People often come to the conclusion that the world is not the way they think it should be because there's something wrong with them. And this deduction makes them feel even worse about themselves.

Ellis suggests some more rational self-talk, such as:

1. I will do my best, but since no one is perfect, I realize and accept that I won't succeed each and every time.
2. You can't please everyone all the time. In fact, there appear to be people you can't please any of the time. I've just got to accept this fact and not allow periodic disapproval to upset me too much.
3. Some people are pretty nasty no matter what you do. I don't like this, but I didn't make the world.

4. The world would be completely fair and just if I were in charge, but the movement to make me Emperor of the World isn't picking up a lot of steam!

5. It's just not realistic to expect that I'm always going to get my way. There are in life periodic reversals. I can either make the best of them or allow them to "blow me away." I'm not going to be blown away!

Ellis' system is in many ways a philosophy of life. It involves elements of self-acceptance and making reasonable demands on ourselves. It also views many aspects of life as being in some ways beyond our control. And we must, in the writers' interpretation, determine not to allow ourselves to be just passively swept along in these currents. We must maintain a certain measure of objectivity in the face of life's inevitable negative occurrences. You've lost your job. You can think of this as a tragedy, a <u>horrible, terrible</u> thing. Or, you can see this as an opportunity to find a better, more satisfying position, a blessing in disguise, if you will. One has to admit that whatever attitude one takes toward having been fired can have no effect on the fact that you were actually canned. But given the inescapability of this, you might as well adopt the rosier attitude. After all, Ellis' approach has a number of advantages over more conventional thinking: 1) it motivates a more positive set of behaviors, looking for a better job, 2) it makes you feel better and 3) it doesn't cost a thing!

Ellis' approach may prove difficult for many of us to learn and use. As noted above, there are millions of people who have, for all practical purposes, been taught to view any negative life event as their <u>fault</u> and as demonstrating that there's something <u>seriously wrong</u> with them. Undoubtedly, society, chiefly through the parents, indoctrinates children in this manner in order to make them law-abiding, responsible citizens. Freud saw this in terms of installing a "super ego." It certainly is an effective social control mechanism, at least in most cases. The problem is that it, like most things in life, can be carried too far. One way to express the results of carrying this well-intentioned process too far is to say that many of us have become "over-socialized." That is, we are left painfully doubting and self-critical, particularly in social situations. We go, for example, to a cocktail party. What we think about at the function is not whether or not we're enjoying ourselves, but whether we have or might commit some social blunder. For should we blunder into a gaff, we might offend someone, or maybe just not live up to our own unrealistic ideal self-concept. And then that person wouldn't love and respect us. That person wouldn't approve of everything we do. And that would be <u>awful</u>, <u>terrible</u> and "The End of the World." One is not going to have a wonderful time at this particular function, quite obviously! And should, Heaven Forbid, the person actually use the wrong fork, the result will be devastation to his self-esteem. Is this example overstated? Perhaps or perhaps not. There are, in fact, many people who view this and similar occasions in just this self-defeating way. They see them as opportunities for something bad to happen to them, and not as chances for a positive outcome, like meeting someone interesting or having fun. They've been taught, "carefully taught," to borrow a phrase.

Hopefully, an understanding of what is going on with these self-defeating self-verbalizations/self-conversations will help one to change one's thinking in a potentially stressful activity, like a speech or a "stiff" social function. Ask yourself some of the following questions:

1. Am I going in with an attitude of avoiding failure or one of looking for success or enjoyment? If the former, how can I change it to the latter? Maybe I should focus on good things that could happen, like meeting someone interesting or learning something new.
2. What horrible or terrible thing is going to happen if I don't perform perfectly on this occasion? Is the world really going to come to an end if something goes wrong?
3. What are my expectations for how I'm going to do on this occasion? How realistic are these expectations? What would a more realistic set of expectations be? Perhaps I should keep repeating to myself that more realistic set of standards so that I won't fall into the old trap of comparing myself to standards that are impossible to match.

It takes a lot of rehearsing of the new ways of looking at things to make a dent in the old ways of thinking. It is recommended that you devote a great deal of time to "analyzing" what's going on in your life. If you feel upset at any point, ask yourself why. Are you upset about what happened, or is the culprit your interpretation of the meaning of the negative event? You might even find it useful to sit down and diagram the ABCs of the matter.

What, you might well ask, is going to happen if you can't change your thinking in a more rational direction on your own? You know that you can't remember everything, but that occasional forgotten form at work persists in sending you into despair. You know that you can't please everyone, but a negative comment made about you by another member of your church causes you a great deal of pain. Despite reading this section, you find yourself wanting to crawl under the table when you make the slightest mistake in table manners, like when a fork falls out of your hand and noisily onto your plate. Unfortunately, such an inability to change these mental habits on your own is not at all unlikely. After all, they were built up and carefully cultivated over many, many years. Changing them is going to be quite difficult. As noted in the preface, you may, in fact, have to seek professional help in order to achieve this goal. But we recommend working with the materials in this section for a while on your own before placing yourself in psychotherapy.

Assertiveness

There is an issue which is also intermediate between stressors and stress. But instead of being a purely attitudinal factor like 'interpretations," this one is both attitudinal and behavioral. The topic being raised here is that of "assertiveness."

The relevance of "assertiveness," which you probably have a general idea of the meaning of but will be defined in more detail later, to stress was illustrated dramatically in a study conducted a number of years ago. A group of subjects were made angry by a series of unfair criticisms which were expressed in a demeaning way. Apparently, the experimenters did a good job of "getting the goat" of the participants in that they observed a significant rise in their blood pressures. This demonstrates arousal in the Sympathetic Portion of the Autonomic Nervous System which meant, as was explained earlier, that they were upset.

Half of the subjects were allowed to express their hostility to their tormenter, to get it off their chest, so to speak. Those who were given this opportunity to vent their anger had their blood pressures return toward normal levels. Those who just "stewed" had to suffer continuing elevation of their blood pressures.

The major implication of the above study seems to be that being put in a position where you are angered and frustrated without an opportunity to respond results in a situation in which the initial anger goes on and on. Obviously, there are times when one simply cannot express her anger and resentment to the person who frustrated her. Service in the military is such an instance, as are some civilian employment situations. But, undoubtedly, there are many more cases in which the silence is self-imposed. But why?

Most of us are taught to not be pushy or demanding or loud. That's fine. But where does that leave us when others don't follow these same gentle rules? It leaves us feeling pretty bad, that's where. Parenthetically, the lack of assertiveness seems to overlap with the earlier-discussed unrealistic self-expectations in that a person who feels compelled to please everyone will be impaired in her ability to confront someone seeking to take her rights away. After all, the would-be rights-taker won't be pleased with her for not going along with his unreasonable demands!

It seems in this set of instances that either we misinterpreted the true lesson or, in fact, the wrong lesson was taught. What we should try to avoid is being <u>aggressive</u>. So many of us have a problem with confusing being <u>assertive</u> with being <u>aggressive</u>. Let's look at the difference.

The underlying concept in explaining the meanings of these two rather easily confused terms is that of "rights." We all have rights. Perhaps the best example of rights is the supermarket checkout line. The rule there is strictly "first come, first served." So no matter who you are, whether you're a janitor or the mayor, your place in the checkout line entitles you to be rung up in exactly that order. Anyone, then, who tries to break in line in this situation, is trying to deprive others of their "rights." Such a person would be said to be "aggressive." We may, thus, define being aggressive as that trait of attempting to take away for one's own advantage the rights of others. This, in reality, is the characteristic that significant others have been trying to teach us to shun.

But what of the individual who allows the aggressor to break in line? That person has not only surrendered his own rights, but additionally the rights of those farther back in line. We may call such a person "passive."

We can now see the "qualities" of being aggressive and passive as lying along a continuum. This continuum ranges from those who take away the rights of others to those who so willingly surrender them. Certainly, neither end, as so often happens, is a happy one. Might there be some mid-point which is more conducive to positive mental health, one that is less likely to cause you to continue to be upset and with chronically high blood pressure, one that won't make others see you as a bully and result in someday getting yourself flattened in the street?

The answer to that question is, to no one's surprise, YES. And that happy medium, as shown in Figure 9-1, is called "assertiveness."

PASSIVE -> -> -> - -> ASSERTIVE -> - -> -> -> AGGRESSIVE

FIGURE 9-1. The Continuum of Dealing with the Rights of Yourself and Others

Now, what is "assertiveness"? It is nothing more or less than the commonsensical idea that <u>everyone's</u> rights are important, valuable and to be protected. Thus, to continue with our grocery store checkout example, the assertive person would never be the one to break in line. That would involve depriving others of their rights, a behavior which is totally unacceptable to the genuinely assertive individual. See how different "assertiveness" is from some of the misconceptions people have about it!

But what about the person or persons who were broken in on? This situation is more complex for the potentially assertive individual. Granted, she's done nothing wrong, so the deprivation of rights suffered by herself and those behind her can't be blamed on any malicious action on her part. But by being "passive" she's quietly agreed to surrender not only her rights but those of others as well.

Now, let's take a little time to consider the "advantages" of being passive. It certainly does have its appeal, so much so that many of us have adopted it as a way of life. It absolutely prevents you from being accused of being aggressive, a charge that so many of us have been taught to avoid like the plague. And it certainly cuts down on the level of conflict in your life. After all, people aren't going to fight with you when you're handing them everything they want on a silver platter!

Sounds good, huh? But there is a price to pay for passivity. The obvious one is that you're subjected to the inconvenience of being delayed in lines, pulling duty for others, etc. But there is a subtler price to be paid for adopting a lifestyle of passivity. It is a price paid in your sense of self-worth and self-esteem. You see, people have a hard time separating who they think they are from how they're treated. In fact, probably no one is ever able to completely "rise above it all" to the point where how others deal with them has almost no influence on their self-perceptions. If you're shoved around day after day and your rights are simply ignored, it's pretty easy to come to the conclusion that you're not a very valuable person. After all, only a "schmuck" deserves that type of treatment. Forgotten at such low moments is the part that you yourself may have played in this particular element of your fate.

And, as we've already mentioned, there is a price to pay in personal comfort and even health. As summarized above, subjects who were angered and put upon without being able to respond in any way continued to suffer elevated blood pressures. This is what the non-assertive, passive person goes through every day. Their rights are taken away and they neither do nor say anything about it. It's no wonder that they feel bad about themselves, that they're chronically upset, and that, through mechanisms to be discussed later, their health suffers.

Well, what do we do about this situation? The grocery store example is reasonably simple and straight-forward. How about flattening the guy? That's really not a very good "solution" when you think about it. The fellow may have done wrong, but violence can't be the answer. Treating violence with violence is like fighting fire with fire; it just creates a lot of ashes. Breaking in line shouldn't, one would think, be deserving of tissue damage! Besides, you might get yourself flattened back into the bargain! That's not going to make you feel better about yourself, now is it? Actually responding to the line breaker with violence would be an act of <u>aggression</u> on your own part. In a strange way, you're depriving someone of his rights. You see, a person has the right to be as obnoxious as he wishes without being physically harmed! But whether or not he should be allowed to get away with it is a different matter totally.

Now, what would be the assertive thing to say and do?

"Gee, I'm sorry but we're already in line here. You'll have to go to the end."

Does that sound too "mealy-mouthed"? Perhaps it is, but we need to recall what we talked about earlier in regard to allowing people to keep their dignity. Besides, the "intruder" could have been genuinely confused about where the line began. The important question centers on whether or not what you say or do works, and not being too accusatory and demeaning often makes others more willing to go along with your requests.

But what if the guy insists on hogging his ill-gotten place in line? Here the situation becomes more complex. One stronger step you can take in the face of the persistence of such aggressive behavior is to appeal to an authority figure. In the supermarket, that would be the checker or a manager. On the street, you can turn to a policeman.

But what if such an authority figure is not readily and conveniently available? In this case, you have a rather difficult and complex question to put to yourself. Is the principle of asserting my rights worth the inconvenience and possible danger it might entail in this case? Obviously there is no simple and always easy answer. Quite a number of factors go into making a decision as to how to handle such situations. Two very obvious things to consider are the degree of rights infringement and the risks involved in making an issue of the matter. But another relevant topic could be how you stand, on balance, in being assertive. If you've been allowing people to take advantage of you of late, it might be a good idea to correct a "little wrong" done to you that you otherwise would let slide. But this decision, in the authors' opinion, doesn't give you permission to take out your frustrations on some poor sales clerk who in haste gave you the wrong amount of change. Make the "correction" with only the force warranted. Even though it's not dramatic, it'll still help convince yourself that you're a worthwhile person with rights.

There are, though, times when it's simply not at all wise to respond assertively. The matter of physical danger has already been alluded to. There are many examples of other reasons in business. Let's say you're about to close a multi-million dollar deal with a wealthy but eccentric client. He's a golf nut, so on a golf course is where you're doing business. You catch him shaving his golf score. Are you going to call him on it? If your answer is "yes," then you should turn in your subscription to the <u>Wall Street Journal</u> and consider a career at Disneyland!

Given that there are situations in which one cannot realistically express her frustrations and demand her rights, what can one do about the inevitable resulting upset? In these cases, we go back to Chapter Three on "Intimacy." It certainly helps a lot if you have someone in your life who will truly and genuinely listen to you. This is the person to whom you can open up and tell about, say, the frustration of dealing with, for example, that demanding person in your business. Admittedly, she may not be able to do anything about it directly, but being able to talk about it, getting it off your chest, is bound to make you feel better. Hopefully, you won't have to pay for this service!

But, and this being a basic theme of this chapter and one that will recur throughout this portion of the book, before concluding that you have to just accept and adjust to a given upsetting person or stressor, consider various possible alternatives:

1. Do you really need this in your life? Perhaps the situation shouldn't be adjusted to. There are just some circumstances which actually need to be gotten out of. To use a personal example, one of us once worked in a mental health setting in which the "boss" was very overbearing and dictatorial. As a matter of fact, he even took pride in calling himself "The Dictator." What was so ironic about the whole

thing, insulting actually, was that this individual had been unable to pass the test to practice his profession in that very state in which he had obtained his terminal degree! Even so, he was directing the minute-by-minute activities of licensed professionals.

You wouldn't think such a situation as is being described could exist. But it can. It did! In fact, the entire "leadership" of that state's mental health system was made up of similarly un-credentialed individuals. This is an extreme example of a demeaning setting, but you can probable come up with similar "horror stories" from your own profession or occupation.

Leaving that degrading institution and going out on my own was not without its elements of insecurity. I had always been able to count on regular paychecks if not on being treated with dignity! But it turned out to be one of the best moves I ever made. The removal of that particular stressor more than compensated for living with a certain degree of financial insecurity.

2. If, in fact, I do have to remain in this job or situation, do I really have to take this abuse? There are several possible ways of improving the situation which, it is argued, one should try before resigning yourself to an acceptance of the unacceptable:
    a. Try asking the person to treat you with more dignity. Admittedly, if your relationship with your "superior" is so bad that it's causing problems, this probably won't work, but it should at least be given a "shot."
    b. Tell the offending person that you're not going to put up with this kind of treatment. You can threaten to complain to higher-ups or some type of grievance committee. Employees often make the mistake of thinking that bosses are all-powerful. In truth, they may actually be on pretty shaky grounds themselves. And particularly in government work, employees are protected from the capricious and vindictive actions of superiors. Check into your rights. You may be able to do something about the mistreatment. You have the right to not work in a hostile environment.
    c. Seek a transfer to another office or branch. This can be a way to effectively change jobs while building up retirement and other benefits in what is technically a single position.

But should none of these "outs" work, then you may have to live with a "bad deal," at least for a while. Try to make things a bit better for yourself by talking with an intimate about what's going on. It will be explained in the next chapter how stress can continue for so long a time that it actually does physical damage to you. No job is as important as your health. Get out before that happens, no matter what the financial or professional cost!

Fear of Fear

The next issue of concern to us is how we react to anxiety itself. Some people seem to feel as though any experience of anxiety is a sure sign that things are falling apart. Given, though, the virtual impossibility of avoiding stress in its entirety, this attitude, quite clearly, leads to a pretty frazzled life! Some possibly more adaptive attitudes toward stress:

1. Well, I'm uptight, but who wouldn't be when confronted by a test prepared by Old Man McCracken?
2. If you're not nervous, you're nuts!
3. Would you rather be on edge or totally out of it?
4. If you weren't anxious, you'd be totally brain dead!

The main message that's trying to be presented here is that there are, in fact, situations in which anxiety is not only not a sign that something is wrong, but is, rather, an indication that you're in touch with reality! The trick is to be able to accept that fact and the inevitable anxiety of life. If you can't accept this, then you are in danger of getting into that cycle of anxiety creating anxiety. There are quite enough causes of "nerves" in this life, so we certainly don't need any more of this type. Try to accept the unavoidable discomforts. Don't let what you can't avoid create even more stress for yourself.

At the risk of being repetitious (again), it is the authors' position that the causes of stress should be addressed before treating the anxiety itself. A helpful reminder here could be to examine "my values" and conduct simple cost/benefit analyses. The specific points at which intervention is possible and the recommended steps are outlined in Table 9-1.

TABLE 9-1. Steps in Dealing with Stress

1. Stressors

     Might you have bitten off more than you can chew? Is it possible that anyone with your lifestyle might be a nervous wreck?

     Well, what you need to do is get your life in order. Chapter Two on the famous "Bowling Ball Theory of Life" is where advice is given on accomplishing that goal.

     See what you can do on your own to make your life one of balance and a realistic work load.

2. Interpretations

     Do you expect too much from yourself? Do you have ideal expectations of yourself that are not reality based?

     Do you insist that you be perfect and that everyone love, respect and admire you?

     In short, are Albert Ellis' irrational beliefs making life, from your point of view, a series of humiliating and painful defeats?

     See if you can "propagandize" yourself into adopting the more realistic set of interpretations presented earlier in the chapter. Good luck!

3. Stressed By Stress

     Do you feel that the least bit of anxiety means that you're losing it?

     Can you allow a little tension to work you into a real state?

     Try accepting the fact that anxiety is a natural, unavoidable part of life. It won't kill you. Look not at what's wrong with you, but rather at what's gone wrong in your life that's causing you to feel this way. Do what you can to correct it

Dealing with the Remaining Stress – On Your Own

After doing all you can with the advice presented in Table 9-1, we move on to an effort to deal with the stress itself.

There are a number of "professionally approved" forms of stress reduction. Chief among these are systematic desensitization and medications. Before, though, rushing into these formal procedures, it might be a good idea to try first some admittedly "homespun" remedies. Here are some. You can probably think of others. The only criterion in evaluating them is what works for you.

1. Exercise. It has been conclusively shown that exercise has tension-reducing properties. This is particularly the case with those activities that involve sustained effort like jogging and swimming. But these are forms of exercise that are not always so convenient when you feel uptight. An excellent and socially acceptable alternative is plain, simple walking. Take a walk during your lunch hour. Between two stressful meetings? Leave the car in your reserved parking spot and walk from one to the other. Tell everyone you're trying to take off a few pounds or "I need the exercise." Get off the bus a few stops early and walk the rest of the way home. It's a great way to unwind and be a more compatible member of the family.

2. Get away for a while. This is a piece of advice psychiatrists have been giving their patients for ages. Sigmund Freud used it himself! Regrettably, it's come to be looked upon with the same derision as, "Take two aspirin and call me in the morning."

   But this can, in actuality and its apparent naivety aside, be pretty sound advice at times. Quite obviously, you can't be on vacation continuously, so that can't be the solution to all of your problems all the time. But there are those points in life when things do pile up to such an extent that you are, literally, in danger of being overwhelmed. We'll talk a lot later about this process and the very real danger of this posing a threat to your health. On such occasions it may, indeed, make sense to get away for a while. The rest and relaxation can, in and of themselves, help to break up the evolving stress cycle. After all, you've been able to get away, albeit temporarily, from the stressors that are putting so much pressure on you. A great advantage of such a rest is that it gives you an opportunity to put things in perspective, to, if you will, figure out how you can get your bowling ball into a better balanced and healthier condition. Armed with a rest and a plan for a more realistic lifestyle, you will, hopefully, return to your workaday world ready to make changes which are needed to ensure that another round of buildup of unbearable tensions doesn't occur.

3. Make it a point to work into your life a number of relaxing activities each day. Obviously, what is relaxing for one person may not be so perceived by another. And there are, of course, differences in schedules between individuals and couples. So the advice that follows can only be regarded as being generally suggestive.

A couple we know found that going out for lunch each work day is a great way to break up stress and make their rather long daily schedule of activities, usually extending to about fifteen hours, go by faster. They are certainly fortunate in this regard to live in Reno where eating out is so inexpensive!

Other relaxing activities are hiking, picnicking, going out for a drink after work, going to the movies and playing cards. The list is almost endless, but the important thing is choosing something that works for you.

It may seem paradoxical when discussing relaxing activities, but it's probably necessary to be scheduled, even compulsive, about engaging in them. With the schedules and sets of demands most of us labor under, it's easy, almost inevitable in fact, that such restorative interludes will be shuffled to one side. "I'll work through lunch and knock out this balance sheet." "Gee, Hon, I'd love to go away for a while, but I've got this big report."

Try to work in some enjoyable, relaxing activity every day. It will help to break up the buildup of stress and thus stave off "burnout." Additionally, it will give you something to look forward to. It's all too easy to fall into the trap of just working without any idea of why or for what.

4. Talk over your frustrations, fears and hurts with an intimate. The importance of this step was explained in the section on Client-Centered Therapy.

Drs. Jacobsen, Wolpe and Goldfried to the Rescue

Let's assume you've been able to get your "bowling ball" as balanced as possible and that your interpretations of your dealings with stressors are positive. And yet and despite your best efforts, you still have stress. What then?

There is a set of nonchemical techniques which work directly on the stress itself. Their evolution began with the work of Edmund Jacobsen, M.D. (1888 – 1983). It was Dr. Jacobsen's opinion that people tended to do a rather poor job of relaxing, and he developed a very nice way to improve our ability to do this. This procedure was applied specifically to the problem of definite and irrational fears by Joseph Wolpe, M.D. (1915 – 1997).

Perhaps the best way to explain and demonstrate this important set of procedures is to give a case history of the therapeutic handling of a patient with a phobia. What follows is an account of a person seeking help for an overwhelming and irrational fear. The reader is invited to review this therapeutic interchange and take from it what might be of value to her or him.

(Note – What follows is a detailed description of a course of Systematic Desensitization. It is included here in order to give the reader enough information so that he/she could use these procedures on one's own. If these techniques are not relevant to your life at this time, you are invited to skim through these pages to Page 115 at the end of this chapter.)

Sam walked into the office and told the nice lady at the desk that he was here for his 10:30 appointment.

The therapist walked out into the waiting room to greet Sam.

"I'm Bill Mason," he announced respectfully.

"Sam Bullock, Doctor," the man said awkwardly as he rose.

"Please come in, Sam."

The two men entered Dr. Mason's office. It was a pretty standard setup, except for all the green plants, most hanging from the ceiling.

Mason "broke the ice" by inquiring as to how Sam felt about the unseasonably cold weather. "We're having a tough time getting Spring started," he remarked.

The amenities aside, Bill asked his new client why he had consulted him.

"Well, you see…uh, I've got this fear of flying. I keep thinking I'll overcome it, but it doesn't seem to work out that way. You see, Doctor…"

"Bill."

"Uh, you see, Bill, I've got to travel a lot in my job. Sometimes I have to drive all night, putting in full days at both ends to get done what the office wants…and all because I hate getting on an airplane. Oh, I know it's crazy. I mean, I've read the books. Actuarially, flying is far and away the safest way to get from Point A to Point B…"

"I'm glad you know that."

"Well, I do. But I'm still afraid of the 'Big Metal Bird.'…This is causing me a lot of problems."

"So I see. Let me ask you this. Did you ever have a really bad experience in an airplane?"

"A bad trip?"

"Quite," Mason responded with a tolerant smile.

"No, not really. At least nothing dramatic… But there was that bumpy ride on the way home from seeing Grandmother and Grandfather… Come to think of it, I wasn't so eager to fly after that."

"Well," the therapist said thoughtfully, "that could have started it. Of course, it doesn't really matter exactly how it got started. I just wanted to make sure there wasn't something really dramatic in your history, like an actual crash…"

"No, nothing so dramatic as that. It just seemed that this flying thing kept getting worse and worse. They made me fly in the Service, but after that, I've avoided it whenever I've possibly been able to."

"Hmmm… I see. Well, given that you know air travel is not so horribly dangerous, we can clearly label this an irrational fear or 'phobia.'"

"Tell me about it!"

"Yes, well, the important thing now is to do something about it. Quite obviously, you get nervous – tense, uptight – in planes. Well, we need to teach you how to relax in that situation. But, you know, for all your obvious talents, it could just be that you're not a great relaxer…"

"A brilliant glimpse into the obvious," I'd say.

"Sam, what I'd like you to do is come over to this lounge chair over here and sit down and relax as best you can. Try to leave your business outside the office."

"That'll be the day. I'm thinking about doing deals in my head all the time."

"I'll bet."

Bill engaged his new client in a short conversation about football. Sam's stocky build and the tie he was wearing which sported the colors of the nearby State University suggested to him an interest in sports, maybe even as a player some years and pounds ago. It developed that the psychologist was correct – left guard, Class of '78. At least it gave Sam a short break from the business rat race and dwelling on his fear of flying.

"Well, Sam, are you relaxed?"

"Yeah, sure, what's to it?"

"We'll see. What I want you to do is make a fist with your right hand… That's it, but tighter, tighter… Tighten it until it aches… Okay, now let your hand relax." Bill's voice was deep, calm and reassuring. "Now, you'll notice something interesting. When your hand goes back to the way it was before you tensed it, it won't just stop there. It'll keep getting more relaxed, even more relaxed than it was to start with."

Bill sat quietly with Sam for a minute or two.

"Now, don't move… Just keep relaxing. But I want you to compare your right and left hands. Can you tell any difference?"

"Well,…gosh, yeah, I can. The right seems heavier and warmer. Does that make any sense, Doc?"

"It sure does. What you're telling me is that that hand is more relaxed than the other. 'Heavy' and 'warm' are the usual ways in which people describe deep muscle relaxation.

"Now, Sam, it seems to me that we've learned something quite interesting and maybe quite important. You see, even though you got your whole body as relaxed as you could on your own, including of course this hand, it turned out that it's possible to get it even more relaxed than that."

"Yes, I can see that."

"Makes sense, doesn't it, that if you can learn to do a better job of relaxing your right hand than you could on your own that we could do the same with all of Sam?"

"Uh-huh."

"And if we can do that, then we've gone a long way toward bringing down the overall level of tension you have to deal with in life. Technically, what we're doing is teaching you to self-stimulate the Parasympathetic branch of the Autonomic Nervous System. That's important because it counteracts, acts against, the part which makes you tense and anxious, the Sympathetic."

"Sounds good."

"Great. We'll start in. But before we do, let me ask you if you've had any injuries or orthopedic problems that would make it unwise for you to tense and relax any part of your body in the manner that we did with your right hand?"

"We'll, I've got a football knee."

"Left or right?"

"Left."

"Okay, let's be real careful when we come to your left leg. Only do that part of the exercise to the extent that you feel comfortable. Understood?"

"You got it."

"Okay, now we'll go back to your right hand and arm. But also tense all the muscles in both your forearm and upper arm…

"Now, tense, tight, tighter."

Sam's arm rose almost involuntarily into the air as the muscles tightened and a mildly contorted expression appeared on his face. Bill allowed his client to remain in this uncomfortable state for only about three seconds.

"Now, relax. Let your arm fall to your lap. Let all those muscles go completely and totally limp. Just completely relax. You'll feel all the muscles in your arm grow heavy. They may feel warm and tingly. That's good. That's all part of the process of relaxing…Just completely relax…Let all the tension in your arm flow out...Allow the relaxation to flow in...The arm just keeps getting more and more relaxed."

Dr. Mason allowed Sam to relax for a few minutes. He periodically interjected comments such as "Just relax" and "Feel the heaviness and warmth...That's good."

The therapist then went on to repeat the process with Sam's left arm. Again, the period of tensing was only about three seconds, and the relaxation was considerably longer. It went on until Bill thought that maximum deep muscle relaxation had been achieved, thirty seconds at a minimum. "This is," he explained, "an exercise to teach you how to relax, not how to get even more uptight!"

The next stop on the anatomical tour was the shoulders. The tension phase asked Sam to "Hunch your shoulders together...tighter...tighter. " During relaxation, the patient was instructed, "Allow your arms and hands to go completely limp. Your lap will support them. ...Just let them get completely relaxed...heavy...warm...tingly."

Next came the chest. Tightening these muscles, obviously, requires stopping breathing. So this phase of the process doesn't last long! The relaxation component very much emphasizes the return of normal breathing. "Your breathing is becoming slower...deeper...more... satisfying...in...out...in...out..."

Then came the abdomen. Sam was instructed to "Poke your stomach out as far as it will go... Now tighten, tighten, tighten...

"Now, remember what I said before. As we move to a new body part, don't tense the part we've already worked with. Just allow them to keep getting more and more relaxed.

"On to the buttocks. Tense...tense...tight... Now relax. Let all those muscles go completely and totally limp. Just allow yourself to settle into your chair. It will support you.

"We're going to work on the legs now. When I tell you to, I want you to raise your right leg from the floor, pull your toes back toward you and tighten all the muscles in that leg..." The relaxation instructions included the words, "Just let the leg flop to the floor..."

Bill reminded Sam to take it easy during their work on the left leg on account of his ancient football injury.

"Now we go on to the neck. 'Scrunch' your head down into your chest and shoulders as far as it will go. Tighten all those muscles... Now relax. Let your head flop back onto the back of the chair...

"And we come now finally to your face. When I ask you to I'd like you to clinch your jaws, furrow your brow and tighten all the muscles in your face… Now, let all the muscles in your face go limp… Just let them sag…

"Okay, you've done great. Now let's put it all together. When I tell you to, I want you to tense at the same time all of the body parts we've worked with, your entire body. Now…tense, tight, tense!… And relax, just let your entire body, head to toe, go completely and totally limp…good…good…" Again, the relaxation part was at least ten times the length of the tension phase.

"Now, we're going to do the whole body again…tense…tight…" After Sam had gone into the relaxation phase, the therapist continued, "Now I want you to imagine that you're lying on the beach. It's a warm day…There's a gentle cooling breeze. You're lying on a blanket on the soft, warm sand. You relax and let your body go limp. The sand will support you…you feel so comfortable. The sand is so soft. The sun and the breeze feel so good… You listen to the waves lapping on the shore, and you can hear the palm leaves rustling behind you. There's the sound of children playing happily down the beach… Okay, at your own pace, please come back from your little 'trip.'"

Sam twisted a bit in the overstuffed chair. He stretched his arms and yawned.

"What's next, Doc?"

"How do you feel?"

"Pretty good, really. Pretty good."

"Relaxed?"

"Yeah, relaxed."

"Glad to hear it! Now I want to see if you can do this on your own. When you're ready, please tense and relax yourself. Then go on your own fantasy trip to wherever you would feel comfortable, happy and relaxed."

Sam thought a minute and then assumed the contorted posture of one in the process of acquiring the skill of relaxation. As usual, the client somewhat overdid the tension side of things, and Bill had to step in.

"Relax, Sam, relax. I'm trying to teach you how to relax, not how to tense."

About five minutes later Sam announced that he was "back" by opening his eyes and looking at the therapist.

"Where'd you go?"

"Oh, we used to have this cabin up in the mountains. Beautiful place."

"Yeah, some people like the ocean and some the mountains. It's usually one or the other, I've found.

"We'll, Sam, I think we're really making progress. You got through the relaxation exercises real well. I'd like you, please, to practice this at least four times a day. It helps to have some structure in terms of when you practice all this…. Uh, I guess that's true of about everything in life, come to think of it. What works for a lot of folk is to do this first thing in the morning, at noon, after work and as you go to sleep at night.

"We're going to do something with your new-found ability to relax that will specifically help with your problem with flying. But first let's talk a few minutes about some of the general uses of what we've learned up to this point."

"Shoot."

"It used to be that people thought that this relaxation procedure was something that could only be used in a doctor's office, kind of like a surgical procedure. But it was learned over time that people who had been taught the technique were using it on their own. So, for instance, a person would come in for help with a specific problem, like an airplane phobia, like you. We'll, the therapist would teach him these procedures in order to help him get over that. Well, it turned out that people were later using these techniques on their own. So if they had something stressful coming up, like an IRS audit, they would relax themselves to help get them through it. At first, this puzzled us greatly because we didn't think anyone outside of one of the 'professionals' could understand and utilize a procedure such as this. But, by golly, they were using it. Then came along a guy named Marvin Goldfried. He said that since so many people were using the relaxation procedures on their own, we ought to make it a point to go out and show them how. That's what I'm trying to do with you right now, as a matter of fact. So from now on, when you're facing something stressful, use these relaxation procedures. Like if you were – forgive the expression – I just know you're going to get over this – if you're flying to that important business meeting, you can use these techniques on the plane. I wouldn't, though, go through the tension phase. People might think you're having some kind of a 'fit.'… Just settle into your chair, relax all your muscles, and go off on a little trip somewhere. This is the kind of thing you can do in your chair right before the big test. Try it!

"Well, let's focus now specifically on your problem with air travel. What we need to do is to develop a so-called hierarchy of things associated with flying that 'get to you,' so to speak. Let me ask you this, when you have a plane trip coming up, when do you first get nervous about it?"

"Gee, I'd say right away. As soon as the boss tells me about a meeting where, you know, from the distance and time it's clear I'm going to have to fly."

"Okay, now what do you find to be the most frightening part of the flight?"

"There's no problem about that. It's the take-off. When that big bird goes rumbling down the runway, I about lose it."

"Okay, now we've got the two poles of our hierarchy. What we need to do now is to arrange events associated with flying along a scale of how upsetting they are to you. The unit we use for this is 'Subjective Units of Distress' or 'SUDS' for short. It's a hundred point scale that we use. Zero is complete relaxation, say when you're home sitting in an easy chair listening to calming music with flying not even on the radar. One hundred is about as anxious as you can get. In your case, we've identified that as the take-off. So we'll make that 100. Tell me, please, in comparison to how you feel at take-off, on a percentage basis, how anxious are you when you first get the word that you're scheduled for a trip that involves flying?"

"Oh…uh, about ten percent."

"Well, then finding out that you've got to fly is ten, and the take-off is 100. What we need to do now is to fill in about a dozen or so spaces between these two extremes.

"What are some of the things associated with flying that aren't as bad as the take-off but are upsetting to you?"

"I'd say waiting to board."

"SUDS?"

"Oh, that's pretty bad. Sixty, sixty-five…"

"What about packing, how would you rate that?"

"Thirty, I'd say."

It took Bill and Sam about a half-hour to come up with the hierarchy reproduced in Table 9-2.

TABLE 9-2

Sam's Hierarchy of Stressful Flying-Related Activities Subjective Units of Distress (SUDS)

Home in an easy chair	0
The boss tells me I've been assigned to attend a meeting back East	10
Driving by the airport	15
My secretary gives me my ticket	25
Packing	30

Driving to the airport	50
Checking in	60
Waiting to board plane	65
Putting on my seatbelt	70
Taxiing	80
Landing	85
Experiencing turbulence in flight	95
Take-off	100

"Now," Bill resumed after the somewhat tedious task of hierarchy construction had been completed, "let's put what we've learned to use so we can really get in there and do something about your problem with flying. What I'm going to do is have you relax. Then I'll ask you to imagine various scenes, some involving flying, some not. If you feel the least bit anxious at any point I want you to raise your index finger." He pointed to that finger, and Sam lifted it slightly as his hand rested peacefully on his lap. "That's exactly right. Now, that'll be my cue that I'm going too fast, and we'll go back to an earlier, less stressful scene. Ready?"

"You bet."

Mason had Sam go through the whole body relaxation exercise.

"Sam, you're home on a Sunday afternoon. You're sitting in your most comfortable chair. You were reading a book, but you got weary and put it aside. There's some nice, calming music in the background."

Mr. Bullock did, indeed look relaxed. Zero SUDS!

"Now, imagine that you hear the distant sound of a plane going overhead..." he watched the finger carefully. Not a budge. Good, he thought. I'm on the right track.

"In the office now. Your secretary brings in the mail. In it there's a brochure about a conference in Philadelphia next month which is just up your line." The finger remains unmoved. "You put the brochure aside and turn to the rest of your mail. Your company's region-by-region sales reports are out. Your team, it turns out, has done pretty darn well.

"Later in the men's room you run into the District Manager. 'Say, Sam,' he says, 'happen to see that notice of the conference coming up in Philly? You know, it talks about moving the product with medical people. That's where we've been losing out a bit to the 'ole competition. Think we ought to pop back there?'"

Still no movement in Sam's index finger. Good.

"Now, you're sitting at your desk, and the secretary brings in the latest pile of things from the mucky-mucks upstairs. On top is the brightly colored folder of an airline ticket."

Up went the finger. Uh-oh, Bill thought to himself, I'm going too fast.

"Okay, cut that off now. No more airline ticket. Just relax for a few seconds.

"You're at a conference table at work. The boss is talking about low sales to hospitals..."

Sam looks pretty calm. The finger is down.

"He mentions the conference in Philadelphia. Turns out a lot of the other guys want to go. As a matter of fact, being asked to accompany the DM there is something of a political plumb."

Sam smiles and settles back into the overstuffed chair.

The session proceeds in this "see-saw" fashion. Bill inches forward toward scenes more and more directly associated with flying. He quickly retreats in the face of indicated discomfort on the part of his patient. Progress is slow, not as slow as in psychoanalysis, but slow nonetheless. Yet, it is made. Session One ends with Sam being able to imagine with relative comfort being presented with a ticket for an upcoming flight.

Session Two gets Sam packed and on the way to City International, all in imagination, of course. But encouragingly and consistent with clinical findings, Sam begins to report some carry-over to his everyday life. Specifically, he is now much less uncomfortable when he considers the inevitability of his business taking him over the jet-way.

The rate of speed of going through the hierarchy slowed somewhat when they got to the airport. So several sessions were required to get Sam from the curb-side check-in and onto the plane. The biggest hang-up was waiting at the gate. Apparently, he had spent quite a number of very uncomfortable hours in that situation, and it took some time to undo the effects of these experiences. As a matter of fact, on the first four occasions when Bill tried to take this step, Sam indicated by raising his finger that he wasn't ready for that. Bill would always take him back to his usual pre-flight visit to the lounge. That appeared to be a relatively safe spot for Sam! But at long last Sam was gotten through the waiting area and down the jet-way.

The part that took place in the plane itself had to be approached very gingerly. Bill used a lot of reassurance, and he constantly reminded his patient to relax.

Sam was now flying high, if only in his own mind.

Two whole sessions were spent relaxing and going through imaginary flights and under different conditions. Bill worked in a little turbulence just to steel Sam against the inevitability of this occurring in real life. The client was able to remain pretty comfortable throughout. Bill felt that they had accomplished about all they could from a technical, procedural point of view.

"Well, Sam," he said off-handedly, "I'm real pleased with what we've accomplished here. I'm particularly happy that our work has transferred or 'generalized,' as we say, to your day-to-day life. For instance, you've indicated, I believe, that in recent weeks talking about air travel has troubled you much, much less than in the past."

"That's true."

"Of course, the 'acid test' will be your flight to Chicago next week."

Sam grimaced slightly, but he managed a smile.

"Well," Dr. Mason continued, "this overlaps with what I've said before, but I want you to understand clearly that what we've done here isn't a definitive 'treatment' in the sense that, say, the use of penicillin may be curative of an infection. Rather, it's more like a skill which, like some kind of athletic ability, needs to be practiced and refined over the years. In other words, you can get better and better at the skill or 'game' of coping with life.

"But I want to stress that word 'practice.' If you leave here thinking you're 'cured' and that's the end of your consideration of the matter, you're really going to be let down. You'll find that, hopefully, initially you'll do quite well at flying, but ultimately you're in danger of being troubled by other fears.

"So what you need to do is keep in condition. And that, of course, means practice. So like I said earlier, go through this at least four times a day. And, whenever you experience one of those panicky feelings, why that would be a good time to pull out that bag of tricks 'Ole Bill Mason taught you.

"You can, you know, go through these exercises just about anywhere. A plane's a good place, actually. Again, I wouldn't do the tension part. People might think you're having a seizure! But you can let your muscles go limp and all the rest.

"And, you know, you can use this to cope with other stressful things that come up in your life. I told you, didn't I, about the writings of Marvin Goldfried?"

Mr. Bullock nods.

"Yeah. He found that people after being taught Wolpe's systematic desensitization were using it on their own. So if they found that they were getting uptight about something, they'd relax themselves and imagine going through what they were dreading. Turns out it worked pretty well. Cheated the doctor out of his next fee!

"But, of course, that's as it should be. It doesn't really matter diddley-squat how well adjusted you are in my office. It's out there that counts.

"Oh, I've had a real go-round with my colleagues on this one over the years. Why, back in graduate school I wrote a paper on generalization, how to make the effects of what you do like here in an office transfer or generalize to the real world. Well, I took it to one of my professors, a very famous man in the field. He finally got around to reading it on a flight to New York.

"Well, when I went to see him the next week to get praised, he handed my paper back to me and said, 'Bill, that's not the point. It's like you go to the dentist and she fixes your teeth. And you say, but I can't see.' Do you know what he meant by that?"

"Uh…no…"

"Neither do I. Never had the faintest idea. But another prof did say something to me that I did understand. Dr. Craddick on the same general issue cited the then in-vogue expression, 'If you see Buddha on the road, kill him.' In other words, if you have something of value, it must survive your death, or the termination of therapy in our case."

Boy, Sam thought to himself, Mason is really getting worked up on this one. Maybe he should see a shrink himself!

"Oh, well, Sam, perhaps that's neither here nor there. But you really do need to practice all this."

Another perspective to this case: Dr. Frankl and Resources of the human spirit

Viktor E. Frankl (1905 – 1997) wanted to compliment the human dimension of *soma* and *psyche*. He introduced into psychotherapy the spiritual dimension *noos* for the purposes of treatment and accomplishing desirable changes. It is within this spiritual dimension, the *noetic* dimension, of a person that we find, he says, the unique resources to deal with a variety of our problems. In Frankl's theoretical framework, he not only assumes the spiritual, the objective world of meaning and values, but he also brings them into play by establishing them as an essential part of the therapeutic process. He encourages clinicians to become sensitive to meaning and values, both of their own and of their patients, and engage their patients' spiritual capacities to be activated in the treatment of specific problems.

If Sam had come with his problem of flying to a Franklien therapist - a logotherapist and existential analysis practitioner - he would most probably have been exposed to the same general type of desensitization or progressive relaxation procedures as described in the above vignette. When they felt confident that his problem of flying was less anxiety-provoking, he might be asked about the importance of holding onto a job that demands frequent flying. The therapist using the Franklien framework of treatment would then invite Sam to spell out and clarify his personal values and embark on aligning his personal values with his employment options.

If this more comprehensive form of treatment had been given to Sam, he would benefit not only from progressive relaxation but also from value clarification. As you can see, the progressive relaxation helps with the somatic or physical dimension, and the value clarification helps with the spiritual or noetic dimension. In order to live his values with authenticity, Sam would need the resources of the human spirit, like courage, patience, sense of purpose or maybe acceptance and humor in order to continue living his life with a meaningful sense of self actualization.

CHAPTER 10

STRESS AND HEALTH

It is, perhaps, important at this point to remind ourselves that one of the announced purposes of this book, as expressed in the preface, relates to an attempted explanation of the relationship between psychological factors and health. Hopefully, an understanding of such connections will make it possible for us to manage our lives in such a way as to avoid health problems and, in fact, to create and enjoy a life of relative fitness. The reader may well complain that we seem to have strayed considerably from that announced topic into a land of psychological mumbo-jumbo and psychotherapy.

The authors are going to attempt to demonstrate that health issues cannot, in fact, be studied and understood in isolation. They must, rather, be dealt with within the context of the person's overall life and lifestyle. It is not argued that such purely physical events as hereditary malformations and physical trauma/accidents either don't occur or are unimportant. It's just that there is so precious little that we can do about such things, at least after their negative effects are in evidence. So it would seem that a more productive use of our time would be to examine and explore those matters which are subject to modification. And this brings us back to style of life.

The preceding nine chapters have attempted to give the reader the necessary background to understand the relationship between psychological factors/style of living and health problems. This chapter will attempt to make that relationship clear and explicit. If the authors succeed in accomplishing this goal, at the conclusion of this chapter the reader will no longer be puzzling over the relevance of the materials presented earlier in this book.

Before proceeding into the bulk of this chapter, one small note, a note of clarification and explanation if you will, needs to be made. This relates to the fact that psychologists typically discuss psychological problems, particularly those relating to health issues, under the heading of "stress." The danger in the use of this term, as emphasized in the last two chapters, is that it might imply to some an overly narrow definition of those psychological states which can have an impact on, say, your health. In other words, we might be tempted to assume that only that state of discomfort and arousal labeled "anxiety" is relevant to health concerns. In actuality, though, any kind of negative (at times even positive, believe it or not) psychological state, particularly when intense, can set the stage for negative impacts on one's physical functioning. Examples here are "hurt," feelings of rejection and inadequacy, depression (about which we'll have more to say later) and even such "existential" concerns as a lack of fulfillment in your work and that haunting sense that life may, after all, have no meaning. Perhaps a good general term to use here would be "upset," but maybe that doesn't sound professional enough! Anyway, there's a great deal of overlap, it develops, between all negative psychological states, anxiety included, and the way they are experienced by the person. As a matter of fact, there are many studies in the literature showing that people are very poor indeed at determining precisely which negative condition they are experiencing. And the predominant manner in which people respond to any kind of negative emotional tone is with that pattern of increased heart rate, heavy breathing, muscular tension, etc. which we have labeled sympathetic arousal and which we have identified with that state called "anxiety." So having gone through all the above, perhaps using the terms "stress" or "anxiety" for those psychological states that get us into mental and physical trouble isn't so far off the mark after all. As Rosanne Rosanadana of Saturday Night Live fame would say, "Never mind."

Seriously, though, the reader is warned not to take the term "stress" too literally in the discussion which follows. We are, in actuality, dealing with a much broader set of negative psychological or emotional states.

Perhaps this will become clearer when we get into the field of addictions and discuss the theoretical formulation of Durand F. Jacobs (1922 – 2013).

Besides, quite obviously, being uncomfortable in its own right, stress, again broadly defined, contributes to health problems through a number of known and well-documented specific mechanisms:

1. Directly through that pattern of neurological arousal know as sympathetic activity
2. Dealing with stress on a long-term basis can result in a "wearing down" of the body's coping mechanisms, resulting in physical or mental illness. This stress-health link will be discussed in great detail below under the heading of Selye's General Adaptation Syndrome.
3. Our attempts to cope with stress may lead us to neglect positive health-producing activities and, instead, to engage in negative, health-destructive behaviors, most dramatically in addictive patterns.
4. There is a mysterious and controversial connection between stress and illness which relates to various theories concerning the functioning of the brain and the auto-immune system.

Before going on to a consideration of the specific ways in which stress plays a role in creating and worsening disease, we need, quite obviously, to demonstrate that such a relationship actually does exist. The clearest demonstration of the negative effect a stressful life can have on one's physical health comes from an early report contributed by Holmes and Rahe.

Dr. Holmes and Dr. Rahe were medical officers in the Canadian Navy. On an extended sea voyage they devised a questionnaire relating to stressful events in life, and they administered it to their captive audience. Interestingly, some of the items on their questionnaire, like "vacation" and "promotion," were positive in character. This inclusion of positive events in the stress scale has caused it to be criticized in that there is general agreement that sudden, tragic events such as the sudden death of a comrade in combat are more likely to produce a posttraumatic stress disorder than are happy events. There is also the matter of the meaning of the series of events to the individual.

Correlating their results with the sailors' medical records revealed some very dramatic relationships. The higher an individual's score, the more likely that individual was to have suffered some form of physical illness in the recent past. In fact, a majority of those who scored 300 or more on their instrument had come down with some form of significant illness.

The relationship between stressful life events and sickness seems clear. What is not clear, though, is the manner, or as we shall see manners, in which the one affects the other. And it is to this intriguing and complex topic that we now turn our detailed attention.

The Direct Result of Sympathetic Arousal

This is the most straight-forward and obvious of the ways in which "stress" has a negative impact on one's physical health. We reviewed in Chapter 5 the specifics of the workings and effects of arousal in the Sympathetic Portion of the Autonomic Nervous System. By way of review, these include such changes as increases in blood pressure and heightened levels of muscular tension. These changes are, clearly, negative and create uncomfortable feeling states in their own right. Further, when they persist on a long-term or "chronic" basis they in and of themselves may produce recognizable medical syndromes. Most cases of high blood pressure are of the so-called "essential hypertension" type. This means, basically, that there is no known cause. It's not a kidney problem, for instance. Certainly, psychological factors such as we have been considering here may play a role in such cases. While perhaps this can't be proven, physicians who treat such cases appear to believe that stress is implicated in their patients' conditions. They routinely advise their hypertensive patients to take a vacation and cut down on their stress levels.

Selye's General Adaptation Syndrome

Hans Selye (1907 – 1982) was a doctor who, literally, had more degrees than a thermometer – M.D., Ph.D., Sc.D, etc. His brilliance caused him to forsake the monetary potential of private practice and led him into a career as a researcher. In his capacity as a scientist, Dr. Selye was conducting a study on the adrenal gland. He had been getting his supply of these organs from one source when circumstances forced him to switch to another supplier. Attendant upon this seemingly inconsequential logistical alteration, the good doctor noted a dramatic change in the quality of the organs he was examining under the microscope. Whereas before they had been healthy and robust, the organs he was now peering into were shriveled and atrophied. A less inquisitive person, in all probability, would simply have demanded a better quality of organs for his biochemical investigations. But not Hans Selye. He wondered what had caused this remarkably consistent change in the specimens he was examining.

Selye's curiosity pushed him to actually go to the farms on which the laboratory animals had been bred and raised. It developed that there was a dramatic difference in the environments in which the two groups of animals had been reared. The breeding farm from which the first set of specimens, the healthy-appearing adrenal glands, had come from was airy, spacious and clean. The other, by contrast, had all the opposite characteristics. It was cramped, and sanitation was abysmally poor. This observation put Selye onto the idea that there was a link between stress and illness.

Years of research, further observations and reviewing the work of others enabled Selye to formulate the general nature of this relationship between stress and the bodily breakdown known as disease. This he termed "The General Adaptation Syndrome." The present writers have adapted the graph in Figure 10-1 to display this theoretical formulation.

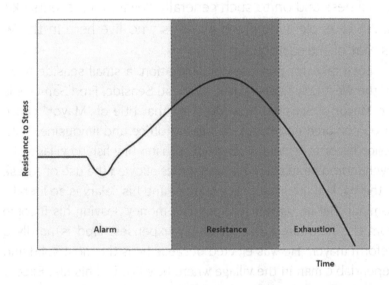

Figure 10-1. The General Adaptation Syndrome

The line drawn on this chart requires a bit of explanation. It shows the depiction of a theoretical concept or "hypothetical construct," as such things are more technically known. The concept being portrayed here is that of "adaptive level," generally one's ability to deal and cope with and adjust to the demands of the world. We presume that this ability is based to a large extent on the efforts made by the individual person. We summarize these various "efforts" into another and overlapping hypothetical construct which we label "adaptive energy." Presumably, different people produce various amounts of adaptive energy at different points in their lives. So, again, what we are charting in Figure 10-1 is level of adaptation of a certain individual which is, put as simply as possible, a combination or interaction of the amount of adaptive energy being produced and the extent to which she or he is being challenged by the world's demands. Hopefully, any confusion remaining in the reader's mind will be cleared up as we go into a discussion of the workings of the General Adaptation Syndrome.

Our graph starts out on the extreme left with a line running along about in the middle of the chart. This shows a person functioning pretty normally in his day-to-day life. Apparently, the demands of this person's life are quite moderate and pose no great challenge. He is functioning well, being required only to produce a very easily accomplished amount of our adaptive energy. Such a person might even be "in a rut," so to speak.

Into this life comes "Trouble," and that starts with "T," and that stands for "Trauma." Trauma may take the form of any kind of overwhelming negative event. These may range from such relatively private affairs as the breakup of a romantic relationship, through professional and financial reversals to illness and on to such generally devastating events like natural disasters. An example with which all of us who live here in the West can identify is that of the earthquake.

Let's take, for purposes of illustration, a small seaside town on the West Coast. We'll call it, why not, Seaside. Fred Samuels is the Mayor of Seaside. Now, don't let that title of "Mayor" cause to be conjured up images of a grand office and limousines with police escorts. Remember, Seaside is just a tiny fishing village of a few hundred people. Fred is sometimes allowed the use of a desk in the back of the little police station, and his salary is so literally nominal that he uses it for spending money, leaving his income from the hardware store for family expenses. Fred is hardly a "reform mayor." He was elected because he is the most solid and dependable man in the village where he's lived all his life. Except for having been drafted during the Vietnam War, it's been a pretty comfortable and routine life for 'Ole Fred.

Fred is, for those of you keeping score, operating in the "normal" (pre-"Alarm") functioning phase of the General Adaptation Syndrome.

And then one day it came, that sickening, unreal rumbling of the earth. Life suddenly became a haze of impossible movements having no constant up or down. No family escaped some injury to a loved one, and no structure was left totally unscathed. Samuels and Sons Hardware Store was a total loss.

They wandered through the rubble, sometimes in search of items like makeup and checkbooks, which were ridiculously irrelevant to the crisis at hand. Thankfully, the National Guard arrived promptly and brought some type of order.

The citizens of Seaside had responded to the trauma of the earthquake by, predictably, entering the "Alarm" phase. As depicted in Figure 10-1, this is the precipitous drop in the person's level of functioning and underlying production of adaptive energy, illustrated by the downturn of functional level in the first portion of the figure.

Some people, fortunately a small minority, will simply not recover from this kind of trauma at all. They may be functionally ineffective for some time to come. For someone like Fred, though, with his record of stability, dedication and service, this is most unlikely to occur. In a rather short length of time, probably from within a few hours to a day or so, he and his fellow citizens will begin to adopt a "We won't be defeated by this" attitude, and they will resolve to "rebuild our town." They may begin to work long hours into the night and accomplish truly heroic and impressive strides in restoring Seaside to, if not its former glory, at least its former hominess.

Because of the tremendous and increased effort required to rebuild Seaside, it's obvious that those involved in this project will somehow have to find within themselves an increased supply of adaptive energy. They will, in effect, have to work overtime. During such periods, people have been known to accomplish things and put in long hours such as they never in the past would have thought possible. How this is done is not exactly known. But it does occur, and this phenomenon is known as the "Resistance Phase" in Selye's theory.

Returning to Fred, as a civic leader, the Mayor, the burdens of rebuilding will fall with particular force on his shoulders. And while if one wanted to be rude one could say with some truth, "Mayor, you're no Abraham Lincoln," still Fred is conscientious and knowledgeable. He is up to the task, which for him involves not only the physical exertion of reconstruction but also the responsibility for much of the planning and the strain of coordinating the activities of various agencies, some of whom, it develops, have "hidden agendas." This is certainly not an easy time for our hero!

Let's overcome the naturally negative impulses of clinical psychologists and allow this story to have a happy ending. After all, Seaside is a small town, and Fred is a big enough person for this particular job. So Fred spends the first few weeks after the quake in overseeing emergency repairs, on restoring public utilities and that kind of thing. Later, his efforts are channeled into long-term projects, like the reconstruction of the seawall and street repairs. He does some speaking around the state on behalf of the fund that was set up to help with hospital costs for the victims.

Gradually, over a period of months, things returned to normal in Seaside. A testimonial dinner was held to honor Fred for his leadership during the crisis through which the City has gone. The Mayor had been having difficulty shaking a minor case of bronchitis during the past few weeks, but his spirits were buoyed by the honors given him by his friends and neighbors. He took his wife to Hawaii for a week. He came back tanned, healthy and refreshed, ready to resume his life as a small business owner and civic leader in the now once again sleepy little town of Seaside.

Mayor Samuels did weather the storm in good form. But Seaside was a reasonably small area to take care of, and the crisis was time-limited. Even so, Fred was willing to admit that at the end he was "tuckered out." But what happens in cases in which the "crisis" turns into a chronic condition? Examples here would be wars, chronic illness in the family and jobs in which the pressure is unrelenting, such as being an air traffic controller.

Persons subjected to long-term stressful conditions may "bear-up" and "overcome" for extended periods of time, often for years. But for most, the "Exhaustion Phase" depicted in Figure 10-1 is inevitable at some point down the road. This is a rapid, sometimes even sudden, decline in a person's ability to cope with life. The individual's ability to produce adaptive energy is unequal to the demands of her or his life, and the whole mechanism shuts down. The specific outward symptom of this process is some manner of disease. Sometimes it's physical, and sometimes it's mental.

The relationship between long-term stress and illness is so clear that journalists have noted this pattern without any "instruction" from the "professors." When Richard M. Nixon was forced to resign the Presidency, a nationally broadcast commentator pointed out that, in his experience, every "sensitive" politician he had covered who had had such a dramatic political reversal had soon fallen victim to some form of significant physical illness. All of this was by way of predicting that Mr. Nixon would soon himself become ill. Sure enough, shortly after leaving the White House, the former president suffered a near fatal attack of phlebitis which required emergency surgical intervention.

What is not clear is why the breakdown takes one form in one person and a totally different malady shows up in another. Why, for instance, does Mr. A develop ulcers, while Mr. B suffers from high blood pressure? Why do some just go ahead and have a nervous breakdown, while other go to the point of physical breakdown and even death? Another facet to our questioning here relates to the fact that there are people who fall apart at the beginning of a crisis and those who are able to hang on to the end. What are the important differences in people that cause them to respond to stressors in such a variety of ways?

While it hasn't been proved, the answer to both of the major questions posed above probably relates to some form of underlying and possibly undetectable weakness in the physical structure of peoples' bodies. Everyone, obviously, has weaknesses, points of vulnerability. Some are easier to see than are others. When more and more traffic is allowed to cross a bridge, at some point the bridge will crumble. And it will be the weakest member that fails first. This may be a crude analogy, but it appears that it will have to do for the present.

Attempts to Deal with Stress through Addictive Patterns of Behavior

Being stressed is uncomfortable. Furthermore, resolving the causes of stress is a long, tedious and inevitably uncomfortable process. Being merely human, we'd like something that's going to make us feel better **NOW**.

Fortunately or unfortunately, there exist a number of chemical agents which are capable of lifting our spirits, at least on a short-term basis. The most obvious and discussed of these is alcohol, but there are others, for instance narcotics. Additionally, there are perfectly legal and acceptable ingestibles which for some have mood-enhancing qualities. Here we're talking about food.

Overindulgence in any of these mood-altering agents has obvious negative implications for one's health. Alcohol can destroy one's liver, although an alcohol-related car crash might prevent this syndrome from achieving clinical significance. Narcotics may have disastrous effects. Even overindulgence in food can prove lethal. Obesity puts a tremendous strain on the heart and other bodily systems, leading to an early demise.

All of the above would appear to reinforce the view that one should seek to avoid excessive levels of stress as opposed to accepting them and attempting to cope through the use of chemical agents.

The Hypothalamus and the Autoimmune System

The last relationship between stress and health is a controversial, indeed even mysterious one. It has never been definitely proved. But it makes so much intuitive sense that, for our purposes in writing and reading this book, we might as well accept it as fact.

There lies deep within the brain a collection of neurological tissue clumped into nuclei called the "hypothalamus." "Hypothalamus," technically, means below the thalamus, but that's neither here nor there. But what is both here and there is the fact that this part of the brain bears some responsibility for the operation of two systems which are of immediate interest to us. The first function that the hypothalamus serves is that of channeling emotionality. The second function is that of overseeing the workings of the Autoimmune System.

The Autoimmune System, basically, directs the healing functions of the body. Specifically, it combats the encroachment of diseases that may invade the body. We are told, for instance, that cancerous cells emerge regularly in our bodies. But we are not usually diagnosed as having the "Big C." The reason for this reprieve is that agents of the Autoimmune System, specifically white blood cells, go out and, as it were, gobble up the diseased tissue.

But what happens when the hypothalamus is preoccupied with dealing with emotional issues, as during some manner of crisis? Well, obviously, there is less time and energy left for dealing with the workings of the Autoimmune System. In other words, times of extreme stress cause the brain to neglect its disease-fighting functions. And when this occurs, diseased tissue is not cleaned up as it should be. Thus, we may see the development of a definite disease process such as a malignancy and/or the development of a chronic autoimmune deficiency syndrome which leaves the person always fatigued and unable to function. One type of this dysfunction may be labeled "Chronic Fatigue Syndrome" (CFS)

The above may, indeed, strike the reader as somewhat fanciful, but some years ago, one of the authors was involved in a study, along with A.V.E. Harris and J. Collins which may shed some light on this matter. Patients with "neoplasms," growths, were given the Holmes and Rahe Scale before the nature of their tumor was diagnosed at the tumor clinic of a VA hospital in Virginia. The resulting data we presented at a conference in Scotland was a comparison of those patients who were subsequently diagnosed as having a malignancy with those whose neoplasms were benign. The graph we drew from these data had almost no overlap. Those who had cancer had much higher Holmes and Rahe scores than those whose growths were nonmalignant.

It seems altogether clear that stress may have a truly devastating effect upon one's physical health. And the inattention to the Autoimmune System controlled by a hypothalamus preoccupied with emotional concerns is a likely cause of at least some of these negative effects.

Summary

As so often happens, we have in the above seen no less than four explanations for the same phenomenon, that of people under stress being more prone to physical illness. To your writers, it isn't a matter of choosing which of these explanations is correct. They are probably all operative to one degree or another. Actually, to us it appears likely that all stress-related illnesses, given a detailed enough analysis, will show all four channels of causation. It may merely be a matter of which source causes the effect first.

Certainly, this chapter argues for the reduction of stress in one's life. Your life may depend upon it!

CHAPTER 11

DEPRESSION AND OTHER MENTAL HEALTH SYMPTOMS

Thus far in this book we have discussed problems in life as though they all flowed rather directly from stress. The reader, one is sure, will not be shocked to learn that this model of things is very much an over-simplification! People are subject to a variety of other problems, some of which are only indirectly related to stress and others which may have almost no relationship whatever to the "anti-hero" of our book. It is the purpose of this chapter to discuss these other problems. And then having done so, we may move on to our primary task of looking at how to deal with health problems which flow from the way in which we conduct our lives.

Defenses against Anxiety

Anxiety, quite obviously, is a highly uncomfortable condition. And people are motivated to try to terminate this unpleasant state when they do experience it and to avoid it when they do not. Some of these anxiety reducing "strategies" take the form of rather active efforts like fleeing from a tension-producing situation and seeking out and ingesting anxiety-relieving chemicals like alcohol. Much will be said about addictions in a later chapter.

Depression

What we will look at here are symptoms people develop, unconsciously if you will, to defend themselves against anxiety. The first among these is a state of low activity, sometimes fatigue, accompanied by negative emotions. This is depression.

The authors are not arguing, we rush to point out, that all depression is a defense against anxiety. There are times when life deals someone such a "bad hand" that a depressive episode become inevitable. And there are physical conditions, such as low blood pressure and certain endocrine conditions, which may cause an individual to experience depression.

But it has been so frequently noted in clinical settings that anxiety and depression occur together that there seems to be a pretty obvious tie-in between the two. Your authors' formulation of that connection is that, basically, the long-term experience of anxiety is such an unpleasant condition that the body will do practically anything in its efforts to escape from it. One coping mechanism seems to be to simply shut down. The individual's level of activity falls dramatically. Sad feelings and thoughts set in. The patient is now diagnosable as clinically depressed.

The fact that this negative emotional state is involved in what we have come to call bodily shutdown should perhaps tip us off to the fact that we may in our discussions thus far have been overlooking a major direction of influence. Up to now, we've been looking at the influence of psychological processes on bodily functioning. Perhaps this emphasis reflects the bias of the authors who are, after all, psychologists. But we need to also understand that things may also work the other way around.

Perhaps the best example of inactivity affecting one's mental outlook negatively is in physical illness. It is frequently reported that people who are injured or sick, particularly in cases such as orthopedic injuries which limit one's ability to get around, become depressed. Here we see the interplay between cause and symptom. A symptom of depression is inactivity. And if people are made to be inactive, they become depressed.

The above described model of the relationship between inactivity and depression may help us understand how a stressed person can lapse into a depression. Living with intense anxiety day after day may become truly unbearable. The body may give up, shut down, or perhaps it's simply a matter of being worn out. We're really not sure exactly what happens. We merely know that it's something akin to what has just been described.

Of course and as is in all probability true of everything discussed in this work, the above presented formulation of the development of depression is both incomplete and over-simplified. For example, cognitive (thinking) factors like negative self-verbalizations can have a strong depressant effect. After all, saying to yourself all day, "I'm ugly and incompetent" sure isn't going to create an up-beat mental state!

Regardless of how depression comes about, it is an important and often serious condition which is well-deserving of our attention in its own right.

What follows below is not intended to be a definitive discussion of the causes and treatments of depression. It is, rather, meant to be a very general guide to what a person him/herself or as a friend or relative of an apparently depressed person can and should do and what such an individual should not attempt. One of the most important things a "layperson" needs to know about depression is when the time comes to call in professional help.

Suicide and Suicide Prevention

It should come as no surprise to the reader that the greatest threat to the depressed person and the reason the frequent need to consult professionals is emphasized is the possibility of suicide. The potentially suicidal represent a genuine mental health emergency. People can and do kill themselves.

But the relationship between depression and suicide is not as simple and clear-cut as one might assume. Not all depressed people, fortunately, are suicidal, and not all suicides are depressed. The underlying and causative factor appears to be "hopelessness."

"Hopelessness" may be defined as a feeling that things are bad and there is no chance of they're getting better. Come to think of it and religious considerations aside, if your life is lousy and you know it will never improve, you might as well do yourself in. A case in point would be a dying person who is suffering from overwhelming pain. Such an individual knows that, realistically, her condition will only get worse and that all she has to look forward to is continuing misery and the creation of more financial problems for her family. Under such circumstances, it would seem that at least a case could be made that taking one's own life might be a reasonable course of action.

But in the "hopelessness" induced by the mental health syndrome of depression, in the vast majority of cases the negative outlook on life is not based on an objective and realistic assessment of the facts. Depression can strike anyone, including young, healthy, attractive, intelligent and educated people who, as they say, have everything to live for. Clearly, suicide is not the rational and appropriate course for a person such as this.

Given that those of us who can be objective about the above-described situation can see clearly that it would be a tragic mistake for such an individual to take her own life, it is, quite obviously, of utmost importance to do all we can to save the person. If we could, we would simply end the depression, thereby making the suicide potential go away with one fell swoop. As desirable as this thorough approach may appear, we will, regrettably, find that the treatment of depression is a long, slow and less than totally reliable process. We could well lose someone to their own hand in the midst of our well-intentioned treatment. Thus, we may have to do something pretty drastic to save a depressed person from a tragic end in order to apply what we know about intervening in this disorder and to assist that person in moving on to that brighter life we know that he is capable of attaining. Here we get into the area of Suicide Prevention.

First of all, how do we identify people who are at risk for killing themselves? Over the years, a number of signs of impending self-destructive actions have been noted. They are not foolproof. In other words, every time you see one of them it doesn't definitely mean that the person is going to kill herself. Further, cases of suicide in which none of these signs were present have been reported. And, admittedly, some of the signs are a "brilliant glimpse into the obvious." But they're still worth repeating here for the sake of completeness:

1. Threats, even oblique mentions of the possibility of taking one's own life. There is the belief, which is absolutely FALSE, that people who talk about killing themselves will never actually do it. As a matter of fact, this has been shown to be the most important danger sign of suicide. So always take such statements seriously!
2. A noticeable lack of interest in future events, as though the person was scheduled for an extended trip, which is not the case
3. The giving away of prized, personal possessions
4. A "devastating" setback to one's prestige, such as the unexpected loss of a political position which was of great importance to the person
5. A notable and prolonged depression

6. All of the above signs are to be taken even more seriously when seen in people who have made past attempts to kill themselves.

This brings us to the question of what one should do when confronted with the above signs or, more dramatically, with someone who announces that he's going to "end it all."

Over the years an informal technology of suicide prevention has evolved. These are the steps that have emerged:

1. Keep the person talking. In the face of this kind of potential crisis, don't, DON'T delay the necessary conversation. Don't, as the old joke goes, allow someone to call the suicide prevention hotline and be put on hold.
2. By all means, stay with the person you're concerned might kill herself. You may, as has happened to your writers, later be called a "nervous nanny," but that's a heck of a lot better than going to the funeral!
3. Allow the distressed person to go over what's got them upset. Chances are things will seem a lot less disastrous when they're "out on the table" than when they just boil and bubble within the person's own mind.
4. Help the person review his resources. Don't do this in a scornful way like, "A young healthy person like you should be ashamed for just thinking such a thing!" Instead, make gentle, supportive comments like, "Well, you know you do have a lot going for you." "You've certainly done well in school/on the football team." In times of crisis, such as the loss of a romantic relationship, people tend to forget the good things in their lives. It helps to remind them.
5. Develop a plan for the future. This could be just a series of appointments with "Dr. What's-his-Name."

A major goal throughout the above process is the development of a no-suicide contract. This, as the name implies, is an agreement on the part of the distraught individual to refrain from any self-destructive behaviors. Asking them to make this promise forever is a bit too much. What seems to work better is to make it time-limited, like "until our appointment tomorrow."

Don't be afraid to use the word "suicide" or the phrase "kill yourself." No one, as best we can tell, has ever been given the idea to kill herself by being asked about this possibility. Certainly with all the press attention given to celebrity suicides, it's extremely naïve to believe that anyone is going to hear about this negative behavior for the first time from you! Besides, we have never spoken to a seriously upset individual who had not given at least some thought to the possibility of self-destruction.

All of the above is a summary of how professionals and volunteer "suicide hotline" workers are trained. What should one do, though, when confronted with potential suicidal behavior if, say, your only exposure to this area has been reading this book? The recommendation offered here is that you pretty much stick with steps one and two, that is <u>stay with the person</u> and keep them talking. Get them to some type of mental health facility, like a community mental health center or the university counseling center. If these kinds of specialized facilities are not readily available, a hospital emergency room can be a good first stop on the way to help. The ER doc will know exactly who to call to handle the situation. Steps three through four may prove helpful in giving you ideas about what to talk about as you steer the person to professional help.

This authors would urge, indeed beg, anyone thrust into the position of dealing with the potentially suicidal to be very, very conservative. Always err on the side of caution. Make sure the professional to whom you ultimately take the person you are trying to help is made fully aware of what statements and behaviors caused you such concern. A little social awkwardness is a small price to pay for saving a life. Remember, people do kill themselves, and lives have been lost because people surrounding the distressed person didn't want to make fools of themselves by "overreacting."

Good luck!

Treating Depression

At this point, it is believed that it may be helpful to discuss the treatment of depression. As is true of all parts of this book, the aim here is not to make you a professional psychotherapist. Rather, the goal is to give you some insights or ideas into how such problems may be dealt with. In this way, perhaps you'll be able to be at least constructive in your relationships with people who are experiencing minor problems in these various areas.

There are, in the authors' opinion, three main steps in the treatment of minor or "garden variety" depression:

1. Attempt to deal with the basic causes of the depression. This step involves two major and yet overlapping considerations.

Firstly, it needs to be acknowledged that some situations are just depressing, period. Might you be in one? Is there any way for you to formulate a plan to get out? Think about it, but more importantly try to do something about it!

The second set of considerations here relates to the general model of this book that stress plays a central role in so many of our physical and mental problems. This, of course, would include depression. If the reader can accept this conceptualization, at least in part, then it becomes clear as we attempt to deal with depression that we must go through all the steps that we have found important in stress reduction. They are, by way of review:

A. Is the person's life one with a reasonable and manageable number of stressors and a sufficient number of satisfactions in life? Or, as it was stated semi-facetiously, is her bowling ball balanced?

B. Are his interpretations of the stressors "healthy"? That is, basically, are they associated with reasonable and achievable expectations?

C. Has the person done all he can to reduce the stress remaining after working as hard as he can on steps A and B above? Does she routinely work into her day relaxing activities, and, possibly, even utilize formal relaxation exercises?

D. Has she developed within herself some understanding of the inevitability of some stress in life and a degree of acceptance of this fact?

Assuming the underlying psychological cause for depression has been taken care of through the "bowling ball treatment" described above, we may now move on to the other purely psychological treatments for this disorder:

2. Increasing activity level. As noted above, both a key sign and cause of depression is inactivity. Depressed people are inactive. They don't get out. They just mope around the house. They let things like the housework go. They may even stop reading and retreat to a life of constant TV watching. In its extreme form, depression may reduce one's life to lying around, drifting in and out of fitful snatches of sleep.

An often overlooked treatment for depression is to attack activity level directly. This may meet with a lot of resistance from the depressed person. What they tend to think and say is, "When I get to feeling better, I'll get out and do more." But it doesn't work that way. In most cases, people get out and start living life again and in the process discover they're less depressed.

One step we've found helpful in working with clients, naïve though it may seem, is to give them the following instructions:

> Every day as you have your morning coffee (assuming, of course, that they're coffee drinkers), I'd like you to make a list of all the things you would do today if you weren't depressed. Then, make yourself do everything on that list!

Despite the obvious simplicity of this "technique," we've seen its use associated with a lessening of depression in a number of cases.

Another variant on this theme is to establish for yourself a regular routine of activities. During periods of stress and discouragement in particular, one of your writers sets for himself a number of daily goals, say a certain number of pages read or written and a fixed amount of data collection. Forcing himself to adhere to this schedule keeps him occupied for a number of hours each day, thereby boosting his activity level. Not just incidentally, these activities help take his mind off such discouraging thoughts as, "I'm not sure any of this is going to pay off."

But what if the depressed person just doesn't feel "up to" a regular schedule of activities. Here's where friends and relatives can really step in and make a difference in the loved one's life. Depending on the specifics of your relationship with the individual, you can somewhere between suggest and insist that she get out and do a couple or three things. Again, please don't do this in a scolding or demeaning manner. The last thing in the world a depressed person needs is to be told, "Look at you, you're just a worthless bump on a log!" Parenthetically, inducing anger is a recognized technique in the treatment of depression, but its use should probably be confined to professional workers. This is because it is a procedure which is not without its dangers, and it will tend not to do your relationship with the person any good!

Use suggestion and gentle encouragement. "I'm going to the store, and I'd enjoy your company." "I need help with a little project I've got on for this evening." Try explaining what we know about the relationship between level of activity and depression. If you're unable to get the person moving through these methods, this is probably an indication that a referral to a professional is in order.

In planning activities, try to work in a number each week that are enjoyable and "fun." For instance, one woman and her husband have a semi-formal routine of enjoyable activities. They include an inexpensive but generous breakfast at a casino each Friday morning. (One can usually get away with sneaking into work a bit late on Fridays). Lunch is along the Truckee River on sunny days where they feed a squirrel they've nicknamed "George." On other days, they have the luncheon special at one of the downtown clubs. They usually go out for a drink about one night a week, and this is often followed up by supper on evenings when their children won't be home. They plan a small day or perhaps overnight trip every few months and a "big" vacation, like to Hawaii, Alaska or outside the country every year. All this not only keeps them busy but gives them things to look forward to.

3. The cognitive side of things. "Cognitive" or "cognition" is just a fancy word for thinking. It is being brought up here because negative thinking is both a symptom and cause of depression. When we're depressed we say down things like, "I'm a failure," "Life isn't worth living," "Woe is me." Less understood is the fact that such down in the mouth statements actually seem to play a role in causing that negative and uncomfortable state we've come to label depression.

Part of the "trick" in overcoming depression lies in ending such "blue" thoughts. Of course, you can't stop one thought without a better thought. What we need to do, thus, is to encourage the generation and repetition of positive verbalizations. As a friend or relative, you can do this in a gentle, supportive manner. Remind the person about past successes and assets. "You know, today reminds me of the day you graduated from OCS. I still have the bars I pinned on you that day." This set of "interventions" flows generally from the work in cognitive therapy of Aaron Beck, M.D. (1921 -) and as carried forward by his daughter Judith Beck, Ph.D. (1954 -).

> One of the authors has utilized with himself a technique which, to the best of his knowledge, has never been scientifically reported or, admittedly, validated. It is reminiscent of reports of individuals who have successfully withstood concentration camps, although he cannot claim to have been subjected to experiences as extreme as these!

What I do every day is <u>try</u> to recall what I was doing on that day, say Monday, each week for the past month. Then I review, as best I can remember, what I was doing on this day of the month for the past year. Finally, I go over what I was involved in at this time of the year for the past decade. During this process, I focus on what I call "good days," days during which I recall experiencing some form of pleasure or enjoyment. The message I try to convey to myself is, basically, if you've had "good days" in the past, then you can have them again in the future. A variant on this theme is to purposefully think of a particularly enjoyable segment of your life. I really enjoy traveling, so this quite often relates to trips I've taken. I try to imagine and re-experience each and every point I can recall about the enjoyable experience. This process is aided, at times, by my collection of photograph albums. By flipping through them, I can be again almost anywhere I might wish, from Hawaii to Europe. You might try this or your own variant of it with yourself. It can buck you up!

The only point to this admittedly rambling discussion is that one should encourage the depressed person, be it yourself or someone else, to think about the positives in life. We have given people cards on which positive attributes they posses, such as "health, "youth," "intelligence" and "attractiveness," were written and suggested that the person whip out the card and review it on an hourly basis. No formal assessment of the effectiveness of this procedure has been conducted, but the informal feedback we have received has indicated to us that it can be helpful.

A general note on Cognitive (Behavioral) (Psycho)Therapy and the special case of "Soap Opera Therapy"

As implied above, cognitive therapy is a set of techniques in which a client is helped to "think through" her or his problems in order to deal with them in more comfortable and successful ways. We have actually seen examples of this general set of principles at several earlier points in this book. Sitting down to make certain that you have only a reasonable number of expectations or "stressors" would qualify here. Albert Ellis' work in developing "rational" interpretations of life's events is another example. We briefly alluded to the work of Aaron and Judith Beck in this field earlier in this chapter on treating depression.

A variant of cognitive-behavioral psychotherapy involves learning from the examples of others. It is quite common, of course, to hear people say,

"I'd like to be more like her," or, "I certainly wouldn't want to be like him!" Such statements may be based on observed outcomes, inspiring us to emulate the characters and behaviors of successful individuals and to shun the traits of those who have been labeled "failures." For example here, in the last chapter of this work, we hold up the lives of Jesus Christ and Richard Nixon as two of those from whom we can learn in structuring and directing our own lives.

But the "people" from whom we can learn do not actually have to be real. For example, people for centuries have learned of the dangers of excessive vanity from Narcissus' drowning. The fable of Midas instructs about the dangers of greed. Looking at more contemporary "fables," JR's hedonistic, free-wheeling lifestyle created "complexities" in his life, including getting shot!

Soap Opera Therapy

As valuable as some of the above-cited classical "fables" may be, they typically present only a single grand lesson, which is not applicable to everyone. And they are usually lengthy into the bargain. By contrast, it turns out that an unending supply of trials and tribulations, triumphs and disasters, romance and heartache flows from daytime TV in the form of soap operas.

One of us made this "discovery," as has been the case with almost everything in his life and career, unwittingly and accidently. I was working in the forensic building of a large southern state hospital. Once a week, Thursday at 1:30 as I recall, we had our weekly staff meeting on the small women's unit. The only place suitable for such a meeting was in the TV room, so the ladies were, unfortunately and to their distress, sent out of that room during our meetings.

Being obsessive-compulsive, I would always go down to the "female unit" on time. However, my colleagues would "straggle in" over the next 15 to 20 minutes. This fact meant that I was able to sit for a while with the ladies and watch part of their soap opera with them. More important, however, was that this set of circumstances permitted me to hear their comments, some of which I eventually came to regard as enlightening.

Some general examples of these comments were, "Don't get involved with that man, Girl. He ain't nothing but trouble" and, "Alexis, don't you remember that Jennifer done the same thing and got herself thrown in jail?" For what it may be worth, I found myself generally agreeing with their psychosocial assessments!

From then on, during commercials and in subsequent therapeutic contacts with these female patients, I would pose the following general and variously worded question, "How is it that you're so good at seeing how the characters in these soap operas are getting into trouble, while seeming to have so much difficulty in recognizing these 'danger signals' in your own life?" The ladies generally agreed that this was a valid question for them. One of the women, who was particularly expressive, literally dropped her jaw when I put this question to her!

Presumably, the women in my Soap Opera Therapy group used this cognitive technique in analyzing and improving their own lives, although, admittedly, there were no follow-up studies conducted. I was, though, asked to describe this "therapy" at a meeting of state-wide forensic mental health personnel, giving some perhaps official "stamp" to my "inventor" status.

Oh, yes, I realize there's probably nothing really new about "Soap Opera Therapy." Bibliotherapy has been in existence for years, and comparisons with others, both real and fictional, are frequently employed in "talk therapy," as implicitly acknowledged at the beginning of this section. But I enjoy being the inventor of Soap Opera Therapy. It enhances my self-esteem. So please don't muddle things with inconvenient facts!

Other Defenses against Anxiety

Depression is by no means the only way the body may defend itself against anxiety. Another important mechanism which may be brought into play involves obsessions and compulsions. Obsessions are thoughts which keep running through one's head despite the desire to end them, and compulsions are behaviors which one has to do over and over despite the recognition that they are unproductive or even harmful. A good example of a compulsion is "tricitillamania," or hair pulling. Some individuals become so caught up in this pattern of behavior that they hair-pull themselves almost completely bald.

Since obsessions and compulsions seem to get worse during times of stress, it would seem that we are justified in relating them also to defenses against anxiety. What appears to happen is that we find that something, like biting our nails or straightening papers, makes us feel more comfortable. Admittedly, we don't exactly know why this is so, but it just seems to work that way. Then in the future when we're stressed again, we fall back into that behavior, apparently in an effort to make ourselves feel better. Of course, we want to feel better, but it's a bit embarrassing not to have fingernails.

As with other types of mental problems, the way we go about trying to deal with obsessions and compulsions is to first of all make efforts to reduce the background level of stress. Here we go back to our "stress cycle" and the points at which we can intervene.

As soon as the general level of stress has been reduced as much as possible, we turn to an attempt to eliminate the specific symptom. Here the earlier chapter on controlling your own behavior comes into play. Again, start by charting. There have been cases in which the mere recording of such negative behaviors as hair-pulling has actually eliminated them. Apparently, the "hassle" of counting each strand of hair was so burdensome that the patient just gave up the whole thing!

But it would not, unfortunately, be realistic to expect such a dramatic and sudden change routinely. Consequently, it's wise to have some type of plan for dealing with an undesirable habit. In addition to the general advice about behavior change, a specific group of techniques applicable to this particular set of problems relates to finding behaviors which are incompatible with the ones which are causing problems. For example, some success has been had by responding to the urge to nail-bite by going into isometric exercises. Doing your relaxation exercises might also prove a good alternative to such problematic habits as nail-biting and hair-pulling.

In dealing with obsessions, repeated and unwanted thoughts, a technique called "thought stopping" may prove useful. Simply stop what you're doing and yell at yourself "STOP" and turn your thinking to a preplanned and positive thought.

As always, if what you try doesn't work, it's time to seek professional assistance.

Professional Interventions for Serious Disorders

Depression is an unpleasant and often dangerous mental state. Professional help is readily available to those afflicted with this disorder. It is the authors' strong opinion that this resource should be called upon much more frequently than is, in fact, the case.

In addition to managing suicidal potential and giving psychotherapeutic assistance, professional workers may have access to antidepressant medications. Unfortunately, these drugs are very much hit-or-miss in their effects. About half of the people who take medications for depression report experiencing unacceptable side effects. And of those who can take them without negative reactions, only about half seem to have their depressed state improved. All this is by way of saying that it would be a great mistake to look to chemicals for a solution to depression. It must be worked on intensely by the depressed person and by those around him or her. The steps outlined above in this chapter were designed to give some guidance as to how to approach this difficult task.

Yet there might be another way to understand depression, which might be unrelated to the amount of stress that we are experiencing. Viktor Frankl recognized in the early 1930s that human beings not only want to know "from what" to live. They also want to know "towards what" to live. Frankl concluded that we need food to live, but also we need a purpose in life. He suggested that the causes of depression may not be only experienced in our physical bodies as tiredness or in our psyche as sadness. He discovered in his research that depression can originate in the spiritual dimension of a person. "In cases where a spiritual problem, a moral conflict, or an existential crisis is etiologically the basis of depression, we speak of spiritual emptiness (existential vacuum) or a sense of meaninglessness, manifesting itself in feelings of boredom and in a sense of indifference."

This surely sounds like typical, common depression that many of us have experienced. Frankl terms this depression Noogenic Neurosis which is an existential frustration that has become pathological. However, when a person discovers a solution in the spiritual dimension, the psychophysical part of us might discover something like contentment and occasionally a deep satisfaction as she or he engages in meaningful and healthy behaviors. This is most acutely true of reactive or situational depression that is based within an unresolved problem within the spiritual level of a person, most commonly known as a conflict of personal values.

As the reader is well aware, this book has presented a model for explaining and dealing with life's problems which very much focuses on the key concept of stress. At this point, though, it must be acknowledged again that not all troublesome behaviors fit neatly into this framework.

One of the main conditions that lie outside of the area we've staked out is a most serious group of mental disorders known as the psychoses. Psychosis is a general term which means "out of touch with reality." In some important and significant way the psychotic person is not participating in the same world as the rest of us. The most prevalent form of psychosis is schizophrenia, and the most dramatic and publicized variant of schizophrenia is the paranoid type. Such people display delusions of grandeur and persecution. They feel that they are some important personage and/or people are plotting to harm them. The TV portrayal of the man who thinks he's Napoleon is an attempt to present this disorder.

But schizophrenia is not the only kind of psychosis. Another type is characterized by mood swings. This is what has traditionally been called "Manic-Depression, "but has now been relabeled "Bipolar Disorder." These serious mental disorders, as well as others, usually require medical treatment administered by psychiatrists and coordinated with ongoing psychosocial interventions.

There are also "character disorders," lifelong patterns of troublesome behaviors which are highly resistant to professional treatment. It is very unlikely that anyone who cares enough about the topic of mental health to get this far in this book would fall into this category.

Regardless of the name you call them by or your theory as to what causes them, these major mental disorders are not merely reactions to stress. They will have to be dealt with by professional workers or there will be serious problems for both the afflicted person and those around him or her.

A Note on the Remainder of this Book

Some explanation for how the following portions of this work have been put together may prove useful to the reader. Further, it is felt that it would help to put this plan within the context of a restatement of the overall organization of the book. It is, after all, so easy to get lost in details.

As the reader will, hopefully, recall, what is being presented here is a model of health and happiness based on stress and our reactions to it. We began by making mention of the importance of an intimate relationship as the basis for a happy and satisfying life on which a pattern of well-adjusted dealing with stress could be based. Suggestions as to how to achieve intimacy were given both theoretically and by way of examples.

We then discussed the points at which one might attempt to bring stress down to manageable levels. These points of opportunity, by way of review, were:

1. Reducing the number of stressors through getting one's "bowling ball" in balance
2. Developing within yourself more adaptive, that is less self-demanding and perfectionistic, ways of looking at how you're dealing with stressors, and;

3. Methods for dealing with stress and anxiety as soon as all that can be done has been done in the preceding two steps

Moving into the announced primary focus of this work, that being health, it was noted that there are four ways in which stress can have a negative effect upon one's well-being. The channels by which stress can affect health are:

1. Directly through the effects of sympathetic arousal, as in high blood pressure
2. Pushing us to engage in negative health behaviors such as addictions
3. Selye's General Adaptation Syndrome
4. Stress can bring about a reduction in the efficiency of the Auto-Immune System, an effect presumably controlled by the hypothalamus at the base of the brain.

It would have been satisfying to the authors' compulsivity, the reader might add "dull" style of writing, to make a separate chapter on the mechanisms of causation in each of these four areas and then another chapter in each area on relevant treatments. Alas however, this neat scheme doesn't appear to fit the reality of things. First of all, the last two stress-disease causes are so theoretical, perhaps one would say even speculative, that there is precious little more one can say about them. These two formulations overlap considerably, additionally and obviously.

The "key" in this area, as in so many others, is prevention. At this point, one can do little more than repeat the pleas that you strive to prevent the kind of buildup of stressors and attendant stress that will result in the Exhaustion Phase of the General Adaptation Syndrome and/or impairment of the Auto-Immune System. Hopefully, an understanding of these health-endangering mechanisms will assist one in short-circuiting their negative actions. For example, during times of crisis, the wise person would request a "break." She would understand that a temporary retreat from the "action" would be not only in the service of her health, but would, in the long run, enable her to make a larger contribution to the cause of resolving the crisis. This is, admittedly, difficult advice to follow when caught up in the "heat of battle," but hopefully it will be at least considered. With the exception of some brief comments to be made about mobilizing the Auto-Immune System in the treatment of diseases, particularly cancer, we will have to leave these two intriguing topics here.

Of the two remaining stress-disease links, the first, sympathetic arousal, is, quite obviously, more direct and easier to understand. But since the emphasis of this book is on prevention and "taking care of first things first," we'll consider cause number two first. This is because negative health behaviors, such as addictions and inactivity, need to be eliminated before we can deal productively with changing the remaining health problems.

The reader may note that up to the present point, an important component, most assuredly the most important component, of the "equation" for successful living has been almost totally left out. This relates, metaphorically speaking, to the "pins" toward which our "bowling ball" is aimed. Here we are considering our long-term, we may say "philosophical," goals in life, which gets us into issues which deal with the very meaning of life itself. Your authors will address themselves to this weighty topic in the final chapter. If the quantity of our writing in that chapter is proportionate to our actual and certain knowledge in the area, this should be by far the shortest chapter in this book!

CHAPTER 12

NEGATIVE HEALTH BEHAVIORS:
The Case of the Addictions

If we've been unsuccessful in dealing with the stressors of life, as detailed above, then we are left with a great deal of what we may call "residual stress." Stress, anxiety, nervousness, being "uptight," as everyone knows, is a most unpleasant state. And people experiencing this unpleasant condition will do about anything they can to relieve it, whether this action is healthy or not. Regrettably, there exist a number of "things," most chemicals, which can rapidly and reliably reduce anxiety, as well as other unhappy mood states such as depression, feelings of inadequacy, loneliness, sense of abandonment, feeling like a failure, etc., etc. The problem with these chemical "solutions" to the problems of living is that they may, and often do, have long-term negative effects upon one's life. DUIs and liver damage are just two of the specifics which come readily to mind here.

While stress is, undoubtedly, a major culprit in the creation of addictions, it is certainly not the only explanation for their cause. This is not at all to dismiss the basic premise of this work that stress and lifestyle, particularly when conflicts in values are involved, are very much implicated in the great majority of health problems we suffer. It is merely to acknowledge that other factors are also relevant.

Durand F. Jacobs was a clinical psychologist who for many years worked within the VA system of hospitals and has advanced a "General theory of Addictions." According to Dr. Jacobs' formulation, there are two factors which predispose a person to the development of an addiction:

1. A state of chronic over- or under-arousal. Here we're talking about either being hyperactive or bored. Clearly, a state of chronic anxiety would qualify as a kind of hyperactivity, so the basic premise of this work is not contradicted by Jacobs' formulation.
2. A state of psychological pain, often based on the rejection by a significant other

Clearly, a person in the throes of these two conditions described by Jacobs is going to be rather constantly uncomfortable. And, as we've seen so many times already in this work, it's most difficult for a person to bear and face a situation in which he's been miserable and feels that he's looking forward to a future in which he can foresee nothing but further misery and unhappiness. The body, certainly, is highly motivated to do something about this unhappy condition. Some people may develop a physical illness. Some may become depressed. Some people may even develop a major mental disorder, perhaps on the scale of a psychosis.

There are those, however, who for one reason or another can't seem to go any of these routes to relieving the misery. Some of these individuals may, happily, short-circuit the process. That is to say they may do something about their unpleasant state <u>before a breakdown occurs</u>. This "short-circuiting" may be positive in nature, as for example when one examines her life in terms of the stress cycle and takes action at one of the possible points of intervention.

Some people, however, discover ways to relieve the distress which are far less positive than reorganizing their lives. Here we get into the matter of addictive behaviors.

When we hear the term "addiction," the thing that jumps immediately into mind is "chemicals." Indeed, the best known addictions are those to alcohol and drugs. But we have learned in recent years that an addictive process can take place in the absence of any substance or chemical agent.

As a matter of fact, Jacobs' clinical work and research focused on the problem of pathological gambling, an interest shared by one of your writers since his move to Nevada over thirty years ago.

One point about addictions which creates both confusion and scientific interest relates to the vastly different effects the various substances and activities have on the individual who engages in them. Probably the two most dramatic poles of this continuum or dimension are alcohol and cocaine. Alcohol, of course, is a "sedative-hypnotic." Its primary effect is that of inducing a state of calmness and relaxation. It also, though, has the effect of inducing a state of euphoria or joy, which somewhat complicates the picture. Cocaine, on the other hand, is a powerful stimulant. It creates a state of hyper-arousal and hyper-vigilance. Its effects, reportedly, in many ways resemble the feelings you get when you drink too much coffee or take allergy pills that make some people "up-tight" and "wired."

The dramatic difference between the two chemicals of alcohol and cocaine even has a striking parallel in nonchemical addictive behavior. In the area of pathological or compulsive gambling, there appear to be some activities which have the effect of increasing the level of arousal and others which do the opposite. Some games, like craps, are exciting and very much heighten the person's level of arousal. Others seem to allow the individual to go into a hypnotic-like trance, which some patients report lets them escape for a time from their troubles into a calm, serene (albeit artificial) world. Slot machine play seems to have this effect on many. A case in point here would be a 30 year-old woman with two children who goes regularly to a small bar to relax after a hard day at work. She finds working all day and going home to small children as well as a cranky husband to be stressful. Going to the bar, drinking and playing the slot machines have a calming effect on her. And this habit gives her artificially-induced confidence in her ability to deal with the difficult situation she will face at home. The obvious problem here is that she is, among other negatives, losing tons of money that she can't afford.

So people engage in addictions both to calm themselves down and pep themselves up. A theory which relies upon a single cause for the addictions would appear to have a lot of explaining to do! This is where Jacobs' theory provides us with so much help. The reader will recall that he tells us that the basic source of underlying discomfort can be either over-arousal or under-arousal. Of course, it may well be that some people are innately or naturally just more up or down than others. In these cases the person has been dealt something with which he or she will have to struggle during the entire course of her/his life. An excellent and, indeed, inspiring example of such an individual was Winston Churchill. From reading his biography, it would appear that Mr. Churchill had a tendency toward depression. He even had a name for it - "The Black Dog." As history well records, Churchill dealt with his problem in a highly constructive manner, at least in the main, through a life of gallantry and public service. In extreme cases, though, such imbalances, in either the direction of being over- or under-aroused, will need chemical intervention, under medical supervision, of course.

At the risk of boring the reader with even more repetition of the same point, the writers would note that it is highly possible for a physically normal individual to create within herself a state of under- or over-arousal through the way in which she conducts her life. A person who commits to a seventy or eighty hour work week is going to end up feeling pretty harried and stressed, a state either resembling anxiety or actually creating chronic anxiety. Alternately, someone who just sits around the house, who has developed neither friends nor hobbies, is going to feel bored, perhaps even depressed. Can the reader tell where the authors are going with all this? That's right, to the matter of balance in one's life, as discussed in the chapter on the "Bowling Ball Theory of Life." Sometimes one simply can't resist the temptation of working something like that in!

But it is being sincerely argued that the issue of balance in life is very relevant to an understanding and management of the addictions. After all, it's hard to believe that a person would wake up one morning and, in effect, say:

> Gosh, what a beautiful day! I feel great because I'm so healthy. You know, I've got a great life. My spouse and I are extremely happily married. Our kids are doing wonderfully both academically and socially. I love my job, and the boss is the most terrific gal in the world. The house is paid for, and we've got no debts to speak of. I have a number of hobbies which really hold my interest...I think I'll...go blow all my money at a "21" table...put my brain to sleep with booze..."mellow" myself beyond comprehension with marijuana...hype myself up with cocaine...etc.

All of the above is simply by way of arguing that what has come to be the "traditional" explanation for addictions just doesn't seem to "hold water." Here we're considering, basically, the idea that they are based on some form of allergy to or, alternately, an intolerance of a certain substance. Firstly, assuming the reader accepts the writers' logic as presented above, it's hard to imagine a happy, well-rounded person developing an addiction in the first instance. Secondly, the allergy/intolerance explanation fails to explain such non-chemical addictions as "workaholism" and compulsive gambling. Compulsive gambling, for example, rather clearly follows the pattern of an addiction in that, like drug addiction, it involves such classic features as the need for increasing amounts of the substance/activity and even withdrawal symptoms.

But, as in the case of compulsive gambling, there is no substance involved in many of these addictions. So, as the authors predictably argue, we must look into the mental/psychological state of the afflicted individual for an explanation or explanations. And before dealing narrowly with the addiction itself, as in going on antabuse or, as is possible in Europe, asking to be barred from the casinos, one should examine his/her life to see that it is truly in balance. If it is not in balance, as described earlier, then one should take the necessary steps to make it so. As always, should your own efforts prove ineffective, then it's time to seek professional assistance.

Before proceeding to the specifics of dealing with a potential or active addiction, a word needs to be said here about the spouse of the addicted individual. Much has been said, and truly so, about the fact that the spouse is not to blame or responsible for the addict's problems and irresponsible behavior. Even so, there are indications from the literature on compulsive gambling, with which one of your authors has been quite familiar, that the spouse of the addict tends to be a rather uninteresting and unsupportive individual. So what does all this mean when we try to deal with the addictive behavior of a spouse or "significant other"? To the writers it means that it is as fruitless for the spouse as for so-called professionals to deal immediately and exclusively with the addiction itself. After all, what have our success rates been like? We can summarize them for you in one word – poor! So such typical actions, usually reactions, as shaming the person, throwing bottles of liquor into the trash and taking the gambler off the checking account, are doomed from the onset. So what is a spouse to do?

The first step is to ask the functionally addicted person if he's happy. You may count on the answer being "no." Nice statements to make at this point are in the order of "Is there something I'm doing wrong?" and/or "Is there something I can do to make things better?" The addict may well be unable to explain what you're doing wrong or how you could improve. In point of fact, this is far and away the most desirable outcome! But this exchange makes the troubled person feel valued and supported and should help to give the individual strength to face and deal with his addiction.

We are now, at long last, prepared to examine the specific addictions. But before doing so, a point made earlier needs to be stressed again here. This relates to the futility of dealing solely with the addictive behavior. We must first make major improvements in the person's underlying and general mental condition. Failure to do so leaves the motivation to use and abuse still there, and we may count on an eventual reemergence of a full-blown addiction at a later date.

Alcoholism

Alcoholism, with the possible exception of overeating which will be considered in the next chapter on weight control, represents the most troublesome pattern of addictive behavior for our society. And America is by no means the only place where "the sauce" is causing difficulties. Some years ago the amount of vodka drunk in the former Soviet Union rose to such a point that an alarmed President Gorbachev mounted a major campaign aimed at reducing drinking.

Undoubtedly, everyone who reads this book is familiar with the drug alcohol, most of us from personal experience. But, hopefully, a short review won't prove too tedious, and it might even bring out some facets of this all so familiar substance of which you were unaware.

First of all, ethanol, drinking alcohol, is a sedative-hypnotic. Its main effect is that of <u>depressing</u> the activities of the brain. This may come as a surprise to some who have seen people "turned on" by booze. There are so many stories of the shy librarian who goes to a party and gets a few drinks in her and becomes outgoing, even seductive. It appears for all the world that the alcohol had a stimulating effect on the typically reserved young lady. What, however, has actually occurred is that the substance has depressed the upper levels of her brain, those very areas which control "judgment," or in the case of the shy person, inhibitions.

The above discussion gets us back to the admittedly dull area of the nervous system. The brain's evolution is clearly seen in its present form. The more primitive "action-oriented" portions are on the inside, and the more recently evolved "civilized' parts are on the outside, specifically the Cerebral Cortex. As is usual in biology, younger, less mature tissue is more sensitive to the influence of chemicals. Thus when we drink it is the upper levels of the brain, those that sternly tell us not to do things which we might otherwise be want to do, that are put to sleep first. Thus, all that "animal energy" pours forth when we're in a state of drunkenness.

As drinking continues, progressively lower levels of the brain become affected, that is put to sleep. At some point, the intoxicated person will lose consciousness. This is, in actuality, a very adaptive reaction. That is because if the numbing process gets deep enough into the brain, specifically to the Medulla, the person will stop breathing and his heart will cease beating. Regrettably, the unfortunate short-circuiting of this passing out mechanism has occurred in the course of college "chug-a-lug" contests, resulting in the tragic deaths of young students.

Hopefully, moving back from the morbid theme reflected above, our understanding of the physiological effects of alcohol consumption will assist us in understanding the motivation for engaging in this health-damaging behavior. It would appear that those most at risk for excessive indulgence in the behavior of consuming alcohol would posses either or more likely both of the following characteristics/problems:

1. A state of chronic anxiety/nervousness
2. Negative, self-derogatory thoughts which keep running through the person's cortex

Alcohol, it is easily seen by reconsidering its actions, would have the effect, reliably but temporarily and sometimes harmfully, of relieving both of these uncomfortable states. As a depressant, it immediately has a calming effect upon our tense, uptight individual. And as alcohol has its most dramatic influence on the thinking part of the brain, it helps to make negative thoughts go away.

From just what we've considered so far, alcohol would seem to be a generally good thing. And, indeed, it is, at least in moderation. There is even some evidence that moderate drinkers are healthier than either heavy drinkers or teetotalers. What, you might ask then, is moderate drinking? Judgments on this vary from one or two drinks a day to three to four over the course of a day. Usually, people are well aware of when they are drinking "too much."

But there are problems associated with the use of alcohol. Some of these are of a long-term kind, and others are more transitory.

But the long-term, disastrous results aside, what do we know about the immediate, short run effectiveness of attempting to deal with anxiety through the use of the chemical agent alcohol? Here, as they say, the verdict is "mixed." Again, the key concept which is emerging is that of "moderation."

Let's use some examples. Fred is an attorney. His life is generally well-balanced and satisfying to him. But as a trial lawyer a certain amount of stress in his daily life is unavoidable. So when Fred arrives home from his current trial after a day of bickering and being on guard about what the other side may have found out, a martini or two sounds pretty good to our worthy solicitor. In fact, to a lot of guys like Fred a belt or two as the sun goes down is something to be looked forward to, regardless of how generally happy and well-balanced their lives may be.

Let's graph Fred's anxiety during the course of his busy, productive day. Because, as pointed out so eloquently by Hans Selye, no one's life can be totally without stress, we've included in Figure 12-1 a blue line which shows a normal or comfortable level of activation, at least for the subject under consideration.

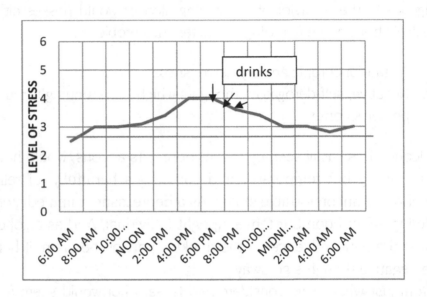

FIGURE 12-1. Level of Stress Experienced by Fred, Esq.

So, as shown by the afternoon section of our graph, our attorney friend got a little stressed-out during the part of the trial that followed the lunch recess. Perhaps his client said something dumb, or maybe he said something dumb! In any case, things got a bit "hot," and our hero is slightly on edge as he walks through the kitchen door. Happily, Mrs. Esquire greets him with a smile and a dry martini. The couple sits down to discuss the day's events and sip their drinks. This is followed by supper accompanied by a glass of wine. Fred begins to relax as he speaks about his frustrations of the day. The martini and wine facilitate, help along, this relaxation and give a little "glow" to his perceptions of the world. He asks Virginia about her day, also and of course. As they rise from the supper table, both Fred and Virginia are more relaxed and enthusiastic about the evening activities they've planned. The effects of the booze have mostly worn off by the time they walk to their neighbors' house for their weekly game of Trivial Pursuit. Certainly, no harm is being done, either physically or socially, by this level of alcohol consumption.

Now, let's change Fred's life just a bit and see what this does to the picture with respect to alcohol. It turns out that our hero is a junior partner in a law firm of rich old coots. All of the tough, mean cases are given to Fred, while the senior partners are out on the golf course. It's gotten to the point that Fred's average work week is about seventy hours. He doesn't always want to work under these conditions, but he'd like to get ahead in life, and he figures that working hard now and gaining some form of social prominence will assist him in doing this. So he's also extensively involved in various civic organizations, as well as being the Junior Warden of his church. All this, naturally, adds tremendously to his work load.

This "put-upon" Fred has gone through the exact same trial as our earlier described protagonist. But because of all of the other demands, "stressors," with which he has to contend he came to it in a much more weakened and "harried" state. Consequently, as depicted in Figure 12-2, he arrives home in a condition that can best be described as a "nervous wreck."

There is no one to greet poor Fred as he walks through the garage door. His wife is in the den watching TV. Fred plops his briefcase on the roll-top desk.

"Hello, Honey," he says in as upbeat a manner as he could muster under the circumstances.

"Hi, Dear," Virginia responds perfunctorily, barely turning her eyes from the screen on which is being played out the high drama of a quiz show.

"Care for a drink?'

"Yeah, just a little white wine."

Fred, now abandoning any pretense of being upbeat, walks back into the kitchen and pours his wife a glass of wine. He pulls a bottle of fine Scotch from a cabinet and pours, oh…a few fingers into a glass and fills the remaining space in the vessel with tap water.

Virginia is so absorbed in *Wheel of Fortune* that she merely nods her acknowledgment of the receipt of the wine. Fred plops, drink in hand, into an easy chair.

Fred is anxious, bored, lonely and miserable. He quickly tires of the game show. After pouring himself another drink, he walks into the living room where he listens to classical music and paces. There's an attempt to read the paper while he works on another drink. There was wine with supper, but he didn't really notice what kind. As a matter of fact, the next day he had to think real hard to remember what they had had to eat.

As Fred shaves the next morning, there's a queasiness in the pit of his stomach. His head hurts. He feels irritable, on edge. Our hero has a hangover. Unfortunately, he often wakes up like this.

All during the morning phase of the trial he keeps looking at his watch. "The Old Fool's gotta call a recess soon," he keeps thinking to himself. "It sure will be good to get some lunch." Fred knows of a place, an Italian restaurant, where everyone, everyone has at least one glass of Chianti with lunch. It was simply the thing to do. Besides, he considered, supposedly as an afterthought, the wine wouldn't do his hangover any harm.

One can easily see that Fred is attempting to deal with an overwhelming level of anxiety and unhappiness through chemical means. He has, of course, succeeded in getting his level of anxiety post-trial below that which is unacceptable. But this was accomplished through artificial means, booze. And once he got comfortable enough through this artificial mechanism, his powers of reasoning were so "gone" that he simply continued drinking. After all, if four drinks make you feel this good, what will eight do? Now, what happened in the morning? Figure 12-2 shows what happened to Fred during the night. What Figure 12-2 shows, basically, is that the "piper must be paid." If our lives are not in balance and satisfying, a chemical such as alcohol may, indeed, make us feel better on a very temporary basis, but this is by no means the solution. We can see in Figure 12-2 that there is a "rebound effect."

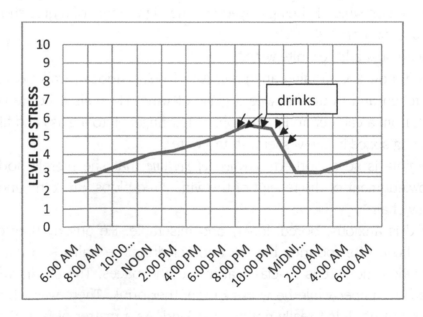

Figure 12-2. A Harried, "Put-Upon" Fred, Esq.

Since our Honorable Member of the Bar had artificially created a sense of calmness and peace, it's as though he now has to pay it back.

During the night, Fred's sleep becomes fitful and disturbed. He is experiencing the process of withdrawal from a sedative. By 6:00 a.m., when he has set the alarm to awaken him, he's extremely agitated, sweating and trembling. But the docket has been set, and there's no getting out of that. So there our learned colleague sits, perspiring in his wool, double-breasted suit.

We can see so clearly from Figure 12-2 where this pattern of behavior is headed; ever increasing levels of alcohol and ever increasing rebounds of tension and anxiety. Thus our embattled hero goes through life at least partially "gassed," thus missing so much of the world's richness. At the same time, he's tense and uncomfortable from the simultaneous withdrawal effects from the sauce. This pattern of abuse, thus, is not contributing at all to an improved quality of life for Fred. It is merely distracting him from taking the corrective actions that he needs to take in order to get his life balanced and satisfying. There are even indications from the research that using alcohol on a long-term basis suppresses the production of brain chemicals which naturally promote feelings of calmness and contentment, thus making the alcohol abuser even more dependent on the ingested chemical and his life even less satisfying.

Home Treatments for Excessive Drinking

Now, what corrective actions should Fred, Esq. take?

Of course, a member of Alcoholics Anonymous (AA) would say that Fred's problem is alcohol, pure and simple. But would, again a person like Fred wake up in the morning and, in effect, say:

> Gosh, my life is so wonderful. I have an attractive, loving wife who is attentive to my needs. My children are doing so well, both academically and socially. My job is great. The boss really goes out of his way to make sure that I'm rewarded for my loyalty. The family finances are secure, to say the least. I think I'll go and put my brain to sleep with alcohol and wake up in the morning with a nasty hangover.

Does this make sense to you? Well, it certainly doesn't make sense to us. So it seems clear that we need to deal with the underlying sources of discontent before we can have any significant impact on the addictive behavior itself. In other words and at the severe risk of repetition, Fred needs to get his life in order. Specifically and most dramatically, he needs to make improvements in his marriage and bring about a more equitable distribution of the workload of his law firm.

Will these changes automatically make his drinking problem go away? Unfortunately, the answer to that question is probably not. Reaching for the bottle has become such an ingrained habit with him. And some stress and sources of discontent are inevitable, even after having removed some of the major stressors. He is still going to have to fight this thing, but now Fred will be in so much better position in that the basic motivation for his excessive drinking has been eliminated.

We're now to the point where we can focus on the drinking itself. Here are some techniques which the Counselor might try:

1. Limit the availability of alcohol. Instead of keeping a well-stocked liquor cabinet, why not, for example, just pick up a quart of beer or a "mini" or two on the way home from work?
2. A lot of the ongoing motivation for alcohol consumption relates to the desire to calm down. Regardless of how well he's doing in so many areas of his life, the practice of law is a stressful pursuit. One is bound to finish up the day a bit on edge. Non-chemical relaxation procedures are in order here.
3. A lot of times people drink whatever they drink simply because they're <u>thirsty</u>. So why not drink a big glass of water before turning to the hard stuff?

So putting all of the above together, we join our hero as he leaves the courthouse about 5:30 in the evening. As is his habit, acquired over long years of conditioning, he's thinking he sure would enjoy a drink. Of course, he could go straight to one of the numerous lounges that adorn the city. There, he could easily find some colleagues who would not only drink with him, but, indeed, encourage him to have another and another. But no, he thinks to himself, he can resist that temptation. He realizes gratefully that he's not as stressed as he had been in the past. He had a real productive "sit down" with the senior partners of his law firm a few months ago. In describing the unfairness of the work load, he wasn't sure whether or not he had succeeded in convincing them that it was unfair, but he got the clear impression that they were scared he might leave! No, they didn't give up their long lunches and golf games. They did, though, give him an assistant, a highly capable young attorney, and that's certainly helped out a lot.

Another reason to skip the bar scene is because he's anxious to get home to Virginia. They recently read a book together, part of which talked about communication in marriage. He had no way of knowing if the shrink who wrote the book knew what he was talking about. He may have been divorced twenty times! But just going through the exercises seemed to help. Maybe that was it, he reflected, perhaps the main thing is just making an effort. And just maybe the advice in the text, like the semi-structured talks, helped. He didn't know for sure, and he, frankly, didn't really care. The important thing was that he and Virginia were getting along so much better and getting closer every day. Gosh, in many ways it was like when they were dating.

He walks to the nearby liquor store and picks out two mini-bottles of his favorite Scotch. "Now, let's see, Ginny said we were having chicken for supper." So two "wine for one" bottles of Chardonnay are put on the counter with the Scotch, that's one for him and one for Virginia.

Ginny is there to greet Fred as he walks through the door. He hugs and kisses her briefly as he puts his little bag of booze on the kitchen counter.

"How are you doing?" he inquires.

"Okay, and you, Dear."

"Fine. There was a snag in this blank-blank trial, something I didn't expect came up. But we can talk about that later."

Having established that there was no immediate crisis with which the Esquire family must deal, Fred pours himself a large glass of water, and he and Ginny walk to the couch in the den. The Counselor removes his coat and loosens his tie. He then does his relaxation exercises, first tensing briefly and then going into the long relaxation phase.

As Fred seems to be becoming quite comfortable, Virginia takes off her eyeglasses and puts her head on her husband's shoulder. Fred reaches out for the glass and takes another sip. They begin their nightly talk about their activities for the day and their thoughts, as Fred puts his arm gently around her shoulders.

When the glass has been depleted, Ginny announces, Well, Hon, let's get supper finished." As they enter the kitchen, Fred asks, "Would you care for some wine now?"

"Oh, no thank you. I think I'll save it for supper.

Fred takes from the cabinet a cocktail glass and fills it with ice. As he does so, he's aware of a feeling of calmness and contentment. That's a far cry from how he used to feel come this time of day, he reflects gratefully. He opens one of the mini-bottles and pours its contents over ice. It makes a refreshing, crackling sound. He takes a sip from the glass, enjoying the taste of the imported sauce. He does enjoy drinking, he realizes, but it's nice not to have to do it to put your brain to sleep on a daily basis. There's just time for the other scotch before supper. He and his wife decided to eat a bit earlier these days. It's better for Ginny's weight, and this step cuts down on the length of the "cocktail hour." The Chardonnay compliments the taste of the chicken beautifully.

Fred is left feeling quite content with his entire evening, his happy hour and particularly the company. And even if something should go "wrong," there's simply no more booze in the house to tempt him. Now, this Fred, just like our "Balanced Fred" described earlier, can go in peace with his wife to the neighbors for their game of Trivial Pursuit.

It's a beautiful day, Fred decides as he pours himself a cup of coffee the next morning. He feels great!

At the law firm now, he pulls a sheet of paper, a graph actually, from under the blotter of his desk. The graph's abscissa (or is it the ordinate?) is unlabeled. He's not keen on the janitor having a written record of his drinking!

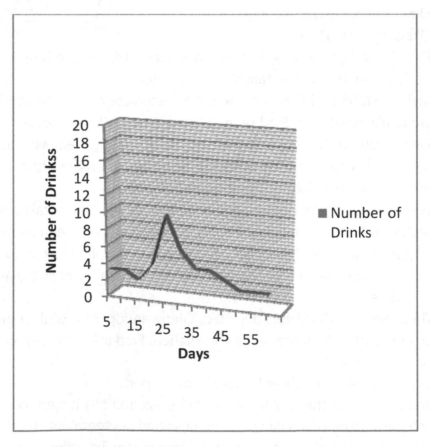

Figure 12-3. Record of Fred's Daily Consumption of Alcohol

Well, Fred thinks to himself, it's going in the right direction, down. Of course, nothing's prefect. He did have that little "slip" on the twenty-third, a Friday night. He and Ginny had gone to a party given by the gynecologist up the block. He had been served two pretty stiff drinks there, probably, he guessed, about three ounces a crack. But by the time he got home, given his "hard won" tolerance for alcohol, he was stone sober. So he got out the bottle he had purchased when the Fergusons had come over the other night and poured himself a two-ouncer. Well, supper was a bit delayed, so, going back to old habits, he poured himself another stiff one. And Ginny, who's on a diet and had gorged at the cocktail buffet, decided to skip supper. So, our hero had both his own *vino* and hers.

The next morning brought back some of the bad old memories of his heavy drinking days, headaches, nausea, irritability. But did Fred succumb to Dr. Marlatt's "Abstinence Violation Syndrome" (The indoctrinated belief that "One Drink = One Slip")? No! Well, not totally. He did have a beer with his hot dog at lunch. And he brought home three minis that night. There's no virtue in suffering! But Fred didn't let this little setback create in him a "What the Hell" attitude. He knows and realizes that his little slip doesn't mean that he's got to go back to a pattern of abuse. No! Fred, Esq. will control drinking. Drinking won't control Fred! Besides, he knows that if he can't control his drinking on his own Virginia will make him go into treatment. And it will probably be one of those abstinence deals. Yuk! Maybe even antabuse.

OTHER ADDICTIONS

We've used alcohol since it is the most common and most studied addiction as our model in discussing patterns of abuse. Now we turn to the matter of other patterns of abuse.

A common thread that runs through all the addictions, even those of a nonchemical nature, is that they have the potential to produce an artificial "rush" of excitement and pleasure. This is true whether we're talking about booze, morphine, power-grabbing or gambling. Of course, taking in these pleasure-creators in this way gives you the illusion of complete control. But what may escape the addict's attention is that she or he has a natural pleasure-producing pump. You see, the brain produces a set of chemicals, collectively called "endorphins." Their structure is very much like that of morphine and other "opiates." In an unaltered human, speaking loosely, these endorphins are released when we need a little boost

But recall from the above that we're talking about an "unaltered human." But what happens if this human is "altered," that is throws chemicals, whether in liquid or tablet form, into his/her system that chemically resemble the naturally occurring opiates? Well it seems that the brain shuts this mechanism off. In other words, it ceases production of these naturally occurring "high-producing" chemicals. So now we're left in a state of total dependency on our artificial agents, again be it booze or pills. And a major problem with both of these artificial agents is that they do the body a lot of harm, like liver damage, just for an example.

So, in summary, what ultimately takes place is that we suppress the natural mechanism that makes us feel good and try to substitute an unnatural external agent. But this artificial agent is cruder and less powerful than the body's own "morphine pump," and these external chemicals may and do create devastating health problems. Who needs them? Well, maybe a beer on a hot Saturday afternoon and a glass of wine with a grilled steak. But not as a routine method of mood control!

If you've gotten hooked into this kind of pattern of addictive behavior, there's no time like the present to begin to get out.

The other chemical addictions are, in fact, so similar to alcohol in their general effects and addicting mechanisms that they can be disposed of rather rapidly. The major differences are that most drugs, unlike alcohol, have no tell-tell signs, like the smell of booze. Thus, addicts are often able to get away with ingesting them during greater periods of the day, and they may delude themselves into thinking that they're "getting away" with the pattern of abuse. But these agents are mind-altering, and there is a price to be paid, as in disruptions in one's personal relationships.

Another compelling reason for believing in the essential similarity of the addictions relates to the tremendous amounts of "cross-addictions" one observes in clinical settings. This relates to the fact that people who have a problem with the abuse of a certain chemical or activity will quite frequently be found to also be indulging to excess in another form or forms of mind-altering activity. Pathological gamblers are frequently also problem drinkers or engage compulsively in "skirt-chasing."

Some anecdotal evidence further supports the contention made here that the various addictions, despite their outward differences, are actually essentially similar attempts to cope with some of the same underlying problems. Some years ago, one of us did an internship in an alcohol treatment facility. Alcoholics Anonymous played a big role in their program, so I frequently attended AA during this time. As anyone who has ever attended AA will tell you, the smoke is so thick you'd think you were in

London, and gallons of coffee are consumed. Leaving smoking aside for the moment, why the coffee? This to me made no sense at all. Alcoholics, according to classic tension-reduction theory, are uptight people who in their quest for anxiety relief become addicted to a depressant "medication." But coffee is a stimulant. You'd think problem drinkers, particularly after long periods of sobriety, would avoid it like the plague. After all, it ought to make an already anxious individual climb the walls!

Undoubtedly, part of my confusion about this observation related to the fact that I had an overly simplistic understanding of the effects of alcohol. But as I listened and watched and did my best imitation of thinking, a very general explanation for what I was seeing began to emerge. THESE PEOPLE WERE UNCOMFORTABLE AND JUST WANTED TO FEEL DIFFERENT. Just about any kind of change in feeling would do, and any way of achieving it was acceptable, just so long as the individual was given hope that there would be some modification forthcoming in her or his discomfort.

Of course, Dr. Jacobs and his theory explain all this in a much more sophisticated manner. But again, the major point is that we need to look at the underlying sources of psychological pain and do something about them. Otherwise, all we're doing is, figuratively speaking, putting our fingers in the dike. So many workers in this area have been frustrated by seeing patients on whom they have lavished so much time and attention go hopping from one addiction to another.

Treatments for Other Addictions

In what follows, treatments for the non-alcohol addictions are lumped together. This way of dealing with things naturally follows from the belief that these various addictions are merely only apparently different ways of attempting to cope with the very same problems. The reader is reminded that much of the information on the self-treatment of excessive drinking is also relevant here, so those materials, by-and-large, won't be repeated.

The first steps in treating these addictions is already known to the reader. This relates to getting one's life in order and attempting to take care of the sources of psychological pain in one's life. The early chapters of this book, of course, were designed to assist the reader in this admittedly complex process. As always, should you be unable to accomplish this or any related goal on your own, professional help is only a phone call away.

The second component of self-treatment flows directly from Jacobs' General Theory of the Addictions. The question here is, basically, whether the addiction is engaged in because the person is over- or under-aroused. Put in more simple and, admittedly, looser terms, is the individual anxious or bored? Some clue to the answer here, obviously, will come from simply looking at the activity indulged in. One is on reasonably safe ground in speculating that the alcoholic and narcotics addict are harried and anxious. The cocaine sniffer and "speed freak" would appear to be telling us that they're bored and under-stimulated. In gambling, slot and video poker players very much tend to be agitated and seeking some kind of hypnotic release from their worries and pressures, an opportunity to "disassociate" as Dewey Jacobs put it. Those attracted to the frenzy of the craps table are obviously "bored out of their gourds" and looking for more action.

One is cautioned that the seemingly common-sense formulation given in the above paragraph is far from fool-proof. Remember, the addict is largely motivated to simply change her or his feeling state and may have gotten "hooked" on something that is actually not all that specific to the true underlying problem. Even so, the assumption that the person has a strong need for the effects of the abused chemical/activity certainly isn't a bad place to start.

Having "diagnosed" the underlying imbalance in activity level through a combination of chemical- and self-analysis, it's time to move on to try to correct it. The goal here is to find and integrate into one's life non-chemical, or as in the case of gambling, non-depleting activities which will provide the feelings formerly obtained from the abused substance or activity.

Anxiety-based Addictions

Mental health professionals are, to be quite honest, much more skilled and experienced in cases in which the underlying problem is one of over-arousal or anxiety. The extensive use of relaxation therapy, as outlined in Chapter Nine, shows how well-developed this sort of technique is. But, surely, one doesn't have to go through this type of ritual each and every time he or she needs to calm down. No indeed!

People in the mental health fields have found that a number of more common activities have relaxing properties. The reader, admittedly, will probably find the list presented below another "brilliant glimpse into the obvious." But sometimes people need to be reminded that they have options outside of getting "gassed." Another point to be made is that some of these behaviors were discussed earlier under the heading of general methods for combating anxiety. They bear, though, some repetition here in that in this chapter they are being presented as specific alternatives to indulging in your addiction of choice. Undoubtedly and hopefully, the reader can enlarge upon what follows:

1. Take a vacation, if only for a day. Get away, if only to a nearby zoo or lake. Sound too time-consuming or expensive? Well, compare it to the expense of going on a "toot,' particularly in terms of the cost to the body.

2. A nice, leisurely lunch out with your spouse or other intimate. Remember here the value of "getting things off your chest" or catharsis.

3. Exercise. Perhaps paradoxically, exercising that involves sustained exertion, like running and swimming, has an overall anxiety-combating function. Another nice feature about this behavior is that it is incompatible with the addictive activity. You can't pull the handle of a slot machine, or your beer will slosh out of the mug!

4. Listening to soft, soothing music

5. Take a nice, long walk.

6. A cool or warm shower, whichever you happen to find more refreshing and rejuvenating

Again, some or none of these suggestions may be of help to you. This is a list tailor-made to be altered and added to in accordance, simply, with what works for you.

The Under-aroused and Bored

As noted above, hypo-arousal, under-stimulation or, commonly put, boredom, is a much more difficult problem with which to deal. Quite frankly, mental health professionals, dull lot that we are, have tended to more condemn people in this category than to try to help them. The idea, crude though it may be at this point, is to try to add to the person's life through some non-abusive means the "spice" or "kick" she's getting from the addiction. This can be accomplished in at least two areas of one's life:

1. At work. It's no wonder you want to get into a hot card game after pulling an eight-hour shift tightening bolt B-12 at the plant. Could you switch to a more exciting line of work? Theoretically, someone who switched from such a ho-hum job to something like being a private detective might have no or at least less need to gamble.

2. At play. How about a more exciting hobby? Or what is more likely, Mr. Addict, how about a hobby to begin with? If boredom's your problem, steer away from things like stamp collecting. One of the authors found cross-country horseback riding, jumping fences included, to give him all the stimulation he needed for a good two or three weeks! But that's just one of many possibilities. Hopefully, your need for excitement won't drive you to such activities as hang gliding and drag racing These hobbies could put you past stimulation, permanently, forever! Better to be at the craps table! Again, it's just what works for you.

The Addictive Behavior Itself

Assuming now that we've taken care of our psychological hurts and corrected any imbalance in our level of stimulation, it's time to move on to dealing with the addictive behavior itself.

The two grand techniques in this area are limiting access to the addictive activity and decreasing its attractiveness.

Gambling provides us with an ideal example of limiting access to the addictive activity. It is truly said that gamblers gamble with not for money. Nevertheless, all the casinos your authors have entered have insisted on "cash on the barrelhead," although and perhaps unfortunately, credit can sometimes be arranged, presenting another potential obstacle to recovery from a gambling addiction. Even so, if one can arrange not to have access to money, one can thereby greatly reduce one's level of gambling. A standard technique in the treatment of gambling, just by way of illustration, is to surrender one's financial resources to another person, typically the spouse. In many of the reports of the successful treatment of compulsive gambling, it is noted that the gambler would turn over his paycheck to his wife. She, in turn, would dole out to him, day-by-day, the money he would need for daily expenses, things like coffee, lunch and bus fare. If the bloke decides to gamble, then he has to forgo his coffee or walk home. It's as simple as that. It's kind of like antabuse for gambling!

Of course, the same general technique will work for other addictions. Reportedly, drug dealers also want to see "the bread up front."

A related technique is to reduce the temptation to indulge in the addictive behavior through avoiding situations and people in the presence of whom it is likely to occur. Quite obviously, after work you shouldn't "hang out" at the home of your dope dealing friend. The "A's" – AA, NA, GA, etc., have recognized the importance of this for years. As a matter of fact, much of the effectiveness of these self-help groups probably relates to the fact that they substitute for your old drinking/gambling/doping cronies a group of enthusiastically anti- all of these things friends. Of course, you don't have to join one of these abstinence-worshiping organizations to have hopes for recovery. Quite obviously, if drinking is your problem you should avoid bars. Gamblers should stay out of casinos, and drug addicts shouldn't frequent those parts of town in which drug deals are commonplace. Why tempt yourself?

In terms of decreasing the attractiveness of the addictive behavior, there are a number of professionally-administered techniques which accomplish this goal quite well. One of the authors used one of these procedures, technically called "covert sensitization," in the treatment of a case of compulsive gambling.

> Paul was a young man, about twenty-two at the time of my contact with him. He was a good-looking fellow with blond, curly hair. His appearance was marred only by the tattoos on his arms, in his case truly a symbol of an antisocial lifestyle. He had been gambling in the casinos of the small Nevada town in which he lived since he was a teenager. The arrests for underage gambling merely added a few lines to his already lengthy juvenile record. His current gambling had escalated to the point that he was forging checks on his sister's bank account in order to "stay in the action." He was facing prosecution for this misbehavior at the time of treatment. My treatment sessions with Paul took the following form:

>> I want you to imagine that you're walking into the Commerce Club. You walk up to one of the slot machines and take out a number of quarters from your pocket. You insert one of the coins into the "one-armed bandit." As you do this, you experience a queasiness in the pit of your stomach. You know you're going to be sick.

>> You begin vomiting all over everything, the slot machine, the carpet, yourself. You're retching right there in the middle of the floor, and everyone's looking at you with disgust. The smell is awful.

>> You turn from the machine and dash toward the casino's door. The vomiting stops as you clear the entrance. Outside on the street now, you're enjoying the fresh air. You feel great!

>> You're walking toward the basketball court. It's a beautiful day. It's wonderful just to be alive!

Sounds a bit rough? Well, maybe it is. But it's been known to work. Like all the techniques discussed in this book, there's no harm in trying to use this one on your own. Just imagine being sick while engaging in whatever activity you happen to indulge in to excess. The more gruesome the better! As always, you're free to seek professional help in order to "fine tune" any procedure you may need.

A less "rough" procedure might flow from a Logotherapy perspective. There is nothing more difficult and produces desires for excessive drinking or gambling, or whatever quick fix to feel better, than a feeling that we are trapped in a competitive rat race that drains our very life energies out of us but does not give us a sense of accomplishment with a sense of purpose and meaning. Each one of us wants to be somebody with a sense of personal identity, meaningful existence, a life with a worthwhile cause. James C. Crumbaugh (1912 – 2001), a clinical psychologist, developed a treatment for addictions like alcoholism. He based his treatment modalities on the research and writings of Viktor Frankl. The following are the five stages of treatment:

1. Self appraisal of where you stand in life: assets, liabilities, fortunes, misfortunes, goals, ambitions, frustrations and failures. Next, you ask yourself about the plans for coping with the present problems and for building a new future.
2. Acting "As If." This second step moves you into the realm of positive action commensurate with personal and meaningful values.
3. Finding Identity and opening yourself up for encounters and closeness with another human being
4. Ongoing search for human values and living them out in your daily existence
5. Self-reevaluation and Commitment to ongoing recovery

The above process, as outlined by Dr. Crumbaugh, is a working treatment plan that has been tested with relative success in the Veterans Administration hospitals where he worked and did his research for many years. His book entitled *Everything to gain: A guide to self-fulfillment through Logoanalysis* is a classic for treating addictions.

The Special Case of Smoking

Smoking, unquestionably, is the single activity which poses the greatest risk to one's health. Certainly, there's no doubt that it is an addiction. There is a drug involved, namely nicotine. Nicotine is a mild stimulant. Also, the smoke displaces oxygen-rich air, thereby mildly suffocating the smoker. Of course, suffocation doesn't sound like much fun, but in a mild form lack of oxygen to the brain has a numbing, euphoria-producing effect. Some people love it!

But in addition to the drug effects of smoking, it seems that simple habit plays a larger role in this negative health behavior than is true with the other addictions. Just from casual observation, it appears that people begin smoking with much less awareness of what they're doing than is true of, say, pouring a drink. Part of the habit-bound nature of smoking probably relates to the fact that the smoker, unlike the drinker, carries the tools of his poison with him or her. You see people pulling out their cigarettes and lighters and lighting up without missing a beat in whatever they're doing at the time. It's that automatic. Another part of the ease with which people start puffing undoubtedly relates to its social acceptability. Obviously, there are so many more places where you can smoke than, say, pop a can of beer. All that's changing, of course. And while these new restrictions on smoking are irritating to the smoker, they will probably help her cut down. She'll have to cut down because, first, there are simply fewer places where she can get by with smoking. But secondly, the need to observe and obey "No Smoking" signs and search for "Designated Smoking Areas" will sensitize her, that is make her more aware of what she's doing to her body, in addition, again, to simply making it more difficult to light up.

All of the above is a long-winded way of saying that in our efforts to deal with smoking, in comparison to the other addictions, we need to work a little more actively with the simple habit elements of this self-destructive activity.

The two grand themes in the self-treatment of smoking, in addition, of course, to getting your life in balance, are 1) increasing response costs and 2) coming up with substitute activities.

1. Increasing response cost

    We met this grand strategy of "increasing response cost" earlier in our discussion of behavioral/learning theory-based ways of changing patterns of life activities. Basically and by way of review, this term means rearranging things in advance so that whatever we're indulging in to excess becomes more difficult in the sense of requiring more effort. Given people's "propensity to conserve energy," a polite way of saying laziness, when we increase the response cost of some activity it typically declines in frequency of occurrence. Some of the specific techniques in this category that have been used in the area of smoking cessation/reduction are:

A. Don't buy cigarettes. As cigarette machines appear less and less common in office buildings, one really has to go out of one's way to get them. If you can just make it out of the store without that pack of weeds, you've gone a long way toward improving your chances for reducing the amount of cancer-producing gunk that's going to enter your lungs that day. Thereafter, you are forced to do one of two things, not smoke or "bum" them from your friends. Bumming involves a certain amount of "work," even though of a disreputable sort, thus qualifying as an increase in response cost. One, in fact, may risk one's friendships in the course of pursuing this particular method of smoking control. So in addition to the increase in response cost, the "bumming technique" through its social embarrassment and threats to relationships, is somewhat punishing. And since, as we saw in Chapter Six, a punishment decreases the future probability of the behavior it follows, this is not an altogether unhappy outcome. We shall see that contriving things so that little punishments become inevitable when indulging in excessive behaviors is a recurrent theme in the psychology of self-control. Aren't psychologists fun?

B. A second technique in this general class relates to where you keep your weeds. Where do you keep them now? In all probability, it's in your pocket or purse, right at hand. How convenient and bad for your health! Let's change that. From now on put them in your socks. That means that every time you want to take a drag you have to bend over, hike up your trousers and unroll your socks. Some effort there, but what's probably worse is having to expose your hairy leg! Again, a bit of social embarrassment which won't, at least in the long run, do you a bit of harm.

C. Substitute Activities

As noted above, the other side of the smoking equation relates to its status as a simple habit. After you give it up, whatever are you going to do with your hands? Kojack, as you may recall, took to sucking lollipops, which would seem to be a pretty reasonable thing to do. After all, it did give him something to do with his hands and in the process provided him with some "oral gratification," as the analysts would say. But this strategy might not have been so good for the old cop's waistline, and it probably didn't add much to his sense of authority either! Some people try "worry beads" as something to do with their hands, but that's a bit "fussy." You could always knit. An ideal substitute for the satisfying hand motions of smoking would be isometric exercises. That's a good example of replacing a negative with a positive. Hopefully, your family and friends will understand and support your efforts at self-improvement, but it probably wouldn't do to try this at a meeting of people you're trying to impress!

As always, use your imagination.

As with the other addictions, it's possible, indeed you're urged, to borrow pages from the books on the treatment of other excessive indulgences.

CHAPTER 13

THE PSYCHOLOGY OF
WEIGHT CONTROL

Many Americans, perhaps most, are overweight. One of your authors once "taught" a class on general psychological issues to employees of the City of Reno. While the announced topic of this series of interactions was "Stress and How to deal with it," the topic that this group, mostly women, gravitated to was weight loss. The women in the group appeared to run about 20% or so over the "ideal" as dictated by the Metropolitan whatever-it-is ideal weight charts.

This situation of being 20% overweight does not, in fact, constitute a medical emergency. People with this form of mild obesity are only slightly more susceptible to the ravages of such diseases as cancer and heart problems than are their normal weight sisters. The sole exception to the above-stated generalization relates to diabetes. Being just slightly overweight, from what we have read, does increase one's chances of developing this complication-fraught disorder. Presumably, this relationship can be accounted for on the basis of those with a family history of, shall we put it, insulin deficiency. In other words, if you have a number of relatives who are diabetic, it probably particularly behooves you to watch your weight. Otherwise, being about 20% overweight is "no big deal," at least medically. It may, though, be a "big deal" psychologically. Your weight can affect your self-concept and hence your self-esteem. As we've seen earlier, particularly in the work of Carl Ransom Rogers, the way you feel about yourself is critical to your ability to cope with the "vicissitudes" of life. So if, for one reason or another, it is your wish to shed a few pounds, how do you go about accomplishing this goal?

First off, let's look squarely at the bad news. The "Battle of the Bulge" is a tough, uphill fight, particularly for women. There are a number of mechanisms in operation which fight your efforts to lose weight. Specifically:

1. The hypothalamus. There is a collection of neurons in the base of the brain called the "hypothalamus," which literally means below the thalamus. As we have seen and will see again, this is a most important structure for those of us who are attempting to understand the relationship between mental life and health. It controls, among other things, some aspects of our emotional lives and the all-important Auto-Immune System which removes disease-causing agents from our bodies before they cause major difficulties for us.

One thing the hypothalamus "does for us" is at times seemingly less beneficial. It regulates our weight by establishing a "set point." When we go above this set point, it exerts pressure to bring us back to it. And what is usually more problematic, when we fall below this weight the hypothalamus exerts pressure to get us to slow our level of activity in order to conserve calories and to eat our way back up to what this little mass of neurological tissue has come to regard as our ideal weight.

The problem is that the hypothalamus hasn't read the ideal weight charts, so it is unaware of what is currently fashionable in terms of figure proportions. It just assumes that whatever weight you're at must be ideal, regardless of what other parts of your brain might believe.

You're very fortunate indeed if your weight is currently in the normal range because that means that the pesky little hypothalamus and its set point are going to be pulling to keep you that way. But if you should happen to be overweight, this little collection of neurological material is going to cause you problems because it's come to "think" that you ought to be chubby. And much to the displeasure of those involved, should you suddenly drop a lot of weight, as from an illness or a "starvation diet," the hypothalamus will try to see that you have a monstrous case of the "munchies" until you're nice and round again.

We've seen examples of the above phenomenon. One of these happened to be a TV personality. People go on starvation diets and lose a lot of weight real quickly. At times, they may look great! But it doesn't last. Why? Because the 'ole hypothalamus is working night and day to get the person back up to his or her usual weight. So back come on the pounds. And your only reward for weeks of hunger is a few photographs of a fleetingly thin you.

You may well ask at this point two questions. One, is it hopeless? And two, if the hypothalamus is working so hard to keep me at one weight, why in the world has it allowed me to put on all this blubber over the years? These are not, in actuality, two independent questions because the answer to the second question assures us that answer to the first is "no."

It appears that while the hypothalamus is unable to adjust to rapid changes in weight, it is perfectly capable of tolerating gradual alterations in fat and poundage. It would, upon thinking about it, pretty much have to be that way. After all, a conspicuous part of the process of physical maturation involves an increase in weight, from eight to ten pounds as an infant to the 150 plus or minus of a young adult. Fortunately, the hypothalamus didn't fight to keep you at eight pounds, six ounces! But notice, please, that the increase in weight was very, very gradual, let's say on the average of about eight to ten pounds a year.

The above account of weight gain during physical development gives us a clue as to how we might go about combating "middle-aged spread." We know that the hypothalamus can't tolerate rapid weight loss or gain, but we know full and depressingly well that it can jolly well adjust most contentedly to gradual weight gain. It seems clear that what we need to do to avoid the meddling of the hypothalamus is to make sure our weight loss is <u>gradual</u>, so gradual in fact that the hypothalamus won't be "offended." What's advocated here is about <u>a pound a week</u>. An additional advantage of this level of gradual weight loss is that, from what we have heard from the physicians with whom we have consulted, this rate of weight loss can be done safely by a healthy middle-aged adult without medical supervision. Obviously, though, you may wish to discuss even this gentle weight control program, or anything else with medical implications, with your primary care physician.

2. The Starvation Syndrome. As noted earlier in the chapter on anxiety, our species was "wired-up" in a very different age and set of circumstances than today's. As we now live in a world of supermarkets and welfare systems, starvation in our society is all but impossible. This was not so in the world of "Ug" and "Og."

Primitive people were totally dependent on the whims of nature. They gathered fruit and hunted game. But food was impossible to obtain when the rains hadn't fallen and the herds failed to appear. There were famines.

Like any other species, our species is adaptable. Over time, evolutionary mechanisms develop to protect the species from extinction in the face of environmental hardship. In the case of famines, the mechanism which appeared to evolve was the so-called "Starvation Syndrome."

The Starvation Syndrome, in a nutshell, is a rather sharp reduction in the use of food, or we might say, the output of calories, in the face of a drastic reduction in the food supply, as occurs in a famine. People under such conditions become less active, and there's probably a lowering of the basal rate of metabolism. The person is conserving energy, which helps to get us through the famine and go on to the further propagation of the species.

Well, Homo sapiens have, indeed, made it to the Twenty-First Century. So far so good! But what happens when Janice Johnson of Middletown, Ohio decides to go on a diet? She knows there's no famine on. She knows she's not going to starve. The problem though is that there are certain primitive parts of Janice's brain which have no understanding whatever of the true conditions of Twenty-First Century life. These ancient control centers will detect the drastic reduction in calories Janice is taking in and conclude, of all things, that there is a famine about! So Janice's brain goes about the task of saving her from starvation, right there in the midst of supermarkets and convenience stores. She becomes lethargic, lacking in energy. Her pace of life slows down. She feels "blah." And does she lose weight? Can she fit herself into that sexy bikini? No! In fact, she may actually gain weight during the course of her diet.

What we're seeing in Janice's case is a special example of the general formula for weight loss/gain:

Calories IN/Calories OUT

The calorie, of course, is a measure of heat, and thus of energy. We take in food, the contents of which can be expressed in caloric units, and burn it for the energy needed to complete life's tasks and activities. Those calories which are not used for energy expenditure, to make a long and complex story short, are stored as fat.

The above formula makes it clear that when we take in more calories than we expend we gain weight, and when the opposite prevails, more caloric output than input, there is a shedding of pounds. There are, according to the physiologists and nutritionists with whom we have spoken, some minor exceptions to this general formula in the case of females. Females, in fact, just have more trouble in keeping their weight under control than do their brothers. But we have been told that the input/output formula is generally valid in the much-discussed "long-run."

The reader should have no difficulty in agreeing with us that most weight control "plans" very much focus on reducing caloric input. In fact, in the minds of most people, losing weight is synonymous with the word "diet," and "diet" is synonymous with the word "hunger." You may also experience headaches and other unpleasant symptoms which probably and primarily are caused by the release of toxins in the burning of fat. It is, indeed, true that if you starve yourself and keep starving yourself the pounds will come off. It's got to be. But who has the willpower to be hungry all the time in this land of plenty? Not many!

And unless you go at this weight-reduction thing with the fervor of one of the Saints, you're likely to fail. Why? Well, the Starvation Syndrome comes into play. The body, sensing a reduction in the food supply, begins to conserve energy. Are you eating less but weighing more?

The way to get around the Starvation Syndrome is to focus on the output side of things. If we reduce input at all, it will only be moderately so. Reduction in the input of calories will only be a major part of the weight-loss regime of those who are obviously "pigging-out." For the rest, we're only going to recommend a slight moderation of one's eating habits. What we're going to stress is an increase in energy expenditure. Yes, we're talking here about "exercise." So, in essence, our weight loss program is going to involve only slightly reducing what we eat but rather substantially increasing our energy expenditure. Combining this with a gradual weight loss, about a pound a week, will mean that neither the hypothalamus nor whatever other parts of the brain may participate in controlling the Starvation Syndrome will become alarmed. And since they won't be fighting this weight loss, they'll let us keep it off!

3. The Gradient of Reinforcement. This is a learning phenomenon which is relevant to all pleasurable behaviors, whether they're engaged in to excess or not. Formally, this concept can be stated in the form of the rule that a positive reinforcer (reward) of any given strength becomes more powerful in proportion to its proximity in

time to the behavior it follows. In other words, the sooner after doing something you get rewarded, the more likely you are to do it again in the future.

The Gradient of Reinforcement causes problems for us in that so many of the things we shouldn't do create pleasure for us right now but problems only in the long run. This is very clearly the case for drinking, for example. The drunk at the bar who is "feeling no pain" tonight is going to feel a lot of pain in the morning! Why, you ask, does he do it to himself? The answer is simple. The enjoyment of imbibing is now, and the excruciating pain of a hangover isn't until tomorrow. After a few belts, tomorrow seems like forever, so why worry about it? Much the same process, although without the booze engendered confusion, takes place with excessive eating. The enjoyment of the food is now. And you can look at the long-term consequences from either a positive or negative perspective. The extra pounds won't show up right away, regardless of how much you consume at this sitting. And that elusive goal of a lithe you is so far off that no detectable progress will be made at this sitting by cutting down on your eating.

So, going back to our definition of the Gradient of Reinforcement, we see that all of the discernible rewards are on the side of eating, of getting as much pleasure as you can from this sitting. The Gradient of Reinforcement creates much difficulty in this and, in reality, in all other areas of self-control. Hopefully, however, if our weight-loss program is gentle enough and we can learn to be rewarded by our compliance with the program as well as the declining number of pounds reflected on our scales and weight charts, the Gradient of Reinforcement can be overcome.

4. The Inapplicability of Abstinence. The final roadblock to losing weight is that one of the treatment options open to those with other forms of excessive self-indulgences is not available to those with weight problems. This option is total abstinence, shunning of the problematic activity. The heavy drugger can not take drugs, and he cannot walk in the neighborhoods in which drug deals are commonplace. And the alcoholic can stay out of bars and shun the "sauce" totally. But the over-eater can't avoid food entirely. Eating is a necessity of life. So the over-indulger in this area is at a disadvantage vis-à-vis those with other types of "addictions." Abstinence, with its comfortable totality and purity, is simply not an option. This means that the over-eater will constantly be exposed

to the "addictive substance." There's no way to avoid it. And there's always that temptation to keep on eating. We'll talk more about this disadvantage of being an over-eater and hence overweight below.

Our Weight Loss Program

Before discussing weight loss, it needs to be acknowledged that this is a part of our general efforts to lead balanced and satisfying lives. If our lives are not balanced, specifically in this case in not getting proper rest and sleep, we will be greatly handicapped in our efforts at weight control.

The above problems having been acknowledged, we now dive into our weight loss program. The first step, though you're undoubtedly tired of hearing about it, is record keeping. Again, as soon as we have an ongoing measure of something we want to change, then it's merely a matter of trying different things until something works. It's as simple as that!

Remembering our general formula for weight status:

Calories IN/Calories OUT

What we're going to shoot for is a modest reduction in food intake, but a more drastic increase in caloric expenditure. We may express this graphically as:

The calorie output side can, but doesn't necessarily have to, involve formal exercise. Any sustained activity will do the trick. Probably the best such activity is the simplest and most commonplace of all, just walking. You can trick yourself into doing a lot of this by such means as letting your spouse keep the car. That way, you've got to walk to those meetings. There's simply no choice.

If your daily graph of how much there is of you shows that your ongoing level of activity isn't having the desired effect, then you've got to get into, shall we say, "contrived channels of energy expenditure." Yes, here we're talking about <u>exercise</u>. And for almost all of us when we get into this area of exercise, we enter again the realm of figuring out how to force ourselves into doing things we <u>really</u> don't want to do. The earlier chapters (6 and 7) on behavioral consequences talk about how we can get ourselves to do things that are not intrinsically enjoyable. The most important weapon we have in this war, in your authors' judgment, is the Premack Principle. This, by way of review, is the use of something we enjoy doing as a reward for those activities we typically shun. Exercise is most definitely in the latter category for all but a few exceptional individuals. This is one way to overcome the Gradient of reinforcement, as discussed above.

At the risk of boring the reader with repetition, the authors can't avoid this tempting opportunity to point out again that most of us live our lives all wrong. We do those things we enjoy doing, like visiting with friends, going out and watching TV, first. All the while we're telling ourselves that we'll do those things we've decided we "ought" to do, like cleaning house and exercising, after we've "rested up." Of course, most of the time we just never seem to get around to these non-fun activities! Nowhere does this very natural human tendency/failing hurt us more than in the area of weight control. If you think about it, perhaps you'll agree that most of the things that are just naturally enjoyable involve very little expenditure of energy. As the amount of energy output associated with an activity rises, most dramatically with exercise, we seem to see a corresponding increase in our dread of doing it and, in fact, in our all too successful outright avoidance of it.

What we need to do, rather obviously, is to make it a rule that, for example, we won't flip on the "tube" until we've completed our exercises. Of course, with exercise you might be able to cut yourself some "slack" here. You can exercise in front of the TV. The rule, though, is that the TV goes dark the moment the exercising ceases.

Should this form of self-management prove unsuccessful, it's always possible to try turning some of the control over to another person. In a good, trusting marriage, the other is typically the spouse. This limited relinquishing of control can be accomplished in one of two ways, directly or through the use of secondary reinforcement.

The direct method involves the spouse declining to engage in enjoyable activities with our weight loser until the prescribed exercise has been accomplished. Examples of such pleasurable activities are going out and various forms of "intimacies." Quite obviously, you need to experience the spouse as enjoyable to be with, or this tactic won't work! An alternative here involves the spouse taking into custody something necessary for your enjoyment, like a component of your TV, your bottle of Scotch or the book you're reading. This item is only released to you following the completion of the exercises.

Secondary reinforcement, you'll recall from Chapter 6, involves the dispensing of points or tokens, valueless in and of themselves, which are later exchangeable for desired goods and activities. A patient of one of the writers used this rather sophisticated technique quite neatly. Her husband awarded her checks, signed by herself, of course, for each mile she took around a track near their home. These checks were exchangeable for articles of new clothing and outings on the basis of a "menu" they had collaborated on jointly.

All of the above are merely ideas for increasing your exercising/output of calories. Try them. Modify them until something works for you. Good luck!

Despite our criticism of the overemphasis conventional weight-loss programs have put on the importance of dieting and our own emphasis on the output side of things, it is at times necessary to restrict one's intake of food.

Some of the specific techniques which have been utilized successfully by people in efforts to moderate their food intake are:

1. Increasing response cost. Please recall that this set of techniques relates to making those behaviors we engage in to excess increasingly more difficult to do. This tactic plays into what an old professor called "the human tendency to conserve energy." He seems to have meant that we're lazy! In any case, making something more difficult to do does, indeed, decrease the frequency of it occurrence.

The results of an experiment conducted several years ago suggest strongly that response cost is an extremely important factor in the psychology of weight control. In this study, students were told that they would have to wait for a time for an "experiment," which was actually fictional (Psychologists can be so deceptive!) to take place. The waiting room was equipped with a bowl of peanuts. For half of the subjects the peanuts were still in their shells, and for the other half the peanuts were already shelled. In each of the groups, "shelled" and "unshelled," the subjects had been carefully selected so that half were of normal weight and the other half were obese. The study's outcome measure was the number of peanuts eaten by the members of the four resulting groups.

The results were dramatic and instructive. There was no difference in the number of peanuts consumed by the normal versus overweight subjects in the unshelled conditions. But when the munchies were available without the necessity of having to go to the effort of shelling them, the overweight subjects ate many, many more. This finding tells us that those with weight problems are extremely sensitive to the response cost of overindulging in food. Make it easy for an overweight person to "pig out," and he or she will. Make it more difficult, and food consumption will decline.

Now, how can we make the effects of response cost work for us? Two major tactics come immediately to mind.

> A. Firstly, only keep on hand foods that have to be prepared with some effort. Pass up the potato chips and microwave dinners. Make yourself "shell" your food. You'll eat less.
>
> B. Our second strategy relates more to the work situation with its snack bars and vending machines. Here we take a page from the treatment of compulsive gambling, that on limiting the availability of resources. Take with you in the morning only bus fare to work, enough for a cup of coffee, a packed lunch of moderate size and bus fare home. Just like the gambler can't put quarters in the slots if they're not in his jeans, you can't put them in the vending machine if they're not in your purse!

Yet another variant of upping the response cost of eating involves a little more in the way of pre-planning and an aversive element. A little technique utilized by two students will illustrate this general strategy. In a course on "Behavioral Interventions" taught at a college in Virginia, two female students appeared. As each student was required to do a project focusing on a real-life "problem" they had, these two particular students chose their weight, hoping to lose some of it during the course. This writer's informal observation of them suggested that their concern about their weight was not just in their imaginations. Both were significantly, one might even say "grossly," overweight. As they both taught in the same school system, they rode together to my class. This entailed a trip of about forty miles, a great, long journey by Virginia standards. The problem for them was that at each of the little townships along the way they would stop for "a little snack," which when described would merit the title of "meal" to your authors. This practice was doing their figures no good at all!

Knowing full well that they could not with "will power" alone end these high-calorie stops, they elected to add a rather unattractive element to the proceedings. They decided that they could, indeed, stop at a fast food restaurant at each and every of the little towns along the way. The only requirement was that before they consumed each had to take out a sheet of paper and write a little letter to herself:

Dear Me,

You're going to eat the mess of junk food you're about to order.

You know what it will do to you. It will only make you FAT. And, as you know, you're already FAT. In fact, you're so fat that you're <u>gross and disgusting</u>! That's why you're not married.

If you keep this up, no man will ever pay any attention to you. You're going to die lonely and alone!

Enjoy your snack,

Me

This requirement that she write this letter to herself before eating did, indeed, increase the response cost of the self-indulgence. It also, it seems clear, detracted somewhat from the fun and pleasure of the activity!

2. Turning some of the control over to others. We all tend to be masters of self-deception, at least in certain areas. This is, perhaps, clearest in the area of the excessive consumption of alcohol. Your friend tells you, for instance, that he has "two," at times "three" drinks each night. You go out with him to a bar, and he complains that the drinks there are "watered down." What he's telling you is that his drinks at home are more than just the standard drinks, by as much as perhaps double. Your friend is deceiving himself.

   The same phenomenon can and does occur in the area of the excessive indulgence in food. One of your authors is well-acquainted with a couple in which the wife had a mild weight problem. Having an informal supper with them one evening proved quite instructive. The Mrs. prepared the plates for both her husband and herself. The mass of food she placed on the plate of her husband, a man of only average height and weight, was truly astonishing. The lady then spooned about half that amount onto her own plate. By comparison with the tremendous heap on her husband's plate, what she served herself <u>seemed</u> quite moderate indeed. At the conclusion of the meal, it was noted that the man had been able to down only about a third of the contents of his plate. And the wife? Her plate was as clean as the proverbial hound's tooth! The self-deception was very obvious.

When what was taking place was pointed out to the woman, she did surrender some of the control to the husband. The rule became that while she would continue to cook (the man had no skills in that area), he would do the actual placing of the food on their plates. Watching him perform this function showed some clear differences. He would put on his plate about the amount that he would, in fact, eat. He placed slightly less on his wife's plate. This little change in family practices appeared to have been a component of her successful weight loss program.

One qualification or warning about this particular technique needs to be pointed out. It tends to work only in relationships which are reasonably strong and healthy. Quite obviously, having your spouse, with whom you are already on shaky terms, measure out your food or booze or give you an allowance from your own paycheck is going to impose an additional and perhaps devastating strain. It's jolly well not likely to work either!

This strategy of surrendering control can be extended to the workplace. So frequently businesses and offices have parties. And what's at the center of these festivities? Food, of course! Also, people will bring in eatables, such as donuts and cakes, on an informally rotating basis. It all provides a lot of temptation for our person with a weight problem.

If you feel comfortable in doing this, you can instruct your coworker on whose desk the "goodies" are being kept to decline to give you more. Or, at the very least, your friend could tap you on the shoulder as you reach for that second donut in gentle reminder that you had set one as your limit. To update an old saying, "No person is an island." We all have areas of weakness in which we need to help each other out. Good relationships can well sustain this kind of guidance which we periodically give each other. Harking back to an earlier theme of this book, though, if we don't enjoy a number of good, solid relationships, we are handicapped in this as well as in many other areas of life.

3. Avoid "food situations." As we've noted before, it's impossible to avoid food altogether. But there are, obviously, places where food is more available than others. And food consumption does tend to increase in rather direct proportion to its availability, particularly

in those with weight problems. Bearing this in mind, where should you take your lunch break with your little prepared meal, in the park or in the food court of the mall next to your office. The answer is obvious. It's all a matter of thinking about it <u>before</u> you go rather than <u>after</u>.

Some "food situations" are all but impossible to avoid entirely. In this category are retirement parties and various other types of receptions. Typically, from your authors' observations, these affairs begin with a period of mingling around and, yes, snacking. This unstructured phase is followed by speeches and sometimes the giving of gifts to the honorees. A potentially useful strategy with such affairs is to arrive late. That way, you put in an appearance, you're there for the pictures, but you've missed a lot of the "grazing." Again, why tempt yourself?

Looking generally at the eating-health relationship and specifically at those who attend church services on a regular basis, you might have noticed the variety of snacks prepared by well-minded members for the after the service gathering. One of the authors wonders about the quality of the snacks. Usually they are either cookies of all kinds with coffee and a variety of sweet breads like banana breads, zucchini breads, doughnuts or something like that. It is all well intended to help church members enjoy visiting after the service. It probably does not, though, help those who are attempting to modify their weight. First, if you had a healthy breakfast and you attend, let's say the 10:30 am service, most probably you will be ready for a healthy lunch by the time the service is over. Second, eating cookies and drinking coffee most probably will interfere with your blood sugar levels and will spike them to a degree that your brain centers will be confused when you decide to have lunch. It is one of your writer's observations that a number of people simply skip lunch after eating cookies and drinking coffee at church. Those who do go to lunch indulge themselves to a degree that requires an extended siesta which might not be conducive to healthy weight management. We are talking here about healthy eating and balanced diet, are we not?

A variant on the avoidance theme is in some ways the reverse of the techniques described above. Here, instead of staying away from "food situations," we're going to try to make places that are now associated with food no longer so. A word of warning needs to be interjected here. This is going to be a difficult thing to accomplish.

Hopefully, the reader at this point will allow the authors to engage in a paragraph or so of social commentary. Obviously, obesity and overeating were not invented in the late Twentieth Century. But some developments in our time seem to have hampered our efforts to eat moderately and thus control our weight. Here we're referring to the increased informality and unstructured nature of contemporary affluent American family life.

In a traditional home, and one of the authors grew up in such a home, meals were served with some ceremony and at specified times and at a specified place, the dining room table. All family members began eating at the same time. Some forty-five minutes to an hour later it was all over. The dishes were cleared, and there was no more eating until breakfast the next morning.

I was surprised as a child, had a little case of "culture shock" you might say, when I was visiting the homes of some of my friends. Instead of orderly meals, these friends and their siblings would raid the refrigerator at will, at various times of the day. They would proceed to take eatables to wherever in the house their fancy moved them to eat. This was usually in front of the TV, but at times it was other locations, such as their bedrooms. Many readers will, I recognize, not find these observations surprising, much less shocking. But to me in the 50s, that's how it seemed.

You're probably wondering at this point what the purpose might be of this little story from one person's childhood. Rather obviously, it speaks to the deterioration of American family life. It's hard to develop good relationships when people don't spend a great deal of time together. And foregoing family meals together is a significant step away from those conditions which foster family togetherness. Telescoping into the future, the failure to develop warm, reciprocal relationships and systems of communication in one's family of origin will hinder the child's ability to form them in subsequent relationships and families. Perhaps the reader will agree that, consistent with this prediction, the conditions described in the observations offered above are increasing in our society. It seems inevitable that we will pay a price for them in that valued commodity known as "interpersonal closeness.'

But the topic under consideration here, your authors obviously have to remind themselves, is weight control. The relevance of this gratuitous social commentary is that the modern American "movable feast" causes many more places and times to become associated with eating. I can, in all honesty, report that as a child I don't recall thinking about eating between meals. This was, I believe, at least partially because the cues for eating simply weren't there. These for me had been restricted to the dining room table and specified meal times. This effect is technically known as "stimulus control." It may be relevant, although certainly not conclusive, that while this author admits to having many problems, overeating is not one of them.

To reduce eating, one strategy which has proved useful and which follows from the discussion presented above is to bring your eating under the control of a narrower range of stimuli or environmental cues. To accomplish this goal, we need to make it a rule to eat in one and only one place in our homes. The dining room table would seem to be a logical place, but, theoretically, any venue would do. And while you eat, just eat. No more bon-bons while you read harlequin novels. No more potato chips while watching TV. After all, since you're going to be eating less, you certainly want to enjoy it more. So don't distract yourself from the taste.

4. There are other miscellaneous "tricks" to help control your eating.

Over the years, a number of ideas on the curbing of overeating have been put forward. By and large, these ideas are more tactics conceived in someone's imagination than the outcome of scientific research. Nevertheless, they are presented for your consideration. If they work, use them. Even if you just think they might work, use them.

A. Substitute taste for quantity. The theory behind this approach is that you eat in an attempt to get gratification, pleasure, from your food. If this is the case, then it makes sense to try to pack as much taste as you can into as few calories as possible. So get out your "haute cuisine" cookbooks. Savor your food!

B. Slow down the pace of eating. It is known that it takes time for the nerves around the stomach to sense that it is full. It must, though, be noted that gastric distension is only a minor factor in eating behavior. Even so, it makes sense to try to get our tummies to be aware that we are sending them what they want before we over-do it. This goal can, theoretically, be accomplished by slowing down the pace of eating. In the past, devices have been marketed on late-night TV which time you're eating. You press a button when you take a bite, and some seconds later, it beeps to tell you when it's time for another spoonful. What would probably work as well is to make a rule for yourself that you'll take a certain number of chews before you swallow. This raises, of course, the issue of the comparison of a mouthful of beefsteak with a mouthful of mashed potatoes! Even so and again, though, if it works for you, use it.

C. Stomach stuffers. This tactic flows from the same idea underlying "B" above which focuses on the importance of a feeling of fullness in our stomachs in alerting us that it's time to quit. In the past biscuits were marketed that would expand when moistened. The idea was that the dieter would ingest them and when he later drank fluid they would expand, giving him that sense of being full. It's untested scientifically, but if you find it useful, use it.

D. Temperature regulation. One can, in fact, regulate the weight of horses by modifying the number of blankets placed on the animal. During the winter, fewer blankets on the horse's back will cause the horse to rely upon its own internal heating mechanisms. Thus, the horse expends more calories and loses weight.

You could, theoretically, achieve the same effect by turning down the thermostat in your apartment and/or putting fewer blankets on your bed. Personally, though, your authors would prefer to do a little extra walking during the day and be "toasty-warm" on a cold winter night. But tastes vary.

E. Snack before meals. This tactic is perhaps the ultimate in paradox. Reportedly, though, some people have experienced some success by eating a candy bar about an hour or so before meals. The theory here is that the candy bar floods the body with sugar, thereby cutting off one of the mechanisms that stimulate eating, a fall in blood sugar.

Intuitively, it would seem that many overeaters could jolly well scarf down a chocolate bar and then go on to eat a hearty meal! But like everything else presented in this work, this "strategy" is set out for your interest and consideration. Use whatever works for you.

To summarize, the general weight reduction strategy advocated here involves an emphasis on the increased output of energy/calories. (By way of anecdotal evidence, this appears to have been the strategy that ultimately worked for Oprah, at least for a long while.) This inevitably involves the dreaded word "exercise." But exercise doesn't necessarily involve going way out of your way. It can mean little more than just walking rather than driving to your next meeting.

SOME CLOSING COMMENTS

Many writers put great emphasis on what you eat. Although it is clearly true that some foods are higher in caloric content than others, and some foods, such as meats, require more energy expenditure for the body to break down, it is the authors' opinion, based on some years of observation, that the more critical issue is how much you eat. Your authors make no pretense of being knowledgeable about nutrition. They merely eat the meals prepared out or at home, which appear to be well-balanced and have kept them in good health. The recommendation to dieters is that you continue to eat a well-balanced diet, just eat a little less of it. The "well-balanced" part of the recommendation is, we think, of crucial importance. After all, what good would it do you if you lost your good health in the process of trying to lose a few pounds?

There is some controversy over the advisability of charting one's weight daily. Some recommend weighing yourself on only a weekly basis, believing that daily fluctuations are discouraging to the dieter. It is your authors' opinion, in contrast, that going full weeks without measurement can allow you to slip into some weight-loss defeating habits. These bad habits could, theoretically, have been nipped in the bud had the individual known about them sooner.

Admittedly, daily weighing will produce a chart which shows fluctuations which may early on be experienced as discouraging or at least confusing. These little ups and downs are particularly a factor in the weight records of younger females. The way to overcome the accompanying "discouragement," it is argued, is for the individual to become familiar enough with the charts to recognize the fluctuations for what they are, "normal" ups and downs with no long-term importance. Hopefully, this experience with measurement and the resulting charting will allow her to look at, say, an upward trend of four or five days and recognize that this exceeds normal fluctuations. Even more hopefully, though, what you'll see is a fluctuating but generally and consistently downward trend showing that you're really losing weight! Thus far, there are, to the authors' knowledge, no studies investigating the relationship between frequency of weighing in and the effectiveness of the weight loss program. So why not try daily weighings? If, though, another system seems to have a better "feel" for you, then use it instead. By all means allow yourself to "savor" the "reward" of a downward moving weight chart. Hopefully, this will help you overcome the negative effect of the Gradient of Reinforcement which places undue importance on the food you might eat right now.

By-the-way, the reason that women are more prone to "hang on" to calories than men is not well understood, at least by the writers. It may, some have speculated, be related to the tendency of women to conserve energy in preparation for child bearing and rearing. Or, speculatively, it could have to do with the use of different mechanisms between the sexes in coping with sudden reductions in the availability of food. Perhaps men become motivated to go out and search for food, whereas women, bound in ancient times to the home camp to care for children, adapted in prehistoric times to famine by conserving energy. Regardless of the explanation, women do tend to have more difficulty with the accumulation of fat. Of course, women even have a higher percentage of their weight in fat than do men. But the situation isn't hopeless. We all know women who have lost weight. And as that Great Philosopher of Science Yogi Berra once said, "If it's happened it must be possible."

This chapter, like all others in this work, has attempted to present a scientifically valid theoretical analysis of a problem. This analysis has been supplemented by the describing of a number of tactics or tricks that may or may not be useful in the case of any specific reader. What is recommended is that you keep a daily record of your weight and keep trying different things, focusing, of course, on the output side, until something works. The battle of the bulge can be won!

CHAPTER 14

EVERYTHING YOUR AUTHORS KNOW ABOUT SEX

There is a strong tendency for sex to be an important part of the life of every healthy, well-adjusted individual. Some mental disorders, like depression, often render people uninterested in sex. And there are physical disorders which make performance either impossible or uncomfortable. Some of these conditions are diabetes and various gynecological diseases.

For those individuals not so afflicted, the range and possibilities for sexual expression and satisfaction are almost endless. One of the most dramatic outcomes of the famous Kinsey Report was the tremendous variability in sexual activity reported. This was particularly notable in females, where it was found that some women would go long periods of time without any form of sexual expression, whereas others would routinely seek out twenty to thirty orgasms a day!

Another factor which prevents one from writing out a prescription for an ideal sex life (not that your authors would be so presumptuous as to attempt to do this in any case!) is the extreme conditionability of human sexual preferences. The reader will recall that "conditioning" refers to the establishment of an association between a cue and an involuntary response. "Pavlov's dogs" is the classic example here, in which by repeatedly pairing food with the sound of a bell, the dogs began to salivate to the bell alone and in the absence of food.

A study illustrating the great modifiability of sexual tastes was conducted some years ago. Male college students were the subjects. This was a "sample of convenience" and one in which the behavior under consideration was strong and active! The subjects were asked what the females who "turned them on" looked like. The experimenters, True Scientists that they were, had a complete file of slides of nude females of various descriptions. It was a fairly easy task to match several of the slides to the boys' expressed preferences.

The subjects were fitted with a device called a "plythysmograph," which was placed on their penises. This instrument, which consists of rubber, tubes, etc., measures the presence and strengths of erections. When the slides were flashed on the laboratory wall, the boys responded with a regularity and consistency unmatched except by Old Faithful.

A wrinkle in this procedure was probably totally unnoticed by the subjects but was of great interest to the experimenters. The nudes were pictured in front of a blue background. Over the course of the session, the intensity of the pictures of the girls was decreased and that of the background was pulled up. But this didn't bother the boys, at least in terms of the measurement being reviewed by the experimenters.

At the end of the session there was, in fact, no nude girl on the screen, only the blue background. But the erections continued! Think of that! We have a group of "normal" college males responding erotically to a blue square. Deviant? No, just conditioned.

Given the above results, it's no wonder that sexual preferences differ so widely among individuals. They may, in fact, change within the same individual over the course of the years. A young man could, for example, begin by believing that his ideal mate would be a tall, thin "statuesque" brunette. But he might fall into the company of a more "full-figured" blond. The subsequent sexual experience and pleasure may totally change our protagonist's views on what an ideal woman looks like. People have spent countless and needless hours, their copies of Freud in hand, worrying about why they are attracted to the people they are. "Wow, my Dad has a mustache too." "Am I attracted to her because my mother also wears glasses?" By-in-large, it's all a matter of conditioning. This, we think, is another good reason for focusing on what's inside the person.

The reader will find no surprise in the authors stating that it is their opinion that a good sexual relationship flows almost naturally from a good relationship, generally and comprehensively speaking. There is, in our opinion, nothing to match, both emotionally and hedonistically, the experience of spending a day with a member of the opposite sex with whom you are emotionally and intellectually close, talking, sharing, say touring historical sites just as an example and ending the day bathing each other and making love...

In the absence of intimacy, sex will be empty and meaningless. It may also be unsuccessful. Within an intimate relationship, though, the only problem can be "lack of success." And that negative possibility is the main topic this chapter will next attempt to address.

Given a good, intimate relationship, what can go wrong? Well, let's pretend this is a textbook and look at it academically. The "list" of sexual problems is detailed in Table 14-1.

Table 4-1

Sexual Disorders

Deviations	Fetishism
	Zoophilia
	Obscene Communication Disorder
Alternatives	Homosexuality
	Transvestism
	Transsexualism
Dysfunctions	Female
	Frigidity
	Vaginismus
	Male
	Impotence
	Premature Ejaculation

"Deviations" refer to those cases in which a person's sex drive is directed to an "inappropriate" object. This statement, obviously, begs the question of what an "appropriate" object for one's sex drive is. Since this is our book, we get to tell you, but only in these pages of course, who an appropriate sex partner is. Perhaps shamefully, our definition is consistent with neither that of the American Psychiatric or Psychological Associations. Normal sex, in your authors' opinion, involves directing one's sex drive to a mature, non-relative, freely consenting member of the opposite sex. This is not to imply that masturbation in the absence of the above-described "appropriate sex partner" is necessarily deviant.

Of course, the members of the Gay Community are offended already! They will point out that, officially, homosexuality is an "alternative" and not a "deviation." And they're right, officially. The authors would simply point out that, over the years they have had many individuals in treatment, including both heterosexuals and homosexuals. It has been noted that while sex was an issue with some of the heterosexuals, it was a major source of distress for all of the homosexuals. Additionally and in our experience, problems in homosexual relationships more frequently display "co-morbidity issues," that is interact with and are exacerbated by other mental problems. There appears, by way of summary, to be a certain naturalness and symmetry in heterosexual sexual relationships that is lacking in those between members of the same gender.

Outside of homosexuality, the major sexual deviation is fetishism. This involves directing one's sex drive to an inanimate object. Here is another area in which people, particularly males, have put in a number of hours of needless worrying. "I sure get turned on by those little shoes with heels, 'candies,' I think they're called. Do I have a foot fetish?" Actually, directing a lot of one's attention to one particular part of the body of the opposite sex is "partialism," not "fetishism." As a matter of fact, one of your authors was involved some time ago in a study in which college students were questioned about what they found attractive about members of the opposite sex. Reliable differences in preferences for different body parts among those sampled were observed. People even differed on such matters as ideal sizes and shapes. Parenthetically, this study got the authors into the Big Time; it was discussed on the Johnny Carson Show! The main point Dr. Joyce Brothers was driving at was that men don't actually wish women to have breasts that are as large as women think they do. But back to my main point, we all have preferences for the way our preferred sex partners look and dress, and these preferences can change pretty dramatically over time and on the basis of conditioning. These desires are nothing to worry about unless they interfere with normal sexual functioning.

An example of the development of a true fetish should help us understand how they are created and the problems they may cause. Thirteen your-old Timmy lived with his parents in an apartment building in a large Eastern city. It happened that a young couple occupied an apartment across an alley from Timmy's bedroom. The wife, a beautiful and voluptuous women, had just delivered a child. The new mother, not thinking about the fact that young males often stare out windows while daydreaming, made it a practice to nurse her child with the curtains incompletely drawn. Not surprisingly, our young friend experienced what he saw as fascinating and highly, highly arousing. As his family and the young couple had established a friendship, Timmy was allowed to visit in the other apartment. On one such visit he had occasion to use their bathroom. In the process, he noticed a dirty clothes hamper. Impulsively, he opened it. Sure enough, there was one of the woman's brassieres. And, it was still damp with mother's milk! Timmy became aroused, experiencing a youthful erection. From then on, he very much looked forward to his visits to the apartment. He would just ask to use the bathroom, and on those "lucky days" when he discovered a bra in the clothes hamper, he would masturbate while fondling it.

About eighteen months later, the couple moved away. He missed his "visits." He discovered, though, that he could obtain some of the same effect with his mother's or big sister's bras. They weren't moist, granted, but with a little imagination he could overcome that problem! He had his sexual outlet!

When Timmy grew up and got a job, he moved into his own apartment, alone of course. He had to resort to buying bras for his "sex life." By now he knew full-well that something was "wrong" with him, and he was made deeply embarrassed and ashamed by the questioning glances of the sales ladies. This, obviously, did his fragile self-esteem no good. He was much too ashamed to discuss the matter with anyone, thus preventing the young man from getting any kind of "help." Here we see a true fetish, one that interferes with normal sexual expression and other areas of one's life as well. This reluctance of people with sexual problems to admit them is, put simply, a real shame. As has been demonstrated in clinical practice, people can even be taught to change their sexual orientation from homosexual to heterosexual and from one specific sex partner to another. These changes in "love lifestyle" are, given that they involve relationships with real, live people, much more difficult to accomplish than to help one terminate his/ her attachment to an inanimate object. It would seem that in this area, as in the addictions, "Silence is the enemy of recovery."

Your authors put before the reader the following story with some reluctance. It may seem a diversion from the consideration of the serious, often agonizing problem of sexual disorders. But it does illustrate, admittedly humorously but also, hopefully, reassuringly, how differently a person educated and trained in these matters may respond to what to others might be perceived as a masculinity-robbing, esteem-lowering "fetish."

One morning while I was a graduate student in the Clinical Training Program at Georgia State University in Atlanta, a fellow student came to sit with another male graduate student and myself. He gave a somewhat startling account of a personal aspect of his life.

"Well, Brien and Bob, I think I've developed a school bus fetish. Yep, yesterday morning I was walking our dog and a school bus went by. Well, I got aroused! Of course, I figured it was some passing thought I had had. You know how my mind goes on! But, so help me, it happened again this morning."

We recognized that this was not a situation worthy of panic. It did not, after all, interfere with his sexual relationship with his wife. But it was, to say the least, intriguing.

A little thought and study into the situation revealed that our friend had been brought up in a rural area of Georgia. As a late adolescent, his parents had brought him to live in downtown Atlanta. Only during this immediately past summer, as a result of some new-found wealth, the result of an unexpected inheritance, had he and his family been able to move from the central city core and out to the suburbs.

Not, you might say, a particularly interesting or relevant story. Well, in response, it may not be interesting, but it is relevant. A peculiarity of downtown Atlanta, at least while this author lived there, is that you didn't see the traditional yellow school buses. School children in the downtown core are transported by MARTA. That's the Metropolitan Atlanta Rapid Transit Authority, which used for all passengers rainbow-striped white buses.

So, you see, from the time our colleague was moved from the country to downtown, he had not really been exposed to the yellow school bus. So, obviously, it seemed some earlier association had been formed between this traditional symbol of early education and sex. What could have happened?

Well, what happened, it turned out, was this. During our friend's childhood in rural Georgia, he had, of course, ridden the school bus to school. His home was situated about half-way back to the school, so he sat about midway back from the front, usually in an aisle seat. Toward the end of the route, a number of older students boarded the bus. One of them was a well-endowed female junior. Since the bus was quite full by this time, the later-entering passengers had to stand. It often worked out that the busty young lady would wind up standing by the seat of our colleague. The road between the point at which she boarded and the high school was under construction, which made for a very bumpy ride. This meant that the fair young lady, with all of her assets, was jostled against our friend in, shall we say, sensuous ways. It goes without saying that this was experienced by him as stimulating and arousing! Of course, all this was taken away from him when his family relocated to downtown Atlanta. No more busty junior. No more yellow school buses. Only concrete, skyscrapers and rainbow-striped MARTA buses – a desert of the libido, an analyst might say. The reader can already see why a move to the suburbs, where the yellow school bus was again in evidence, would re-invoke a sexual response.

The point here is that our colleague was neither upset nor disturbed by his seemingly abnormal response to school buses. He was, in fact, bemused by it. And when, as inevitably occurs, his exposure to school buses *sans* reinforcement caused the extinction of his "fetish," he actually came to miss the morning "excitement."

Other deviations are zoophilia, literally "love of animals," and "obscene communication disorder," which would appear to be self-explanatory.

The alert reader will note that there is a category of sexual patterns to which your authors have given short shrift. This is the so-called "Alternatives." The idea here is that there are patterns of sexual adjustment which are different from those of a majority of people but are not necessarily psychopathological (mentally sick). The most prominent "alternative" in this category is homosexuality, the directing of one's sex drive to a member of one's own sex. But we also find here transvestism, dressing up as a member of the opposite sex, and trans-sexuality, the seeking out of gender reassignment.

Prior to 1970, homosexuality was considered a sexual deviation, a mental disorder. Then the Committee on Nomenclature or something of the American Psychiatric Association, under pressure it seems from gay rights groups, voted to delete homosexuality from the Diagnostic and Statistical Manual as long as it was "ego-syntonic," that is to say that the person was satisfied with his/her life as a homosexual. Voting diseases in and out in this fashion is not a standard medical/scientific procedure, of course. And the way this matter was handled has certainly held the mental health professions up to a lot of ridicule!

The authors have already made some perhaps unenlightened statements about homosexuality. Please understand, though, that these comments do not represent any kind of rejection of the individual homosexual or any form of discrimination against "gay" people. As a matter of fact, one of the finest people with whom we ever worked was an openly "gay" man. The issue is not one of acceptance of the individual, but whether any given lifestyle is consistent with optimum adjustment and happiness. The fact that your best friend is a diabetic or has a conditioned phobia does not make these desirable conditions to have.

Actually, homosexuality seems to have more than one cause and manifestation:

1. From lack of availability of members of the opposite sex, as in one gender-only colleges and certain religious institutions
2. This cause overlaps with number one above, and relates to experimentation with homosexuality, as after having read about celebrates "coming out," such experimentation seeming to be particularly likely when deprived of contact with member of the other gender.
3. Genetic. The genetic "born gay" explanation seems to present problems in that homosexuals, by definition, are not seeking to have sexual relations with members of the opposite sex, a usual prerequisite for reproduction. One would, therefore, predict that this "trait" of homosexuality would be evolutionarily deselected over time from the gene pool. As a physician who attended the group trial run of the use of this manuscript noted simply, "This (homosexuality) is not an evolutionarily adaptive trait." However, we are aware of no decreases in rates of homosexuality over time. Puzzling, don't you think?

The authors have already shared their observations from the psychotherapeutic situation that homosexual relationships appear more problematic than do those of a heterosexual nature. Beyond this, a relevant and, we think, fascinating thing occurred during the course of the training of one of us:

> This author had in treatment a homosexual male. This psychotherapy was conducted under the supervision of a senior clinical psychologist whose basic orientation was Jungian. (We'll briefly discuss Jung's work in a later chapter.) The client was a leader in a homosexual church and affected an attitude of pride about his "gayness." During one of our sessions, Trevor told me that he had had a dream. He pressed very hard for me to listen to it right away.
>
> > "I got up one Sunday morning to go to church. But as I drove up to the church, I was shocked at how dilapidated it had become. The paint was peeling, and boards were falling

off. I was so appalled at the way my old church looked that I just kept on driving. Around the bend I came to another church. This one was gleaming and freshly painted."

Trevor looked at me searchingly, expectantly. He was obviously awaiting some enlightenment as to the meaning of a dream which to him clearly had some great intuitive significance. As I make no pretense of being a dream analyst, I told him I would take the dream to my supervisor and report back to him what Dr. Craddick had to say.

I recounted the dream at my next supervisory session. Dr. Craddick sat back a moment and thought. And then he looked at me and adopted a highly uncharacteristic air of authority. Emphasizing his words with a pointed finger he said:

"I want you to go back and tell Trevor this: The old run-down church represents his current life as a homosexual, and the bright new church symbolizes his future life of fulfillment as a heterosexual."

My response to his instruction, knowing my client's pride in his "gayness," was to take a big gulp.

I chose my words carefully at the next session. I told Trevor that I had taken his dream to my supervisor. Then slowly and raising my voice slightly, I said, "And Dr. Craddick told me to tell you this." I then dutifully and in a monotonic voice repeated word-for-word what my supervisor had instructed me to say.

Well, to put it mildly, Trevor had a "fit." "All this time," he lamented, "I thought we had such a good relationship. And now I find out how negative and prejudiced you are about gayness." It took a number of sessions to reestablish anything resembling a working rapport, and then it was time for me to move on. Fortunately, most of the client's presenting problems had been resolved prior to the "blow-up."

Every time I returned to the city of my training, I would make it a point to drop in on my old friend and senior colleague. On one such visit, Dr. Craddick remarked to me, "You know, Bob, you remember Trevor, don't you? We'll he's come back into the clinic several times about minor problems since you left. Each time he's come in he's said, 'I want to see Dr. Craddick or someone supervised by Dr. Craddick'!"

What does this little story prove? Well, it <u>proves</u> nothing. But it may suggest a lot!

So much for homosexuality as a "normal sexual alternative." And if you think that a man struggling into a brassier and girdle or a woman seeking to have her breasts removed and her vagina converted into a penis are normal sexual behaviors, then perhaps you should consider the lack of evolutionary adaptation involved in taking these paths, as discussed earlier in this chapter.

As the reader has surely gleaned from the lines written above, and in the unlikely event that this hasn't been discovered from personal experience, probably no part of life outside of sex has been responsible for both such pleasure and ecstasy and also such pain and suffering. There is, on the negative side, the obvious factor that sexual relationships tend to give people "power" over each other, and this power may be used in manipulative and hurtful ways. It must be admitted that novelists have done a better job of describing and explaining this phenomenon than have psychologists! Additionally, there has been a tremendous amount of self-doubt and self-berating, most of it absolutely needless, over such issues as sexual preferences and practices.

The Sexual Dysfunctions

But the part of sex which has, undoubtedly, caused the most amount of pain in human lives is the one to which we turn our attention now, the sexual dysfunctions. A "sexual dysfunction" is a situation in which a person is attempting to direct her or his sex drive to an "appropriate" person, that is a mature, non-relative, freely consenting member of the opposite sex, but is unsuccessful in this effort.

At the risk, or more probably at the certainty, of boring the reader with more of the "sermon" on the interdependence of all things and the importance of balance and intimacy in one's life, the authors can't resist the urge to warn about the danger of dealing with sex in isolation and as an end unto itself. In the absence of a close, sharing, intimate relationship, it's a pretty empty activity. And, as we shall see, most "sexual problems" are actually interpersonal problems.

But it is, theoretically, possible for a sexual dysfunction to exist even within a loving, intimate and comfortable relationship. We say "theoretically" because the details of the connection between intimacy and sex, at least in your authors' opinion and particularly during the "performance is everything, every female owes herself an orgasm NOW, and a real man is always able to go on forever" decades of the 60s and 70s were very much ignored. Of course, the 60s and 70s are over, but many of us got our "training" during that era, and much of the era remains with us.

As noted in Table 14-1, there are both male and female sexual dysfunctions. We shall see, however, that despite *la difference* female and male sexual dysfunctions are remarkably similar in their causes. As will be developed, the basic underlying cause of these problems in both sexes is anxiety. But there are some differences as to how the dysfunctions operate in each sex, and these will be discussed in turn.

Female Sexual Dysfunctions

Following the old and probably chauvinistic rule of "ladies first," we'll take up the matter of female dysfunctions before going on to those which afflict their brothers. The two most commonly found dysfunctions in women are vagainismus and frigidity. The former is much, much simpler to understand than the latter.

Vaginismus is the involuntary contraction of the muscles surrounding the entrance to the vagina. We have, of course, already seen that muscular tension is an almost invariable accompaniment of anxiety, formally called activation of the Sympathetic Portion of the Autonomic Nervous System. Reportedly, some females experience this disorder during their first attempt at coitus. After years of having the virtues of virginity extolled, it should not at all strike us as surprising that a young woman would respond with anxiety to the process of depriving her of this "asset," biological cul-de-sac though it may be. More experienced women may, though, suffer from this same dysfunction if they are upset and anxious about something, particularly if it concerns their sex partner. It is truly said that "drinking and driving don't mix." Similarly, sex and being upset, anxious don't, well you know... This would be the "perfect" disorder for a woman to have who is unhappy with her partner, particularly if she is in some way threatened by him. It is, perhaps, a "brilliant glimpse into the obvious" to say that vaginismus is a sign that a woman is less than happy with the sexual arrangements that have been made for her!

Frigidity, as noted above, is a much more complex issue. The basic idea is that the woman is unresponsive sexually. Imagine, though, if you will, a man having been humiliated on the golf course, hot and sweaty at this point, coming home to the "little woman." He decides for reasons of his own, that it's time to assert his masculinity. He tells his wife that he wants to make love. They go into the bedroom and undress. He enters her and thrusts for about a minute until he ejaculates. Well, he has succeeded in asserting himself. But what has he done for her? Not much. Katherine was neither aroused nor did she experience an orgasm. So during that particular encounter she met the definition of frigidity, whatever criteria one might employ.

That wouldn't be such a "big deal" if it were only an isolated incident. But at least from what we have been told by woman in psychotherapy, many, many sex partners are routinely insensitive in this general manner. First of all, such sex acts are lacking in intimacy. And for most women and some men, intimacy is the most important, indeed the basic, component of sexual responsiveness.

But even with the effects of a lack of intimacy aside, the "little woman" in this case would still have had difficulty with sexual responsiveness. You see, there's a difference between males and females in latency to orgasm. On average, a male can achieve orgasm after about a minute of penile stimulation. A female, though, requires about three minutes of vaginal/clitoral stimulation to come to an orgasm. So it's easy to see that in a sexual "relationship" in which the male partner is interested only in satisfying himself in the most rapid manner possible the woman will not receive enough stimulation to climax. And these repeatedly unfulfilling experiences will certainly not contribute to her desire to engage in sex, at least not with that particular male. We have been told by sex therapists that the most common case on which they are consulted is one in which the husband and wife appear, the male very self-assured, the female clearly deflated. When asked what the problem is, the man points to the wife, announcing, "She's frigid." The woman hangs her head as though to acknowledge, "Alas, it is so."

But investigation of the matter reveals that there is, in fact, nothing "wrong" with the female. The husband in his haste to self-satisfaction is simply not giving the woman enough stimulation to achieve pleasure, much less an orgasm. What this couple needs is a few lessons on the Importance of Good Timing.

The focus of Good Timing is to help a couple arrange their sexual relationship so that she receives enough stimulation to find love-making satisfying. The first step in this process is educational. The couple needs to fully understand the difference in latency to orgasm for males and females. It doesn't reflect anything "wrong" with her, or him for that matter. That's just the way people of both sexes were wired up. Clearly, this biological fact is not as widely known as an academic might assume. In fact, one of the authors once asked a class of upper division college students how many of them were aware of this. Not even one student raised his or her hand!

Of course, the most obvious way to go about providing the female with the needed amount of stimulation is for the male to simply delay ejaculation until his partner has climaxed. There are, though and as we shall see in the later section on male sexual problems, dangers involved in a man attempting to greatly prolong the length of time he has intercourse. Fortunately, it is not necessarily critical exactly how the stimulation is delivered to the female partner. Oral or digital stimulation may be quite effective in getting the female to the point at which the man's "range" can bring her to climax during intercourse. This is a matter which a couple needs to discuss, to "work out" as they say. One of the major conclusions to emerge from this general discussion is that most sexual problems are couple problems, not individual problems. And it takes both members of the couple, working together and in an atmosphere of intimacy, to solve them. Unfortunately, studies show that couples tend to discuss their sex lives and how to improve them very, very little.

Assuming there's not a timing problem and, as we need to keep reminding ourselves, assuming there's no relevant medical condition, a woman's lack of responsiveness in all probability is caused by some form of anxiety. The reader will recall again, please, that anxiety is mediated by the Sympathetic Portion of the Autonomic Nervous System, which, among other things, inhibits sexual responsiveness in the female. This anxiety can relate either to past events and problems or to something that is going on in her current life.

A dramatic example of anxiety originating from past events would be a case in which a woman was sexually abused as a child or had at some point been the victim of a sexual assault. Trauma of this seriousness will probably need to be dealt with by a mental health professional. Systematic Desensitization, the relaxation procedure discussed earlier, may play a major part in this type of treatment, as well as giving the lady a chance to talk things out. The husband can help by being understanding, supportive and, perhaps most difficult of all, patient. Try not to push or rush her sexually. She may love you madly, but she's having a rough time showing it.

Other causes of sexual anxiety relate to what's going on in the woman's current life. A pretty good way to tell the difference between a sexual dysfunction based on past trauma and one relating to an ongoing problem is to look at the timing of the appearance of the disorder. Typically, a problem rooted in the past will show up very early in the relationship, if it's not apparent immediately. The woman appears to want a good, comprehensive relationship, including the sexual component, but she simply can't respond. She's been too seriously traumatized to do so. On the other hand, an ongoing source of anxiety will tend to show up later, and it may come and go.

The source or sources of ongoing anxiety may lie either within or outside the relationship. Examples of outside anxiety would be the illness of a loved-one or job-related stress. An increasingly common source of stress these days is the need to care for elderly parents, placing the individual, usually the daughter, in the unenviable position of having to try to both participate in her own marriage/family while at the same time increasingly managing the affairs of her physically and cognitively impaired parents. Worries over health matters, hopefully, will be of a short-term nature. Again, understanding and patience on the part of the husband are called for. Job-related and other outside sources of stress, as, for instance, in a woman's relationship with her family of origin, may be either of a short-term or long-term nature. If it goes on for more than a week or so, that's a sign that something may be rather basically unbalanced in your life. Here the reader is referred back to the "Bowling Ball" chapter.

If the stress resides within the relationship, on the other hand, the resolution of the problem is going to be a bit more "touchy." We all want to be right, and it's difficult to admit that we're wrong about something. The key here would appear to be to put the marriage before our own self-conceit. "How do you think we could make things better?" "Specifically, how might I improve?" are two good questions to "get the ball rolling." The simple fact is that most women and many sensitive men are simply unable to have a good sexual relationship when there are unresolved issues in the marriage. As an actress said in a movie many years ago, "You can't argue about money all day and then jump in bed and make love."

The problem, though, could be more narrowly in the sexual area. Perhaps the partner had been impatient or rough in sexual intercourse. Now she needs to be "babied" a bit. Put the emphasis on stroking and cuddling for a while. Wait for her to ask for intercourse when she's ready. Unless a more basic problem has gone unnoticed, a loving, sensitive male can help his partner and himself as well to overcome this kind of minor difficulty. We'll have more to say about this general approach at the end of this chapter when we discuss ways that people, as couples, can go about improving their sex lives.

Male Sexual Problems

Let's turn now to the male side of sex. Please recall that the major sexual dysfunctions in men are impotence and premature ejaculation. The reader will probably be surprised at how similar males and females are when it comes to their sexual functioning and the problems they may encounter in this area of life.

"Impotence" is the inability of a male to obtain or maintain an erection long enough to satisfy his partner.

The phrase "long enough to satisfy his partner" is highly significant. First of all, it shows how interpersonal, couple-oriented our definition of sexual problems is and, the authors would add, well it should be. And it explains some of the male motivation for labeling women "frigid." After all, if we look at it from a purely negative, disease-oriented point of view, if a man's wife doesn't climax, then, "Either I'm impotent or she's frigid… Yep, she's frigid." But our stance is that couples, not individuals, have sexual problems. In fact, toward the end of the chapter we're going to be very positive about this matter. We'll focus not so much on curing sexual disorders as on improving a couple's sex life.

But, back we go now to the diagnostic category of sexual dysfunction known as impotence.

There are two types of impotence, "primary" and "secondary." Primary impotence is related to some medical condition. Men afflicted with this disorder never have erections. They don't have erections during the night, for example. Primary impotence may be a complication of diabetes, and it may also, among other things, be a side effect of certain medications for high blood pressure. The treatment of primary impotence is a matter for your physician.

Secondary impotence is found in males who do have erections but may have difficulty in doing so at the "right" times. In other words, the man may wake up with an erection, but when he and his wife wish to make love, to be quite blunt about the matter, nothing happens. Or if something does happen, it doesn't happen enough or long enough. This is not just an object of academic study. It is a truly distressing situation for our hero. It's a "revolting development," to quote a famous line from a pioneer sitcom. The great, great majority of cases of impotence are of the secondary type.

Now, what is the cause of secondary impotence? It's very much the same as the cause of frigidity in females. Our culprit once again is anxiety.

The erectile response in the male, just like sexual responsiveness in the female, including both receptivity and such mechanical changes as lubrication, is mediated by the Parasympathetic Portion of the Autonomic Nervous System. Anxiety, as has been so often pointed out, is the product of activity in the Sympathetic Portion. Since the two divisions of the Autonomic Nervous System are "opposite and antagonistic," it's quite obvious that Sympathetic arousal, anxiety, is incompatible with sexual arousal and performance.

As is the case with his sisters, a man's anxiety can relate to either problems within or outside the relationship. In looking at the "outside" causes, it's not at all unusual for men who are under a great deal of pressure at work or facing painful/dangerous medical procedures or who are in legal difficulties to experience transient episodes of impotence. It's tough to be sexy tonight when you know you're going on trial for income tax evasion in the morning! Understanding and support on the part of the wife/girlfriend are of critical importance in helping the man get though this rough spot and hastening the end of the temporary impotence. Such comments as "Most men under the kind of pressure you're dealing with wouldn't even be able to think about sex," are helpful at these times.

Pressure arising from within the relationship is much, much less likely to go away on its own than is that relating to external events which are either time-limited or potentially resolvable "out there." Although rarer than in the female, a man who is upset and angry with his mate may experience some difficulty in sexual relations with her. Here again, what is needed is an open dealing with and resolution of the underlying conflicts. The couple can then move on to the establishment or reestablishment of intimacy, which will have the effect of greatly enhancing the sexual relationship.

There is a particular form of anxiety which afflicts males which partakes of both specific problems within the sexual relationship and also a more central problem which the man may carry with him from relationship to relationship. This is the so-called "performance anxiety."

If the authors could again be allowed to indulge in a bit of social commentary, we would put forward the undoubtedly highly oversimplified position that decades ago there was the general, popular view that women engaged in sexual activities as a duty, in order to satisfy their husband's carnal needs. It was something they had to so in exchange for the financial support they received from the male. This was not at all an accurate view of female sexuality, as shown by the Kinsey Report, but it is merely argued that was the general perception.

During this time, males very much tended to see females as sex objects and to view sexual relationships pretty narrowly in the focus of their own satisfaction. As a matter of fact, one of your authors, part of whose childhood was spent in a rural area of Georgia, can recall girls having been spoken of in this very manner. But during the 60s, a number of books appeared which emphasized, many in quite exaggerated form, the importance women attach to their own sexual satisfaction. Parenthetically, it is undoubtedly true that someone more knowledgeable about the history of literature would point out that there have been previous instances of the emergence of this type of writing, so here I'm only speaking from my own experience. In any case, many males, particularly the "yuppie" college boy type, began to take a great deal of pride, perhaps we might say an inordinate amount of pride, in their ability to give their partners satisfaction, "The Big O." And it was felt necessary to accomplish this with what Albert Ellis referred to as "Your Sacred Penis." One fellow, reportedly, went so far as to place a clock by the bed and time how long he was able to carry on intercourse! Male bull sessions in college dorms shifted the focus of bragging from the charms of their conquests to their own performance.

The problem with the above is that it makes sex for the man not so much a pleasure but a performance, a show. And whenever you put on a show, you rather naturally become concerned about the quality of your performance. You experience "Performance Anxiety." Now, professors of homiletics maintain that a touch of anxiety will help a seminarian preach a better sermon. And that may well be true. And coaches will tell you that being "worked up" will assist one in running faster and throwing farther. And that may be true too. But anxiety will <u>not</u> help you in bed. Anxiety will counteract the Parasympathetic arousal necessary for penile erection.

One of the principal keys to overcoming secondary impotence, whether you're working on your own or with a professional, is to shift the focus of your attention from <u>"how well I'm doing"</u> to <u>"how good this feels."</u> An understanding, supportive partner with whom you have an intimate relationship can be a tremendous help in this process.

But even if a man is able to obtain an erection and doesn't lose it spontaneously, he may still have sexual problems. Here we enter the discussion of the second major male sexual disorder, that of "premature ejaculation." This is the name we apply to cases in which the husband is able to obtain and maintain an erection but climaxes, ejaculates, before either he or the woman, usually both, are satisfied with the sexual experience.

A seeming paradox in the structure of the nervous system may help us understand premature ejaculation. This is that while the erectile response is Parasympathetically mediated, the ejaculatory response is of Sympathetic origin. It is as though the intensity of the Parasympathetic activation, "pleasure" we may informally call it, becomes so great that it "spills over" into the Sympathetic system and the whole Autonomic Nervous System experiences an explosion of pleasurable stimulation. The overall significance of this fact is that an anxious man who can still, somehow, obtain an erection may find that the anxiety manifests itself in an all too early climax. The answer to this problem, again, is an attempt to resolve one's general conflicts in life and those specific to the relationship.

A number of, shall we say, artificial techniques have been put forward to "assist" males in producing Herculean sexual performances. Available on the market are creams which will, purportedly, deaden feeling in the penis, thereby reducing the functional amount of stimulation the man receives and delaying ejaculation. There is also the so-called "Squeeze Play" in which the woman literally squeezes the shaft of the penis. This reportedly, delays ejaculation. It's not at all surprising that pain would have that effect! The problem with these contrived methods is that they are based on a reduction in the amount of pleasure received from sexual intercourse. And that's exactly the opposite of what we wish to bring about in our efforts to improve sexual relationships in ways which will increase the satisfaction and intimacy experienced by both partners.

Some men report the temporary usefulness of some internal "mind tricks" in attempting to overcome self-diagnosed premature ejaculation. Some fraternity brothers may advise you, for instance, to think about garbage during intercourse until such time as your male ego advises you that it would be "cool" to ejaculate. Then, and only then, do you turn your mind to sex. The proposed result of this technique is that the young lady will later tell you admiringly that you're "The Best." What probably, though, is going to actually happen is that you're going to come to associate sex with garbage and begin to have erectile difficulties!

The most successful case of "mind control" over sexual functioning known to your authors was related to him by a colleague. This man, then in his mid-30s, had a wonderful, intimate relationship with a certain lady. He told us that during intercourse he would think about the quality of their relationship. He would recall the long talks they had had and review in his mind experiences they had shared, such as the extensive traveling they had done together. He found these thoughts, plus, of course, the physical closeness of his very attractive partner, to be quite sufficiently stimulating to permit him to make love to her for long periods of time. When the lady signaled to him her contentment, he would, he told us, shift his attention to the more directly sexual aspects of the relationship. Ejaculation would shortly follow, and the couple would be left holding each other in a state of satisfaction and pleasant exhaustion.

The above case may be described as more ideal than usual. The gentleman was blessed with an exceptionally close, intimate relationship with his partner. A fellow and thus a couple experiencing a lack of sexual satisfaction resulting from the brevity of intercourse might try this approach, but one shouldn't, it is cautioned, be surprised if it fails in the absence of such ideal conditions. In the face of such failure, a couple needs to fall back on the general procedure of negotiating ways in which they can both achieve satisfaction within the boundaries of any limitations either of them may have. In other words, alternatives to a total reliance on penile-vaginal stimulation need to be explored and agreed upon. The importance of open communication in this process cannot be over-emphasized.

A NOTE ON AIDS

No authors who allow themselves to indulge in "social commentary" could leave the subject of sex without some mention of Auto-Immune Deficiency Syndrome, AIDS. Regrettably, your authors have nothing to contribute in terms of solving what has come to be termed the "AIDS epidemic." It is another "brilliant glimpse into the obvious" to point out that AIDS certainly doesn't increase the level of comfort of either the male or the female in sexual relationships, and thus through the already much-discussed mechanism of Sympathetic arousal may have the effect of impairing sexual adjustment. All your authors can do with respect to this matter is to join their voices with that of others in stating that AIDS is a powerful argument for stability of lifestyle and discretion.

THE LOVE CURE – CHEAP

Help is available to couples with sexual problems. Masters and Johnson, for example, founded a sex clinic in St. Louis. The couple pays their fee and checks into a motel in that city for a week or so. The basic idea here is that the couple gets away from things in order to have an opportunity to work on their relationship. We don't know about you, but we know of a lot of places we would rather get away to than St Louis! Sexually, the operative word in the work Masters and Johnson do with the couple is "non-demanding." The man and woman focus on the pleasure of each other's company. They cuddle, stroke and "pleasure" each other. Intercourse occurs only when it comes spontaneously, almost as though they <u>must</u> make love. Fortunately, this almost always happens sooner or later!

With all due respect to Drs. Masters and Johnson, it would seem that a lot of what is done in their program could be accomplished by a couple on their own. And this type of self-help can save you from having to pay a fat fee and a trip to St. Louis. Have fun!

In general overview and to bring sexual aspects into the perspective of the core of the relationship, it is important, we believe, to recall that truly human sexuality requires devotion to and concentration on the partner. The words of Elizabeth Lukas, a German clinical psychologist and Logotherapist, are highly explanatory here. She said, "Just as love does not allow itself to be coerced, delightful intercourse as a physical expression of love between man and woman does not allow itself to be forced."

CHAPTER 15

TREATING MEDICAL DISORDERS:
What We Can Do for Ourselves

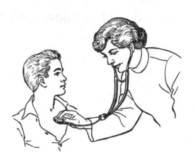

It may, perhaps, strike the reader as rather strange that in a book whose title begins with the word "health" we have gotten this far into the work and are just now taking up the topic of how to deal with physical disease <u>per se</u>. This structure of the book was dictated by the basic idea that <u>the best way to take care of your health is to not get sick in the first place</u>.

The final sentence of the last paragraph is so simple and self-evident that the reader may feel that her intelligence has been insulted by its inclusion. And yet, many factors in the way we conduct our society suggest that we do not, in fact, truly understand this basic principle. For example, we lionize and our insurance companies pay huge fees to the heart surgeon who unblocks our arteries and provides new sources of blood for our hearts, but the person who urges in her writings that people eat sensibly, avoid various excesses and exercise regularly, behaviors which would help one avoid the necessity of such dramatic unclogging missions, is usually passed off as a "kook." There are TV shows making heroes of the emergency personnel who go out and rescue individuals from the grips of horrible accidents. But as deserving of honor as these brave women and men are, did it ever occur to you that the guy who urges safety behind the wheel and the correction of potentially hazardous conditions in the workplace is often dismissed as being fussy, obsessive-compulsive or a "weak sister"?

And yet, prevention is clearly the key to health. One simple demonstration of this fact should help us understand the truth of the above statement. No disease has ever been eradicated through treatment. New cases of malaria kept appearing until the swamps were drained. And despite the doctors' best efforts to help the victims of polio, children continued to be crippled until Jonas Salk developed his vaccine. Some years back, smallpox was declared "eradicated." This dramatic feat was accomplished through preventive measures. Children today are not even inoculated against this formerly dreaded and disfiguring disease.

This book has, of course, placed great emphasis on <u>stress</u> and its negative impact on health. This work and complementary writings and applied work on the part of your authors' colleagues are not so dramatic as, nor do they reflect the genius of a Walter Reed or a Jonas Salk. But stress and its reduction to manageable proportions continue to be important if not attention-grabbing topics. After all, the Surgeon General of the United States some years ago estimated that of those Americans who escape "traumatic" deaths, such as in accidents, murders and wars, a whopping 80% will go on to die of stress-related diseases. It seems obvious, thus, that helping people resolve this underlying problem which undermines health would contribute to increasing both the length and quality of life for almost four-fifths of the population.

Another set of issues in the prevention of disease, outside of the above-mentioned stress reduction and accident prevention, relates to matters such as exercise and nutrition.

"Proper" nutrition is a controversial area of study and practice. And the "consensus" of professionals in the field, such as it is, is constantly changing. In view of the above, it is your authors' judgment that the long-term usefulness of this work would not be advanced by rigidly specifying at this particular point in time the "Proper Diet." Besides, your authors know practically nothing about nutrition! We simply eat the meals prepared for us or we cook ourselves, which are well-balanced and include all the "food groups," and take a multi-vitamin each morning, just in case some needed nutrient may have slipped by. And, as the authors keeps stating – knock on wood – they enjoy now past mid-life amazingly good health. Of course, one of the writers has to admit that he has been assisted in this "achievement" by a number of factors. Firstly, my tastes in food are "wide-ranging." Being a classic omnivore makes it so that I don't automatically shun certain foods which might contain nutrients which I need. In addition, there are, I'm sure, hereditary factors at work here. Anyone not blessed with the above-described "qualities" of heredity and broad food preferences might wish to consult a source of nutritional information which is more extensive than that contained in the present work!

The second major prevention step a person can take in her attempts to avoid physical illness relates to the…shudder…shudder…E word. That's right, exercise! This word conjures up images of sweating, huffing and puffing and pain. But, as we're seeing, exercise in the service of health need not necessarily be either taxing or aversive.

There are two main types of exercise. The first is designed to build muscle mass. The clearest example of this is weight-lifting. Traditionally, this is an activity in which males have engaged in order to make themselves attractive to members of the opposite sex. From what we have heard from women, however, there appears to be a clear parallel here between male physique and female bust size. Just as women tend to overestimate the size of breasts longed for by men, males seem to very much overshoot the mark in their predictions of the value that females place on the bulging and rippling muscles of the "Mr. Worlds" who stride self-consciously along the beach. For most of us, the primary benefit of this type of exercise relates to our self-esteem. We want to have bodies we can be proud of, meaning, basically, not appearing flabby for the girls and the avoidance of the "90 pound weakling" image for the boys.

The type of exercise of most interest to us in this book on "health" is the type of sustained but not unduly stressful exercise which brings about improvements in the functioning of the Cardio-Vascular System. This type of activity creates an increase in heart rate and puts additional pressure on the lungs. It does this, though, in a way which not only doesn't harm the heart and lungs, those organ systems which are most central to the maintenance of life, but actually increases their capacity, in effect conditioning them. This is the type of exercise which has come to be called "aerobic." Examples of aerobic exercise are jogging and swimming. Some fast-paced athletic contests, like handball, may also bring with them these important health benefits. So those readers who have an aversion to exercise for its own sake, a not at all uncommon attitude, may wish to schedule themselves for a match or two with a colleague.

There exist tables for computing the maximum, safe heart-rate that each age range should strive for in order to obtain the greatest benefit from aerobic exercise. And, of course, it's pointed out that it is always wise to check with your primary care physician before embarking on such a program. Even so, those of us who have, to one degree or another, shunned a totally sedentary lifestyle and have no major ongoing health problems are encouraged by a recently published report. This report indicated that maximum health benefits can be obtained from just walking briskly two to three miles about three times a week. For many of us, this means that just walking to work and back twice a week will do the trick. Speaking of tricks, there are a lot of relevant "tricks" you can play on yourself. For example, leave the car at home, or change to a parking garage farther from your office building. Take the steps instead of the elevator. Should these expedients, however, prove ineffective in getting you the exercise you need, then please look back at the chapter on behavioral interventions in order to get yourself to do something you really don't want to do.

But despite our best efforts, health problems may and do develop. This chapter talks about these problems and what we as non-physicians can do to improve our own status in this area. The nature of the following material almost necessitates that it be presented in a rather technical fashion. The authors apologize in advance for this departure from the overall "chatty" form of presentation of this work.

Cardiovascular Disorders

It is here that we see the classic example of a psychosomatic disorder. Anxiety, arousal in the Sympathetic Portion of the Autonomic Nervous System, as has already been pointed out, creates increases in blood pressure and heart rate. The chronically anxious individual is going to have chronically high blood pressure in many cases. Physicians call this "essential hypertension," and it creates strain on and damage to many organ systems of the body, such as the arteries, the kidneys and the brain.

Several decades ago, a number of studies were published which seemed to demonstrate the actual conditioning of heart rate and blood pressure. In other words, it was shown that a person could be taught to reduce both his blood pressure and heart rate. Follow-up studies, though, failed to demonstrate any superiority of this specific type of conditioning over the effects of general relaxation training. So going through the deep muscle relaxation procedure described earlier in this book will do as much for your blood pressure as any specific psychological treatment. One of us has demonstrated this general effect for himself at blood pressure stations which one sees in grocery stores. By using relaxation procedures, I can reliably bring my blood pressure from an initial 135 over 80 to around 115 over 70. Obviously, leading a balanced life which keeps stressors at manageable levels is important in blood pressure control in that it prevents the build-up of those conditions which lead to the development of essential hypertension.

Headaches

There are two main types of headaches, vascular and muscular.

Vascular headaches, which tend to be of the "sick" or migraine type, are, as the name implies, products of the circulatory system. The primary explanation for these types of headaches is reasonably straight-forward. The reader will recall, please, that one of the actions of the Sympathetic Portion of the Autonomic Nervous System is to withdraw blood from the outer portions of the body, such as the hands and feet, and concentrate the blood in the body's central core. This step would reduce the loss of blood we would suffer should we actually be physically injured, and it explains the cold hands we experience when we're nervous.

Obviously, this blood which has been withdrawn from the central core of the body has to be kept somewhere. Unfortunately, in many cases that blood engorges and distends the vessels in the brain. As the skull is closed, this can only have the effect of putting pressure on and thus irritating surrounding neurological tissue. The results of this effect may be dramatic to the point of being frightening. People having migraine headaches have reported flashing lights, blind spots, nausea, dizziness and extreme sensitivity to light, among other symptoms. Doesn't sound like much fun does it?

Your authors will now say, or really re-say, something that the reader is probably quite tired of hearing. This is that clearly the best way to avoid migraine headaches is to manage your life in that well-balanced fashion which will prevent the build-up of excessive amounts of anxiety or Sympathetic arousal in the first place.

If one does, though, suffer the misfortune of having a migraine headache, it is self-evident that employing the previously described progressive relaxation procedure might be helpful. After all, we have strong reason to believe that at least one of the culprits in migraine headaches is Sympathetic arousal, and relaxation training rather directly combats that.

But here we encounter in migraine headaches one of those rare instances in which a more specific procedure is useful in combating a so-called "psychosomatic disorder," that is a physical complaint whose main cause is believed to relate to psychological problems. The story of the discovery of this simple procedure is both interesting and illustrates the sometimes strange way in which science progresses.

As noted above, some of the early work suggested that certain activities of the Autonomic Nervous System could be directly conditioned. This is to say that for a time it was believed that a person could change such bodily functions as heart rate and blood pressure, which had previously been thought to be totally autonomic. This pioneering work was done by a psychologist named Neal Miller (1909 - 2002). Subsequent research, however, demonstrated that the conditioning was not, in fact, direct. To put it technically, the observed changes were "mediated" through the Skeletal Nervous System. In other words, the individual could be taught to relax or excite himself/herself, and the associated bodily changes would occur as a matter of course. Despite the disappointment felt by the boys in lab coats over this failure to demonstrate direct autonomic conditioning, we shall see that it detracts not a whit from the clinical usefulness of the techniques which flowed from this program of research.

A psychologist at the Menninger Clinic by the name of Elmer Green (1917 -) was involved in a research project that was part of this general chain of studies. The particular topic of interest to Green was the ability of people to modify skin temperature. Quite obviously, a convenient part of the skin to work with is the hand. So he attached to his subjects' hands a device called a "thermistor." "Thermistor, by the way, is just a fancy name for a thermometer. Well, it turned out that they could, in fact, exert a powerful effect upon skin temperature when they were given a readout of the ongoing thermistor measurements. This effect could go either way, up or down.

It just happened that several of Green's subjects were migraine sufferers. On several occasions when they had served in the hand <u>warming</u> condition, these individuals remarked that they had had a headache before the session but now it was gone. This happened enough times for Green to notice.

The hand warming exercise actually involved people learning to move blood out to their hands, and presumably other extremities, and away from the center of the body, particularly for our purposes the head where it was causing problems. The question of whether this exercise reflects the learning of the specific skill of transferring blood within the body or merely illustrates one of the effects of the general relaxation response is going to be of little importance to a Kansas housewife who has just been relieved of her "sick headache."

This is something you can use at home. Little thermometers are, of course, commercially available. Migraine sufferers would do well to acquire one of these and practice with it by taping it to a finger. Sit down in a comfortable chair and <u>relax</u>. You should see the red mercury go up in a pretty steady manner. You'll learn ways to hasten this process. Going through the deep muscle exercises is one. Another involves the imaging of comfortable scenes, such as the beach or a cool, tranquil mountain top. It is recommended that you practice this skill in advance, much like an athlete preparing for a big competition. The next time a migraine rears its ugly head, you may not have a thermister handy!

Another disorder in which the hand warming technique may prove useful is Raynaud's Syndrome (or Phenomenon). In this disorder, the blood vessels in the hand become severely restricted, causing the hand to become cold, numb and useless. There have been cases in which gangrene has set in and the hand had to be amputated. A standard medical technique to try to prevent this disastrous outcome is to clip some of the nerves leading to the hand. Surely a course of hand warming should be given a try before this surgical step!

Green's findings motivate your authors to make three comments, all by way of parenthetical remarks. First of all, the use of a thermister in treating migraines is inconsistent with the overall finding that such specific treatments have no demonstrated superiority over general relaxation procedures. At this point in the development of the field, perhaps the best we can do is to say that the validity of the general rule is granted. But this appears to be one of the much-discussed "exceptions to the rule."

The specific benefits of working toward hand warming, that is to say a more even distribution of blood throughout the body, is illustrated by and is consistent with the observations made by a woman known to one of the authors. She noted at a time before she had had any formal training in such matters that her migraine headaches were relieved by running very warm water over her hands. This action, of course, had the physical effect of expanding the blood vessels in the hands, allowing more blood to enter them. There was, also and undoubtedly, a general relaxing effect at work here. We shall see other exceptions to the principle of general relaxation being as good as anything else below.

The third comment the authors wish to make is that Green's work, the use of a thermister and the specific training of a bodily response, introduce to us a new technology and, inevitably, a new term. The new term is "biofeedback." That name is, quite evidently, a combination of the terms "biological" and "feedback." In other words, biofeedback means that feedback is given about a biological process. It develops that people can learn to change quite a number of aspects of their biological functioning if they are simply given feedback on the status of these bodily activities. That's basically all "biofeedback" is. It gives people a read-out of what's going on inside them, and that affords them an opportunity to practice ways to change these functions in desirable directions. We will discuss other specific uses of biofeedback below.

Turning now to muscular or the so-called "tension" headache, a closely related but slightly different tact is taken. Obviously, from what we have discussed in great detail earlier, muscular tension is a component of Sympathetic arousal, anxiety. Thus, deep muscle relaxation would appear to be the treatment of choice. This process may, and the word "may" is used because this has never, at least to our knowledge, been established through research, be aided by attaching a device to the skin above the muscles surrounding the skull. This device is called an EMG, which stands for "electromyograph." Electromyograph, in turn, means a graph or record of the electrical activity of muscles. This is most definitely not to argue that the frontalis, the major muscle of the forehead, is, as some have claimed, a so-called "master muscle." It is simply to say, as was indicated in the story of the blood pressure apparatus discussed earlier, that some type of feedback may have the effect of assuring the person that she's on the right track. Again, the major focus in the treatment of "tension" headaches is one of general tension reduction.

Neuro-Muscular Disorders

Neuro-muscular disorders are those in which some muscle group which is activated by the Skeletal Nervous System is paralyzed or weakened. Good examples here are limps that people might acquire after suffering strokes and muscle atrophy or wastage following spinal cord disease/injury. The common "slipped" or herniated disc if not treated in time or if treated inexpertly may leave a patient in this situation.

In the presence of such disorders, your physician will, as a routine matter, refer you for physical therapy. The goal here, of course, is to restore as much function as possible to the weakened limb. If traditional physical therapy alone does the trick, GREAT! You may consider yourself very lucky, indeed. But what if it doesn't? Well, you might do well to discuss with your doctor a referral to an expert in biofeedback. You may have a bit of explaining to do to her in that this is not a standard medical procedure, nor are there competent practitioners in this field in every community.

How, you ask, would biofeedback help if the nerves to the afflicted muscles have died? The answer relates to the fact that the functioning of the nervous system is not so straight-forward and simple as that portrayed in the charts and models in your physician's office. In actuality, muscles are served not by single nerves but by overlapping patterns of them. Thus, a given muscle may, indeed, be enervated by a major primary nerve. But it also has some connections with and thus receives some stimulation from nerves which are principally directed to other muscles.

The above outlined structure of the Skeletal Nervous System opens up the possibility that an apparently completely paralyzed muscle may, in fact, continue to receive some input from other nerves. This stimulation isn't apparent because it is so relatively small and has no relationship to the patient's efforts to move that muscle. So when the afflicted muscle of our, say, failed discectomy patient is connected to an EMG, he and the biofeedback expert may hear some reassuring "click-click-clicks." They're not so strong, to be sure, as those coming from the same muscle on the other side of the patient's body. But they're there, and that's a start!

The feedback from this very small amount of stimulation can be used to increase that stimulation and thus promote the return of functioning to that body part. To simplify matters greatly, what basically is done is that the patient and the therapist try and explore different ways to increase the number and/or intensity of the sounds giving feedback. This represents the acquiring of a new skill in that sending messages to the weakened muscle(s) through these new routes may be experienced by the patient as totally different from the way he "sent commands" to, say, his foot for his entire preceding life. So a lot of experimentation and practice will be necessary. But it may all be worth it in that a combination of learning new ways to stimulate the weakened muscles plus physical therapy to strengthen them may combine to give someone whom the doctors in years may have given up as a helpless cripple a pretty normal way of walking and style of life.

Before leaving this general topic, it may be well to note that there are times when it's desirable to use an EMG to <u>decrease</u> rather than increase the activity of muscles. An excellent example here is "wry neck," technically called "torticollis," which in Latin means "twisted column." In this distressing disorder, a major muscle on one side of the person's neck is rather constantly in spasm. This pulls the individual's head down toward the shoulder on that side, thus leaving the patient's neck, literally, a "twisted column." This over time is, quite obviously, painful, and the social embarrassment leading to lowered self-esteem are added problems with which those afflicted by wry neck must deal.

It's little more than yet another "brilliant glimpse into the obvious" to note that wry neck is most frequently a product of anxiety. Why the anxiety expresses itself in this particular manner is not known. Perhaps it has some symbolic significance, like in vaginismus which we discussed earlier under the heading of sexual disorders. Of course and as noted above, we don't really understand why one person responds to stress with heart trouble and another with ulcers, so our confusion in this area shouldn't surprise us.

The first step in the treatment of wry neck, obviously, is going to be for your physician to try a course of muscle relaxers. Should this step fail, you might move on to tranquilizers and/or general relaxation training. These measures failing, one would then go on to biofeedback training utilizing the feedback of an EMG of the electrical activity of the offending muscle or muscles. This general strategy may also be employed with spasms in other muscle groups, such as in the back and legs.

Gastric Disorders

A relevant concept in our attempts to understand stomach and intestinal disorders is that of "Parasympathetic Rebound." This is a rather common defense against anxiety in which the body manages to "kick in" the Parasympathetic system. This excessive activity creates problems by, for example, constricting the bronchi as in psychogenic asthma and in causing too much activity in the gastric system, such as in the excessive secretion of gastric juices which may contribute to the development of ulcers.

There is a group of gastrointestinal disorders, like colitis and ileitis, which appear to partake of this Parasympathetic Rebound. The problem here is caused by excessive waves of contractions, called peristalsis, which move material through the intestines too rapidly for proper absorption to take place. This leads to painful diarrhea and may make that part of the body susceptible to the later development of cancer.

The key to the biofeedback treatment of gastric disorders, again assuming that brief, conventional medical treatment and general relaxation training have failed, is to be found in the fact that movements of the "gut" make sounds. You can actually hear these noises with the unaided ear, such as by putting your head up against a horse's side. What you hear are called 'Borborigmy' (We're told that the word "sound" is included in that name.) Obviously, the number and intensity of these Borborigmy will correspond in a general way to the level of ongoing activity in the intestines. When amplified, they provide our "trotting" patient with a form of feedback which he may use to learn ways to reduce the rate of peristalsis in the gastrointestinal system, thus bringing about clinical improvement in the condition.

Ulcers appear to be caused, at least in part, by the excessive secretion of gastric juices which may be a component of Parasympathetic Rebound. Obviously, the general discussion in this work on bringing down one's level of stress has some relevance to the treatment of ulcers.

Gynecological Disorders

The basic treatment of gynecological disorders is, of course, a matter for gynecologists. There are, however, emotional or psychological/psychiatric consequences of gynecological imbalances. At times, problems in this area, most notably Premenstrual Syndrome (PMS) and menopause, may produce veritable "hormonal storms," leaving a woman with almost no control over her own mental life.

The first step in the control of such problems is medical. Your doctor needs to do what she can to remove the source of the internal upheavals, whatever it may be. Unfortunately, it appears that Medical Science has not yet progressed to the point where such distressing physical conditions for females have been completely eliminated.

Given that such "endocrine upheavals" will, regrettably, be a monthly occurrence in the lives of many women, it would seem that the relevant concept in the control of this problem is not "cure" but rather "training." One of your authors had a client once who was, three weeks out of the month, a wonderful cultured and sensitive lady. The fourth week or so, however, was given over to PMS and her period itself. During these times she would vent her discomfort on her husband, an equally cultured gentleman of some means who expressed his adoration of her both physically and emotionally, in addition to providing her a powder blue Jaguar for her transportation convenience. A consultation with the woman's gynecologist revealed that he had done all that he could for the basic disorder itself. These apparently medically untreatable outbursts had, to put it mildly, placed a strain on what was an otherwise excellent marriage.

Having been assured by the lady's gynecologist that everything that could be done from a medical standpoint had, in fact, been done, it appeared that the relevant concept here was, again, training. In other words, we would prepare for the time preceding and during her period much as a long-distance runner would prepare herself for a marathon. The specific steps involved were:

1. Cognitive Restructuring: This, in the present instance, is just a fancy term for if not "giving credit where credit is due," at least "not putting the blame where the blame isn't due." Alise had to be very clear about the fact that her negative feelings were the product of her hormonal condition and not the result of some transgression on the part of her husband.

   She would rehearse again and again the statement that this is how she feels prior to her period – "This is what happens every month. It has nothing to do with anyone else, particularly not Ted. It will pass, it will pass, it will pass. And when it does, I will still have a loving husband and wonderful family." She repeated these statements much like a student of Eastern Mysticism would a Mantra.

2. Training: Obviously, a major problem with these hormonal storms is what may loosely be called "being upset." During the time surrounding her period, she would utilize relaxation exercises to reduce these feelings of being upset and to create within herself a sense of warmth and well-being.

3. Marital Therapy: The focus in helping Alise get through her hormonal storms was very much on working <u>with</u> her husband. He was, one might say, her "coach." He was the one who was actually with her as she went through the distressing experiences. It was most important that they have a solid, mutually supportive relationship. Great stress was put on communication, like, "Let me tell you what's going on inside me right now. I love you, and I know it's my condition that's upsetting me and not you."

What needs to be emphasized again in this case is the "training" nature of the treatment. Alise would prepare for the times around her period by talking about what she knew she would be going through. In this way, she could go ahead and experience a part of what it would be like, but she could do this in small, easily handled doses. This training made the rush of hormones, when it finally did appear, less frightening, and she felt that she had some tools, some power, to help her through it.

Premenstrual Syndrome is hardly the only area in which this kind of training model is applicable. Any kind of unpleasant or frightening experience, a painful medical procedure or a court appearance, as examples, may be prepared for in this manner.

This general strategy opens up the topic of "Stress Inoculation." This is a set of procedures for preparing either yourself or someone else for some upcoming stressful event. An example, far from the gynecological area, will illustrate this general approach which has been introduced by the treatment of "Alise."

Ralph is an accountant who for some years had been doing the books for a chain of local, small town loan companies. His competence and conscientiousness had led him to discover that "skimming" was going on in the company. Specifically, some of the profits were being "taken off the top," that is not reported. This practice is highly convenient in that it allows a company to avoid paying a lot of taxes. But it is highly, highly illegal. So when the time came for him to certify the books, his ethical standards prevented him from doing so. Ralph, naturally, was fired and replaced by a less "rigid" and more "cooperative" accountant.

Later the IRS audited the company. The agents suspected that something was "fishy," but they couldn't prove it. Noting the change in accountants, they went to question Ralph, who, of course, told them what he knew.

Sometime later, an indictment for income tax evasion was handed down against the owner of the loan company chain. Our Ralph was slated to be the chief prosecution witness at next month's trial. Ralph had never been comfortable speaking in public, and the thought of testifying in the conflict-full atmosphere of what would be a highly publicized trial filled him with dread, actually with terror and panic! So Ralph sought out the services of a psychotherapist who specializes in anxiety-based disorders.

The therapist spent a little time at the beginning getting to know the man he would be working with, establishing "rapport," as they say. He assured him that while his problem was unique and dramatic in Ralph's own life, perhaps in the life of anyone, the general class of difficulty which was being brought to the office was not at all unique or new. A great deal is known about helping people with such problems, Ralph was assured. He was taught the progressive muscular relaxation procedure described earlier, specifically in Chapter 9. This was done in order to bring about some general relief from the excruciating anxiety from which Ralph was suffering. In particular, it assisted him in sleeping better, which was important in helping him maintain his balance in life. Relaxation training was also, as we shall see, an important skill that the client would need for the future work Dr. Stewart would be doing with him.

The next step in the process of treatment was one that could best be described as "cognitive restructuring." The first component of this step was one of emphasizing the importance of what Ralph was doing. A crime had been committed by people who were trusted by The People. It was a good citizen's duty to come forward and help to right the wrong which had been done! The second aspect here is one of emphasizing that his "performance" in court need not be "perfect" (Remember here the writings of Albert Ellis.). Yes, Ralph may be uncomfortable on the witness stand, and his voice may tremble a bit. But his not being a "professional witness" will make his testimony all the more believable. It also adds to the amount of courage required for him to be doing what he's doing!

Then we see the use of systematic desensitization enter the therapeutic process. First of all, a hierarchy of "subjective units of distress" was constructed by Ralph and Dr. Stewart. This ranged, of course, from things that bothered the client not at all to the elements of the upcoming ordeal that he dreaded the most. The top of the scale, "100," not unexpectedly, was the rough, personally-directed cross-examination he expected from the "Kingpin's mouthpiece." In office systematic desensitization was then conducted along the lines described earlier in the chapter on the general treatment of anxiety-based disorders.

Lest the reader be left with the impression that the process being described here consists of completely different segments, it needs to be pointed out that what we're describing is more a matter of shifting emphases as therapy progresses. The working on the relationship and the verbal assurance continue throughout. What actually happens is that additional procedures, like systematic desensitization, are "woven into" the fabric of the treatment process as time goes forward.

The last phase of the treatment being discussed is technically known as "*in vivo* desensitization." As used here, it means, basically, that we're going to take the desensitization procedures out into the "real world." Dr. Stewart arranged for he and Ralph to have access to the courtroom in which the trial will be held. The client became a bit anxious as they entered the courthouse, so they sat down on one of the benches out in the hall, and, without attracting attention, went through the relaxation procedures. After about fifteen minutes of this, they were able to enter the courtroom itself and go through the relaxation process there. The next day, our accountant was able to sit in the witness chair and answer Dr. Stewart's questions relating to his upcoming testimony. Of course, they had to stop periodically for the therapist to instruct Ralph in going through additional muscle relaxation. But by the end of the session he was feeling reasonably comfortable in recounting what he had observed and his conclusions. The next session proved long and difficult but successful. Steward got an attorney friend of his to join them in the courtroom. Mr. Jones, Esq. played the role of the defense attorney and cross-examined Ralph. The lawyer and his friend had conspired that the questions put to the accountant got increasingly harsh as the session progressed, part, of course, of the gradual "turning up the heat" which is a component of desensitization therapy.

It wasn't without discomfort that our hero got through the trial. But he did get through it. And his testimony was judged by others to have been crucial in bringing down a conviction. Everyone in town was proud of the self-effacing accountant. And to be honest, Ralph was pretty proud of himself too! Certainly, he got through the experience with less "wear and tear" on his body than would have otherwise been the case, thus protecting his health and bringing this vignette back to the central theme of the present chapter. And he learned some skills he could use in facing other difficult situations which life throws at one.

Old Age

Like PMS, old age is not a disease as such. It is, hopefully for most of us, an unavoidable and inconvenient part of life. As they say, it's not good, but it beats the alternative!

The numerous aliments which attend advanced age are of a general medical nature, and this work has no specific contribution to make in terms of their management. The problem we do, though, wish to discuss here is failing memory.

Deficits in "short-term memory," that is difficulty in remembering what happened yesterday or what you're supposed to do today even though you can recall vividly what you were doing when Pearl Harbor was bombed or the day President Kennedy was assassinated, is an inevitable accompaniment of growing older. Since it can't be avoided, the question becomes, "How can I live with it?" The answer here appears to be found in two words, "system" and "order." Those who grow old successfully appear to be those who have established routines in life. They've fallen into what we might call "comfortable ruts." They just know automatically what comes next in their day, so they really don't even have to think about it. The lively octogenarian next door takes his walk at eight-thirty each morning. You can set your clock by it. He always has two martinis at six and a glass of wine with supper. Inflexible? Rigid? Perhaps. But he knows, he has learned, or maybe just senses that a more freewheeling lifestyle isn't going to work for him. He'd become confused, disorganized. So why put yourself through that? Stay in that nice comfortable rut.

Another component of successful aging is record keeping. The old memory is not as good as it used to be, so you've got to supplement it somehow. You'll see a lot of older business leaders carrying note pads with them and making notations on their calendars. They're substituting a "prosthetic device" (Eyeglasses, hearing aids and artificial limbs are also prosthetic devices.) for what used to happen inside them with no assistance. Regardless of your age, it wouldn't be a bad idea for you to start getting into the habit of adopting such tactics. When you truly need them, you may not be able to recognize that you need them, nor might you then have the ability to devise a system that is workable. As a colleague of ours once said, "Old age is where the future is."

In addition to the above devices, increasingly research indicates that mental exercises can be effective in preventing or slowing encroaching senility/dementia. In fact, electronic game-like exercises are being sold on TV informercials. Whether they are superior to just remaining mentally active, as through reading and staying involved in life, has not, to our knowledge at least, been demonstrated. But it does seem reasonable to assume that the brain, like so many other body parts, partakes of the general rule of "use it or lose it"!

One of the most difficult tasks for people growing old is to (continue) to say "yes to life." When medical problems become overwhelming or when bank accounts are depleted, they become discouraged and forget to look for resources and activities which might still be satisfying and meaningful. We should recall here that Victor Frankl's most famous book, *Man's search for meaning in life* in English, was titled in German *Despite everything, say "Yes to life"* (*Trodzdem ja zum leben sagen*). "Despite everything" is the key expression here. For Frankl, it expressed his unconditional acceptance of life on life's own terms. He explained that only while living can we create experiences, transcend difficulties and experience meaning in life. He always emphasized one's spiritual commitment as being central to a person's role and purpose in life.

Engaging in activities that produce meaning and fulfilling experiences, accordingly, should be one of the most important goals toward which we strive, particularly as we grow older. Unfortunately, many elderly people cease engaging in meaningful activities. They seem to expect that others will give meaning to their lives. When lives of chronic illness and limited mobility seem to smother the spirit, older people should look to the example of Sisyphus, as described by Camus. The gods wanted to punish Sisyphus for betraying their secret and rebelling against their will. They at this point desired nothing less than to break his spirit. So they condemned him to rolling a stone up a hill, at which point it would simply roll back down again, requiring Sisyphus to have to endlessly repeat the same meaningless task. The gods thought, and with good reason, that condemning someone to such a repetitive and meaningless task would be demoralizing. And, as discussed above, we should strive to work toward meaningful goals and not just mindlessly perform routine activities. But Sisyphus had no choice here. He had been condemned to this "job" by the gods themselves! But the gods did not break Sisyphus' spirit. He found meaning even in his suffering and won a moral victory over the gods!

As we grow older, we should become more determined to pursue meaningful and transcendent goals, goals which are more important than just ourselves. But even in the most trying and debilitating of circumstances, we, like Sisyphus, can discover deeper resources of the human spirit which allow us to find meaning and joy in even our suffering.

Compliance

"I've given 8.5 million dollars of advice in my life, but people have only taken a buck twenty-five of it," is a rough quote from the late Senator Sam Ervin of Watergate fame. It's a safe bet that your family doctor feels a lot like that too. After all, she's been telling you for years to stop smoking, reduce your booze intake, lose weight, exercise, take this pill until the vial is empty, eat more of this, etc., etc. This brings us to one of the most vexing issues in the practice of medicine, "Compliance Problems."

What follows assumes that you believe what your doctor is telling you. If you don't, you may need a new doctor! But in the great, great majority of cases we know "in our hearts" that the doctor is really right. After all, not many of us truly believe that we should smoke and drink more and exercise less! So once the advice is given and understood (Make sure you do!), the issue becomes one of getting yourself to do something, or some things, you don't really want to do. Here the reader is referred back to the chapter on behavioral interventions for guidance on how to change various aspects of your lifestyle to promote better health.

Another potential resource in dealing with compliance problems goes back to the very opening theme of this book, the importance of an intimate relationship. Studies consistently show that married people are healthier than their single counterparts. And despite all the griping about the "Old Ball and Chain," this relationship between marriage and health is particularly strong for men! Many workers speculate that the difference is caused by the spouse's involvement in the treatment process. She reminds Herb to take his pills and do his exercises for his back. Additionally, it's just more difficult to engage in negative health behaviors, like excessive drinking, when someone else is around and expecting you to hold up your end of the relationship.

We noted earlier in the area of substance abuse that, "Silence is the enemy of recovery." So it is also with any kind of medical disorder in which complying with your doctor's orders is important in recovering. The patient, in order to maximize a tremendous potential resource, needs to let the spouse know exactly what medical problems they're facing and what will be needed to overcome them. Spouse, get involved! Inquire, talk about it, support, lovingly push your wife to do those things that are important to get over this. These maternalistic /paternalistic actions won't hurt a good, intimate relationship. You'll see that they will actually enhance it. There is no better investment of your time!

Pain

Despite its unpleasantness, pain is actually a very adaptive mechanism in that it signals the need for change in life, whether to stop pounding a hammer into our thumb or to go see the doctor about an infection. However, some "chronic conditions" cause "chronic pain." The best example of such chronic pain relates to a "bad back," from which so many of us suffer as we get older. In such cases, the pain gives no clue as to how we might improve our lives. It merely reminds us that we're getting older, hardly something for Headline News, or should we write HLN?

A proposed "key" to dealing with such chronic pain relates to its similarity to depression. If you think about it, the depressed and those in pain share many similarities, inactivity, complaining, etc. Further, there are a number of medications which doctors use both in the treatment of depression and pain. In fact, so much of what we've learned about the treatment of depression, particularly forcing yourself to stay active, is also applicable to dealing successfully with pain.

Another component to handling pain relates to cognitive focus. If we have meaningful interests and projects in life that engage our attention, we are less likely to simply wallow in our pain. We know this can happen, since we once heard a woman who complained about her bad back almost constantly exclaim after attending a personally relevant court hearing, "I got so wrapped up in that that I forgot all about my back!"

Extraordinary Healing Powers of the Body/Mind

Increasingly in the literature on health one reads the word "holistic." As a matter of fact, this term appears in the very title of the book you're holding. The word "holistic," as used here, means, basically, that the mind and body are not viewed as two distinct and separate things. They are seen as different expressions of what we may call the "same organismic essence." For the philosophically-minded, we may summarize what is attempted to be said here by saying that the holistic approach represents a rejection of Cartesian Dualism.

An early expression of the holistic approach is contained in the statement of a noted physician that often, "It is more important to know what patient has the disease than to know what disease the patient has." In other words, people vary considerably in the way they respond to contracting a disease. And a part of the way they vary relates to what we may generally call "mental attitude." Mental attitude, as the term is used here, includes a variety of factors. We're talking about the person's general psychological approach to life. Is she cheerful or down, optimistic or pessimistic? Does he take an active role in life, or does he just passively accept what the world has to hand out? And what is the patient's reaction to the current illness? Is she going to "fight it all the way" or "just roll over and die?"

The idea that the development of and recovery from disease is in some way or ways related to mental factors is controversial, even heretical to some. But it has been reliably observed that those individuals who are subjected to great mental stress become more subject to disease. And a mechanism for this connection, the hypothalamus which controls both the auto-immune system and emotions, has been proposed. So this proposed link is not purely the product of some science fiction writer's imagination. And while, admittedly, the emotion-hypothalamus-sickness connection has not been "written in stone" in the same way as Einstein's

Theory of Relativity, other possible connections between mind set and physical condition have not been ruled out. Indeed, they have largely gone unexplored.

There have appeared in recent years a number of credible reports of people having recovered from "hopeless" illnesses through the use of their mental powers for recovery. Norman Cousins (1915 – 1990) has provided us with the most noted example in this category. Stricken with a life-threatening disease, he decided to try to overcome it with a positive mental attitude. He thought "happy thoughts" and brought more laughter into his life through such means as watching old Marx Brothers films. Despite the prediction of his doctors, Cousins recovered fully.

Also relevant here is the well-received book on recovering from cancer through mental imaging by the husband and wife medical team (Carl Simonton [1942 – 2009] was an M.D.) of Simonton and Simonton. They had their patients actively imagine the white corpuscles in their blood stream gobbling up the cancer cells. The patients visualized these body defenders in the manner of the Pac Man creature that goes about the maze eating up little enemies in the video game. They cited a number of cases in which recovery exceeding all expectations was achieved through the use of this innovative and unconventional technique.

The connection between mental attitude and illness, principally on the recovery side, is promising. But it certainly hasn't been documented fully. So use it to the fullest, but it wouldn't be advisable to throw out your arthritis medication or insulin!

Speaking of diabetes, many people with this disorder find that they are able to reduce their level of insulin intake following the learning of deep muscle relaxation. What appears to occur, basically, is that the amount of "stress hormones" in the body is reduced. These stress hormones bear a chemical resemblance to insulin and other secretions. The decreased secretion of some of the chemicals related to stress leaves, we might say, more of the body's resources available for the production of other chemicals, including insulin. A similar process seems to be at work in the numerous reported cases in which "infertile couples" conceive shortly following adopting. Now that they have "The Baby," their level of stress is reduced. Down come the stress hormones, and up go the others, including those involved in reproduction.

So don't just dismiss this psychology-health thing as merely the ravings of a "crackpot." We have enough evidence that it's real to make us all try to find more and better ways to make it work for us!

CHAPTER 16

Setting Up Your Bowling Pins

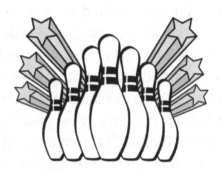

Or

A Stab at Figuring Out the Meaning of Life

This book began, the reader may recall with a yawn, with the analogy of life as a bowling ball. The image was developed of a sleek, shiny black orb streaking down the alley toward the pins. Up to this point, the writing has focused almost exclusively on the "art of bowling ball maintenance." In general, we've talked about keeping the "ball" healthy through balancing it, with the core of our "bowling ball" being an intimate, sharing relationship with another person.

The reader will note that your authors have left untouched the issue of the "pins, "the ultimate goals in life. There are several reasons for this delay in addressing this topic. The first is that this is the matter which your authors, admittedly, are least qualified to discuss. The second is that setting goals is a highly personal thing. Everyone must do this for himself or herself. What is meaningful and important in life for one person may not be so for another. Probably the best we can hope for in our efforts to understand this most important part of life is to find general trends, a direction which appears to offer a bit more hope and light than others.

Hopefully, we can obtain some guidance in this matter from the great religions of the world. Their theologians have been grappling with this matter of the meaning of life for centuries. And many religious leaders will tell you, with varying degrees of certainty, that they know The Answer. The fact that they so frequently quarrel with each other and their pitches for money on Sunday morning TV cause one to shy away from a blind acceptance of the pronouncements of these men of the cloth, in our personal view. But with all their tatters, it's the best we've got, so here goes.

As your authors see it, standard or "mainstream" religions of the world share a number of things which are relevant to the matter of goals in life. In summary form, they appear to us to be:

1. A belief in a benevolent power or spirit which, to one degree or another, guides or at least influences the course of life
2. A belief in the desirability of doing "good works"
3. A belief in the importance of being "kind" to your fellow creatures

Let's now take these three components of religion and see how they might assist us in setting up our "bowling pins of life."

The first religious element, a belief in a great power or spirit, is important for a number of reasons. In fact, a key principle of the theory of one of the founders of Psychoanalysis, broadly defined, was that people could actually develop rather serious mental disorders should they lose touch completely with spiritual elements in life. Carl Jung was born into a family in which almost all of the males, his father included, were clergymen. So it should come as little surprise that he would go on to very much emphasize the spiritual or religious side of people's efforts at adjustment.

Jung accepted Freud's idea of an unconscious, a part of one's mind which influences what an individual does but of which the person is unaware. Jung referred to Freud's unconscious, roughly speaking, as the "Personal Unconscious" in his theory of personality. But to that he added another layer of mental activity of which we are also largely unaware. This he called the "Collective Unconscious." This is a "repository of racial experiences," as Jung termed it, which has been built up over many generations. In it, he theorized, was contained the collective experience of the species. Jung observed that people very much enjoyed looking into crackling fires, almost as though they were watching modern TV sets. People will also go far out of their way to visit the ocean, even though they have no practical purpose for doing so. He felt that the attraction of fire and water related to the importance of these forces, evolutionarily speaking, to humanity. Mankind, according to evolutionary theory, emerged from water. And we return to an "aquatic environment," in our case within an embryonic sac, in order to reproduce. And fire was a critical component of Man's at least apparent rise to dominion over the Earth. Thus, fire and the sea, by virtue of their importance in the evolution of our species, have been stamped into a specific part of our unconscious, our "Collective Unconscious" to use Jung's phrase. And we respond to them with a sense of meaning, almost reverence.

An even more important component of the Collective Unconscious, according to Jung, is a feel for what is eternally significant in the universe. Here we get into the matter of a Great Purpose or Spirit, or, as they say in 12-step programs, what we may "choose to call God." Cutting ourselves off from this Great Spirit can have the effect of making us feel incomplete, dissatisfied with our lives. Perhaps, after all, we can't live completely in the "Secular City."

And it certainly would be depressing to think that we are merely acting out biological processes and urges. Much more comforting is it, indeed, to believe that there is a purpose in life and that our individual lives play a role in the fulfillment of that overall purpose. Of course, the specifics of that overall purpose will depend very much on which religious leader you happen to ask! Ultimately, everyone must make a judgment on this matter for her-/himself. Your writers are forced at this point in their lives to live with a great deal of fuzziness on this topic. But just a general belief in this mysterious principle is enough to get us by, at least for now.

The matter of "good works," or, as your authors like to put it, "making the world a better place," is also highly individual in nature. There certainly is no end to the number of "good things" that need to be done. There's finding a cure for cancer, whipping prejudice and discrimination, building housing for the poor, promoting peace around the world, preparing for earthquakes... Well, you get the idea!

With this richness of causes to pursue in life, one would think that everybody would be gloriously engaged in some form of work for the betterment of mankind. That such is not actually the case is, your authors believe, because of a number of difficulties associated with efforts to actually make the world a better place

The first is that not everyone even cares about doing anything to improve the human condition! We have encountered those who are only concerned with their own comfort and pleasure. And when asked, they will freely admit that such is the case. All that can be said here is that it is your authors' very definite observation that those people who are engaged in projects aimed at helping others in some way appear to lead more satisfying and fulfilling lives that those who are not.

And if you are concerned about improving the world, there's the highly complex question about <u>exactly how</u>. And when you see a direction for your efforts, you're bound to run into opposition and resistance. A Life of Service is, in many ways and to use an old Southern expression, "A tough row to hoe."

At the risk of descending from the "heights" of theology back to the "depths" of psychology, your authors can't help themselves from pointing out that one of the classic personality theorists came to a position that stressed the importance of goals in life and making the world a better place. Alfred Adler, who worked closely for a time with Sigmund Freud, was most noted for his concept of the "Inferiority Complex." In actuality, though, feelings of inferiority are not things that just afflict "sick" people. We are all born feeling helpless, powerless and inferior. That's because the human newborn is totally dependent on others and incapable of meeting any of his needs on his own. That's pretty inferior! And that's where we all "came from."

Given this shared background of inferiority, it's little wonder that the emphasis in Adler's theory relates to the way people attempt to overcome their sense of inferiority. In analyzing his patients, Adler observed and made notes of a number of strategies people often employ in attempting to get over the feelings of inferiority that haunt them. Among those he saw were Attempting to be Perfect, Using and Manipulating Others and Gaining Power over Others. All of these ways of trying to overcome inferiority are unworkable in the long-run, "maladaptive" we might say. Not only do they not make the person feel better about herself, but they actually confirm her sense of inferiority and thereby ultimately condemn her to the pits of despair.

Probably the most common and best illustration of a lifestyle intended to overcome a sense of inferiority which doesn't work is that of trying to gain power over others. This way of attempting to triumph over our feelings of powerlessness might well make sense at first. After all, one might "reason," "I feel inadequate and inferior now. But if I could arrange things so that hundreds, perhaps thousands, of people were at my beck and call, then I'd be a pretty powerful and important guy. AND then I wouldn't feel inferior!"

There are, though, obvious problems with gaining power as a way to make yourself feel better about yourself. First of all, it ties your entire sense of self-worth and self-esteem into whatever office you might hold. So whatever might threaten your office, like the upcoming election, threatens you personally and basically. One thinks here of Richard Nixon during Watergate. The Presidency certainly seemed to offer him little pleasure or comfort during this period of time! And even, to be generous in granting success to your pursuit of power, if you rose to the Presidency and weren't voted out like Jimmy Carter or "scandled out" like Nixon, there would still come the inevitable end of the second term. Then you'd no longer be at the center of things. There'd be no more hotlines to answer or vetoes to exercise at your personal will. What then? Reportedly, a number of Presidents have had a difficult time adjusting to post-White House life. Little wonder! Efforts to be Perfect or the Most Talented or the Smartest or the Most Beautiful or the Richest in the long run meet similar fates.

According to Adler, and one must add, consistent with the pronouncements of most religions, the best way to deal with one's inferiority feelings is to merge your life and efforts into some grand scheme or project aimed at improving the lot of mankind. This could be a political movement, whether of conservative or liberal stripe, whose progress will, you believe, lead to better lives for those residing in a particular political jurisdiction. Or it could be a campaign to stop the mistreatment of certain individuals, like fighting racial discrimination or the abuse of animals. Or it could be involvement in a scientific project aimed at finding a cure for this or that disease or a series of studies which, hopefully, will help us do a better job of controlling some problem, like air pollution. Again, the list goes on. But the point here is that submerging yourself in such worthy projects with others virtually insures against the devastating, inferiority-confirming failures suffered by those who devote themselves to purely competitive activities. After all, if one of your experiments doesn't "pan out,'" you can always say to yourself, paraphrasing Thomas Edison, "Well, at least I found something that didn't work. That'll save the next guy from having to waste her time on Formula BC1907." And when, as inevitably occurs, you become too old or infirm to carry on yourself, you at least have the satisfaction of seeing "The Work" carried forward, by others, but it carries on nonetheless. And that's a whole lot better than having your telephones and dispatch cases suddenly snatched from you by a rival and then being sent home on a plane "bound for nowhere."

Now, just because an old shrink says something is so doesn't make it so. But it is interesting, perhaps comforting, to see a point in which classical religion and classical psychology are in such agreement. After all, if something comes to you from several directions, it would probably be wise to pay attention!

There is another Viennese person we want to briefly here reintroduce to you. He was born, raised and lived most of his life in Vienna, Austria, just like his before-mentioned fellow countrymen Sigmund Freud and Alfred Adler. He studied and associated with Sigmund Freud. He also became a member of the circle of Alfred Adler. His name was Viktor Emil Frankl. The importance of introducing him to you is not because of his medical career or his neurological achievements or his psychiatric success stories. In our minds, he is uniquely qualified to talk to us about further discovering purpose and meaning in life, adding yet another and higher dimension to living a socially useful life. His book, entitled in English *Man's Search for Meaning*, is a classic best seller. The book is a moving account of his life amid the horrors of the Nazi death camps. This experience convinced Frankl that life is meaningful under all circumstances because in the most difficult situations the forces of the human spirit could be activated. The resources of the human spirit, he believed, are the storehouse of specifically human strengths within ourselves that could restore and maintain our mental health.

Frankl suggested that discovering meaning in one's life is at the very core of living a satisfying life. The opposite is lack of meaning, or as Frankl called it "existential vacuum." Frankl believed that every person is motivated to discover meaning in his or her life. The belief in meaning, the will to find it and the freedom to search for it, are the tenets of his school of therapy that he named logotherapy and existential analysis.

Life consists of numerous meanings of the moment for each and every one of us. The meaning of the moment is intensely personal and value laden. We are, indeed, called by our personal questioning of our existence to find it and follow it, for this means to lead a more meaningful life.

Frankl was also concerned about the ultimate meaning of life. In fact, he wrote a book entitled *Man's search for Ultimate Meaning*, which was published in English in 2000. He talks in it about personal spirituality. He said, "Religion will have to become profoundly personalized which allows any human being to speak a language of his or her own when addressing himself or herself to the ultimate being. Usually, such a mode of speaking to God is called praying. Truly, prayer is a person-to-person call. Indeed, it could be considered the highest expression of the 'I-Thou relationship'..."

While we argue here for some awareness of meaningfulness in life in terms of setting and moving toward worthwhile goals, according to Frankl it is actually not helpful to speculate excessively on the ultimate meaning of life because it is beyond out human comprehension. In fact, glimpses of understanding ultimate meaning can only be attained by us "by reaching in faith into the transcendence of God."

Your authors would note here that we, too, believe that it is useless for us to intellectually ponder why senseless and tragic things happen. Many theologians and philosophers, by contrast, have attempted to deal with these questions, and they have had conspicuously little success! Here we must, in our view, return to the overall theme of this chapter of goals and ask ourselves what particular task(s) in life might be calling to us to help overcome such tragedies and senseless suffering in life in order to do what we can to try to prevent such unfortunate events from occurring again.

Frankl's work, thus, helps us further understand and appreciate the importance of our "bowling ball pin" goals. Frankl teaches that, in addition to the pursuit of worthy aims, we must find the "meaning of the moment." We should view the "pins," therefore, within the specific meanings of the moments in which we find ourselves and within the context of the goals we have set for ourselves. It is this kind of meaning that we can repeatedly discover in our ability to review and reflect on the specific meaningful contents of our daily lives. It is this type of meaning that we may discover and even project by loving someone and/or some worthy goal that we are dedicated to pursuing. The relevance of this "meaning of the moment" is that it is anchored in someone we love, in a situation that is vital to us and time specific. Maria Marshall, Ph.D., a Canadian psychologist and logotherapist, express this concept best: "In other words, it is unique, personalized and unrepeatable. It is relative to our values or universal truths." It is, therefore, not actually necessary for us to achieve great goals in life to live meaningfully. Victor Frankl helps us find meaning in our daily struggles even within our limited stores of resources and talents.

The third and last "Principles of the Good Life" is that we be kind to each other, that we treat one another with dignity and respect.

To find someone who lives her or his life dramatically according to this principle is, regrettably, a rare occurrence. One demonstration of this is the way people drive their automobiles. They run others off the road. They follow their fellow motorists by feet if not inches! And pedestrians crossing the street must, at times, feel that they are, quite literally, under attack. Do they not recognize that they're handling a lethal weapon? Have they no regard for their fellow creatures? One can only guess that the answer to these questions is a resounding "NO." While driving style is used here merely as an example, we are intrigued by the fact that the report of a past conclave of American Catholic Bishops included the way we drive in their list of concerns about violence in our society. There are actually so many ways in which people are cruel to each other. One can so easily observe people yelling and screaming at each other. Why would you treat a fellow being in this manner? One is at a loss in his or her attempts to understand. And yet it happens every day. One, indeed, may have to acknowledge, sadly, that it is sometimes even the norm.

So how, how can this be? Why do people deal with each other in this fashion? Can they not feel that which their fellow creature feels? Do they not experience that which is felt by the individual who stands so close to them? Apparently not.

So it would seem that this book is, as they say, "irrelevant" to most of you out there. But those of us who feel something of that which is experienced by those around us, "empathy" is the technical term, may take some pride in this attitude of caring and sensitivity. It would, we would argue, be a better world if there were more people in it like you.

Probably the best known example (at least for those of us in a country where most of the people say they are "Christians") of a caring, giving life is that of Christ. To follow this example does not, at least in your authors' judgment, require a belief in the literal divinity of Jesus. In so many ways, we know little about the man. And much of what we "know" about him proves not to be true. In Bishop Spong's book, *Rescuing the Bible from Fundamentalism*, it is pointed out that Christ certainly was not born in Bethlehem, and there's no real reason to believe that he was born of a virgin, to give just two outstanding examples.

The startling, perhaps heretical assertions contained in the preceding paragraph are not at all threatening to your authors. What we have in the life of Christ, and other religious leaders for that matter, is an example of how to live a life of meaning and service. The question of the validity of various claims about them thus becomes irrelevant. Nor is it important which was "greater" than the other. What is important is that we learn from their examples and try to make ourselves better people and the world a better place.

So, in summary, leading a <u>balanced</u> life merely makes it possible for us to take advantage of various opportunities. A <u>fulfilling</u> life is one in which you devote a substantial part of yourself to improving the world. We all qualify for some type of search for meaning in life. It is, indeed and alas, true that not all of us have the talent to help find a cure for AIDS or dispatch people to Mars. But we can volunteer for cleanup crews or pass out blankets at emergency scenes. Those whose careers have brought them material wealth can give of that, although some "hands on" work would probably contribute to an increased sense of satisfaction. The point is that all of us are capable of making a contribution, and our lives will be enriched considerably by making an effort to do so. There are also the feelings of warmth and satisfaction you experience when you make a positive effort to treat everyone you encounter in such a way as to make them feel better about themselves and the world.

If the reader is disappointed by this little chapter on "bowling pins" or The Meaning of Life she or he should be aware of the fact that we are no less so. You were warned not to expect too much. It was the best we could do.

But perhaps it will give you something to think about.

THE END

Printed in the United States
By Bookmasters

Printed in the United States
By Bookmasters